CAMBRIDGE TEXTBOOKS IN LINGUISTICS

General Editors: B.COMRIE, C.J.FILLMORE, R.LASS, R.B. LE PAGE,
J.LYONS, P.H.MATTHEWS, F.R.PALMER, R.POSNER, S.ROMAINE,
N.V.SMITH, J.L.M.TRIM, A.ZWICKY

SEMANTIC THEORY

SEMANTIC THEORY

RUTH M. KEMPSON

LECTURER IN LINGUISTICS
UNIVERSITY OF LONDON

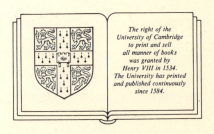

The right of the
University of Cambridge
to print and sell
all manner of books
was granted by
Henry VIII in 1534.
The University has printed
and published continuously
since 1584.

CAMBRIDGE UNIVERSITY PRESS

CAMBRIDGE
LONDON NEW YORK NEW ROCHELLE
MELBOURNE SYDNEY

Published by the Press Syndicate of the University of Cambridge
The Pitt Building, Trumpington Street, Cambridge CB2 1RP
32 East 57th Street, New York, NY 10022, USA
10 Stamford Road, Oakleigh, Melbourne 3166, Australia

First published 1977
Reprinted 1979, 1980, 1984, 1986

Printed in Great Britain
at the Alden Press, Oxford

Library of Congress Cataloguing in Publication Data

Kempson, Ruth M.
Semantic theory
(Cambridge textbooks in linguistics)
Bibliography: p.
Includes index.
1. Semantics. 2. Semantics (Philosophy)
3. Languages–Philosophy. I. Title.
P325.K44   410   77-70948

ISBN 0 521 21613 3 hard covers
ISBN 0 521 29209 3 paperback

CONTENTS

To Mark and Hugh,
who were born during the time in which this
book was written

PREFACE

As a bridge discipline between linguistics and philosophy, semantics poses a considerable initial problem for anyone new to the subject as much of the literature to be grappled with is written by philosophers not linguists. And even when the particular details of the arguments in the literature are understood, it is only too easy to fail to realise the theoretical consequences of agreeing, or disagreeing, with the arguments in question.

With these difficulties in mind, I have had two aims in writing this book. The first aim is to introduce the reader not only to topics such as componential analysis, semantic universals, and the syntax–semantics controversy which are familiar to linguists, but also, without assuming any knowledge of either philosophy or logic, to introduce the reader to problem areas in the philosophy of language which are relevant to linguistics. So, among more linguistic topics, I have included an explanation of the concepts of logical form, truth condition, truth table, analytic truth, entailment, and presupposition, and I have attempted to make clear the relevance to linguistic theory of such philosophical topics as Tarski's theory of truth, analyticity, speech act theory, and presuppositional logic.

My other aim has been to show the reader how arguments can be constructed in semantics by putting forward a series of arguments, following the conclusions through from argument to argument. I have hoped in this way to give students an over-all perspective of the subject as a part of general linguistic theory. During the course of the book I have in fact argued that semantics is best approached by adopting a truth-based analysis, excluding from what we might call central-core semantics all concepts relating to the speech situation – concepts such as speech act, illocutionary force, utterance meaning, etc. I have furthermore argued that such an analysis is not incompatible with componential analysis of the type familiar to linguists, despite Quine's famous attack on meaning and analytic truth. In connection with the detailed specification of the semantic component within a transformational framework, I have argued for the more traditional interpretive semantics view, since in my opinion the evidence available suggests that while syntactic and semantic generalisations are partially interdependent, there is by no means a one-to-one correlation between these two types of generalisation. Finally, despite the large number of semantic analyses in terms of presupposition which have been suggested in the literature, I have argued that a semantic concept of presupposition has no role to play in natural-language semantics.

Since my exposition is argumentative rather than descriptive, much of what I say may seem to the more experienced reader to be contentious. This possibly rather doctrinaire approach is however deliberate. There seem to me to be two distinct types of introduction to any subject which students should be given. The first is the comprehensive introduction summarising all the major points of view which have been advocated in the literature. The second is the introduction to the procedure of argumentation, which by its very nature has to be more selective than the first type of introduction. In other areas of linguistics both types of introduction are well represented in the literature. But in semantics it is only the first type of introduction which is at all well represented in the current literature (see in particular Lyons' two-volume introduction to semantics – Lyons 1977). The second type of introduction to semantics is virtually non-existent. For this reason I have not even aimed at writing a comprehensive introduction to the subject, and students should not be encouraged to read this book uncritically. Indeed I would think it a pity if the readers of the book agreed with every detailed argument I have put forward. My hope however is that this book will evoke in the reader an educated and critical enthusiasm for the subject so that he will be able to grapple with the wide range of literature with some hope of managing to evaluate it for himself.

At the end of each chapter I have given a list of detailed recommendations for further reading on each topic covered in the chapter, and references are only included in the text and its accompanying footnotes in the case of quotations and other such specific purposes. Students must therefore refer to these recommended reading lists for the relevant supporting references to the text. The recommendations are sometimes given in a general list for the whole chapter, sometimes with reference to particular sub-sections. In each case, I have specified author and title only. For full details of the reference recommended, the reader should consult the bibliography. In view of the introductory nature of this book, I have tried to restrict the references I have given to material which is easily available to students. Accordingly, I have not referred at all to mimeographed literature which might be in circulation, and have in general referred to material circulated by linguistic societies and other non-commercial or student organisations only if there is no other relevant literature in print.

This book owes its present form largely to Professor John Lyons, whose detailed and often critical comments caused much of the book to be entirely rewritten. It is therefore him that I have to thank in the first instance, though I hasten to add for his sake that he should not be held responsible for any of the arguments I have put forward. Other colleagues to whom I am grateful for comments on various sections of the book include Dr Peter Cannings, Dr Anita Mittwoch, Dr Neil Smith, and Dr Deirdre Wilson. In connection with the preparation of the book for publication, I would like to thank the staff at Cambridge University Press for their unfailingly efficient help. On a more personal note, I need to thank my husband and children who have kept me alive and well by, in their different ways, preventing me from thinking only about semantics twenty-four hours a day. But perhaps most of all I have to thank Miss Eileen Stewart who with her loving care of my children enabled me to spend more of those twenty-four hours each day working on this book than I ever dreamed would be possible.

I

Introduction

This book is concerned with semantic theory, and its relation to general linguistic theory of which it is a part. The problems involved in theory-building will therefore permeate this book, from the first page to the last. In particular, we shall be concerned with semantics as part of a general linguistic theory that is scientific in the sense that it makes empirically testable predictions. For if, on the contrary, a hypothesis is stated in such vague terms that there is no way in which one could test whether it be false or not, then we have no means of assessing it against the evidence of the data. Such a theory ceases to be an empirical one and from the scientific point of view is vacuous. Not only this but, as Popper in particular has emphasised, a theory can only be tested by attempts to falsify it, for while it is possible to prove that a theory is false by a given set of facts, it is logically impossible to prove the truth of a theory in this way. Facts either are or are not compatible with a theory, but their being compatible can never *prove* the validity of that theory for it may be false for some independent reason. In general therefore scientific endeavour is not concerned with evidence which seems to show theories to be correct but only with evidence which might show them to be false. Linguistics, like any other science, is concerned, then, not with the mere collection of facts, but with the construction of a system of abstract concepts which will account most adequately for the particular properties which languages display. And, in the spirit of Popperian scientific methodology, the development of linguistic theory has generally followed a particular pattern: (i) constructing an abstract system (a theory) to account for a certain part of language structure, (ii) investigating the consequences of setting up such a system, and (iii) rejecting the system if it predicts certain facts which do not in fact obtain, and (iv) substituting an alternative system which is compatible with the facts.

Introduction

Now semantics has, until recently, been the Cinderella of linguistics, a branch of the subject which many scholars thought was not amenable to such rigorous methods of evaluation. Happily this pessimism is not as widespread as it was, but despite the renewed interest linguists are showing in semantics, there is still no one semantic theory which enjoys widespread acceptance, even in bare outlines. As a result, the subject remains at present a very fragmented one. The primary aim of this book is to show how this state of affairs could be improved, by assessing the problems which arise in semantics in the light of the two general requirements: firstly that a semantic theory, like other theories, must be falsifiable if it is to be empirical and secondly that any such competing theories be evaluated by attempts at their falsification. This over-all aim will be carried out by first of all considering the various prerequisites of any theory of semantics as a fully specified part of a general linguistic theory, secondly assessing various approaches to semantics in the light of these prerequisites, and finally considering in detail within a particular framework a number of problems which must be solved by any theory claiming validity as an explanation of semantics.

The first step in this forbiddingly large task is to collect together those preliminary properties of language which all linguists would agree that a semantic theory must explain. So let me start with some basic data. All languages depend on words[1] and sentences having meaning: every word and every sentence is conventionally associated with at least one meaning. Accordingly, for any one language, our semantic theory must be able to assign to each word and sentence the meaning (or meanings) associated with it in that language. In the case of words, this essentially means writing a dictionary (though we shall see that it is rather a different task from writing an ordinary dictionary). But in the case of sentences, the problem is more complex. In all languages, words can be arranged to form sentences, and the meaning of those sentences is dependent on the meaning of the words it contains. But this is not a simple accumulation process. *Cats chase dogs* and *Dogs chase cats* do not mean the same, though the words in each sentence are identical. And sometimes word-order will change meaning, but sometimes not. *The opera house had never been closed before* and *Never before had the opera house been closed*, like *Cats chase dogs* and *Dogs chase cats*, contain identical words but in a different order, but, unlike the latter, this pair

[1] Cf. 6.1 below for a detailed discussion of the different interpretations of *word*.

do not differ in meaning. Thus a semantic theory has not only to capture the exact nature of the relation between word meaning and sentence meaning, but it must be able to state in what ways this relation is dependent on word-order or, as we shall see, other aspects of the grammatical structure of the sentence.

Not only this but both words and sentences can be ambiguous, and in different ways. *I went to the bank* is ambiguous by virtue of the ambiguity inherent in the word *bank*. But the sentence *Washing machines can be tiresome*, though ambiguous, has no ambiguous words in it. In this case the ambiguity is due to the structure – dependent on whether *machines* is understood as the subject of the verb *washing* or as the object. Thus again we come up against the interdependence of the syntactic structure of a sentence and its meaning. Moreover, as we shall see in chapter 8, the concept of ambiguity is itself far from clear, and yet, as part of the problem of the interpretation of forms of a natural language,[1] the explanation of ambiguity is an essential task of a semantic theory.

In constructing such a theory, at least one further task is also agreed upon as the special task of semantics. Not only do words and sentences have meaning, but these meanings are related to those of other words and sentences. For example, the words *man, woman, girl, child* are related in meaning in a way not shared by the words *man, mirror, enumeration*. In an analogous way, *John murdered Mary, John killed Mary, Mary died* are related in meaning in a way that *John murdered Mary, John greeted Mary, Mary sniffed* are not. In this connection, the problem of synonymy arises: and synonymy is just one of the relations between words and between sentences. Other relations are entailment (or implication), and contradiction. Each of these are logical relations which, as we shall see later (3.4.3 below), are defined formally. But, as a first rough approximation, we can say of entailment that one sentence entails a second sentence if saying that first sentence implies that the second sentence is also true. For example, the sentence *John murdered Mary* entails both *John killed Mary* and *Mary died*, for saying that John murdered Mary implies that John killed Mary and that she died. A similar relation holds for the pairs *Edmund has just finished building our house, We have a house; Bill ran home, Bill moved; Susie did a strip-tease,*

---

[1] The term *a natural language* is used to refer to any language which is or has been used by human beings as their primary means of communication, in contrast to *a formal language*, which is an abstract system drawn up for a specific purpose (for example by a logician).

Susie took her clothes off; Robin is about to give birth to a baby, Robin is pregnant. The corresponding relation for words is logical inclusion (or hyponymy). The meaning of the word *dog* logically includes the meaning of *animal*, because to say that something is a dog implies that it is an animal. Similarly with the pairs *waltz, dance; run, move; nightmare, dream.* Contradiction is the converse of entailment. *John murdered Mary* is in contradiction with *John did not kill Mary* and *Mary did not die; John has just finished building our house* and *We do not have a house* contradict each other; and so too with the other pairs. Now all these relations clearly depend on the meaning either of the words or the sentences, and so in characterising the meanings of the items of a language, a semantic theory is also committed to characterising these relations.

So far then, we have seen that in order to have any claims to adequacy, a semantic theory must fulfil at least three conditions: (i) it must capture for any language the nature of word meaning and sentence meaning, and explain the nature of the relation between them; (ii) it must be able to predict the ambiguities in the forms of a language, whether in words or sentences; (iii) it must characterise and explain the systematic relations between words and between sentences of a language – i.e. it must give some explicit account of the relations of synonymy, logical inclusion, entailment, contradiction, etc. Any theory which fails to capture these relations, either at all, or in particular cases making the wrong predictions, must be inadequate, either in principle or in some detail of the theory. There are also some general properties of language which any part of a general linguistic theory must take account of. Perhaps the most important is that each human language is made up of a set of sentences, and this is not finite. This property of natural language was first emphasised by Chomsky and the attempt to capture this aspect of natural languages lies at the heart of Chomsky's transformational grammar of natural language. For, as Chomsky pointed out, if one of the goals of a linguistic theory is to characterise the various properties of all sentences of any language – syntactic, semantic or phonological – then this cannot be achieved by listing sentences and giving a description of each one, as had always been the linguist's implicit procedure. As an alternative, Chomsky proposed a procedure common in mathematical or formal languages, whereby an infinite set of objects can be described by a finite set of rules. We need not concern ourselves with the details here. What is important is that any account of any aspect of natural languages should be in terms of a finite set of general statements or rules characterising an infinite set of sentences. Now in the case of semantics, this property of natural languages does not affect the statement of word meaning. For all languages contain only a finite set of words. So word meanings can be given in a finite list. It is with our account of sentence meaning that we meet the problem of the non-finite nature of natural language. For if we are to give an explicit account of the nature of the relation between word meaning and sentence meaning for each and every sentence of any language, then we must do so by a finite set of general rules. The same problem arises in accounting for synonymy, entailment, etc. The accounts of these relations must be in a rule formulation which automatically predicts the relations involved in the particular cases.

So we already have certain criteria by which to judge any account of the semantics of natural language: since any complete account of a language must give an interpretation to an infinite set of sentences, it must be in the form of a finite set of general principles, and it must by these means account for word meaning and sentence meaning in a language, capturing the systematic nature of the relation between them; and it must moreover account for ambiguity, synonymy, entailment, contradiction, etc. While these conditions may seem simple, even in some cases obvious, we shall see as we proceed that few accounts of meaning can fulfil them, even in principle.

Before we get into the details of any particular account, it is worth taking a step back from the morass of detail we have already taken a glance at. For the nature of all linguistic arguments hinges on the central aim behind all theoretical linguistic inquiry. What is it that we are hoping to achieve in our inquiry into the nature of linguistic structure? One global aim of linguistics – and arguably the most important – is to set up a general theory of linguistic structure which captures exactly those features of human language which are both unique to human languages and shared by all of them. On this view, the contribution of linguistics to our knowledge about the world lies in its attempt to characterise explicitly those aspects of human language which are our unique heritage. One might well at this point wonder how this global perspective can be made consistent with the detailed study of individual languages, also claimed to be one of the goals of linguistic inquiry and among the conditions for an adequate semantic theory. To see that the two are not inconsistent, recall the dictum that theories can only be tested by attempting to falsify them. In the case of linguistics, and purported universal linguistic statements, falsification is very straightforward. For any universal claim, provided that it is expressed sufficiently precisely, is falsified by facts from any one language. As an example let us take one possible claim about the nature of semantics in natural language. We have assumed previously that all languages have words, which have a meaning associated with them, and moreover these words can be arranged in different syntactic structures to form sentences. Let us then suppose the existence of a theory which captures these two levels of generalisation in the form of two different components: a syntactic component containing all the general statements about the principles of sentence formation, and a semantic component which contains a statement of word meanings and a set of rules predicting sentence meanings. This theory, let us assume, states no relations between the two components. But unless some such relation is characterised in the theory, it will encapsulate the negative claim that there is no relationship to be stated between syntactic generalisations and semantic generalisations. However we have already seen that there is an interaction between syntactic properties of sentences and their semantic properties. For sometimes re-ordering affects the meaning of a sentence and sometimes not. In English, the sentence *Never before had the opera house been closed* means the same as *The opera house had never been closed before* because the items moved (*never* and *before*) are adverbs of a particular kind; but *Cats chase dogs* and *Dogs chase cats*, where the subject and object are interchanged, are very different in meaning. So the prediction of sameness or difference of meaning between sentences (a matter for semantics) depends on grammatical labels such as adverb, subject and object (a matter for syntax). Any theory, then, which does not incorporate some account of the relationship between syntactic generalisations and semantic ones, whatever that relationship may be, must be wrong. Thus in this way, simple self-evident facts about the nature of word and sentence meaning in just one language, in this case English, can be used to falsify an abstract formulation of linguistic theory attempting to capture the general properties of natural language. More generally, linguists *are* concerned with constructing grammars for particular languages, but the theoretical justification for such grammars lies in the evidence they provide for specifically formulated universal claims. And ultimately the individual language is but one testing-ground for predictions made by setting up a universal linguistic theory. In this spirit, the methodology adopted in this book will be along the following lines: I shall consider some general hypothesis and test it against the particular evidence provided by any one language. Incidentally, we shall see in the later sections of this book that the exact nature of the relation between syntactic structure and semantics is one of the still hotly debated issues in linguistic theory. However at this point, all I hope to have demonstrated is the importance of the methodological principle of refutation of general principles of linguistic theory – by any single language.

There is one more methodological preliminary before we can consider any detailed semantic arguments: what is the nature of a linguist's evidence, for or against any putative theory? This question is already partly answered. In arguing that syntax and semantics are not independent, I assumed as agreed English data that the sentence *Never before had the opera house been closed* meant the same as the sentence *The opera house had never been closed before* and conversely that the sentences *Cats chase dogs* and *Dogs chase cats* did not; and this assumption was made merely on the basis of my own intuitions as a speaker of English. Indeed throughout this book, I shall use data which are culled solely from the intuitions of one English speaker – myself. This is parallel to the use in work on syntax of a speaker's intuition about which are the grammatical sentences of his language and which are not.[1] Now this use of a speaker's intuition has sometimes been ridiculed as a source for empirical refutation for a theory, on the ground that such evidence can scarcely be considered objective, reliable data. Moreover in semantics the problem is compounded by the fact that speakers often do not have clear intuitions about synonymy, ambiguity, entailment, etc., and yet it is these intuitions which are used as data. Despite this problem, there are good reasons for using a speaker's intuitions as data. In the first place, any language contains an infinite number of sentences, and all speech events are finite. A collection of recorded speech events can therefore never record more than a subset of the required set of sentences. In any case a recording of any set of sentences however large would never yield data about what a sentence implies or whether a sentence is ambiguous, even about that finite set of sentences, for it

[1] Since the grammar a linguist devises is set up to characterise all and only the sentences which a speaker recognises as belonging to his language, *grammatical* as a technical linguistic term is used to describe those sentences which are generated by the grammar.

7

would only provide the sentences themselves. More seriously, in actual communication, a number of factors combine to determine what is actually said by a speaker and how what a speaker says is understood by his audience, as we shall see in detail in due course (chapter 5). Environmental influences, social influences, perceptual ability, psychological make-up, constraints on memory and linguistic ability all interact to determine what is said and how it is understood on particular occasions. In other words, the knowledge of a language that we possess as speakers of a language is only one of many factors which have to be accounted for in a general explanation of the way in which we actually communicate as speakers of that language; and it is arguably just this one factor which it is the burden of linguistic theory to explain. But we have no means of isolating this one factor except by access to the speaker's intuitions, for the production and comprehension of any actual utterance[1] or sequence of utterances will always be determined by the conflation of factors which influence communication and not solely by the linguistic ability the speaker and hearer of that utterance have. This problem of the data on which linguistic theories are based remains an important one, which continues to concern linguists, but it is not within the scope of this book to consider all the ramifications of this particular area of controversy. So for the remainder of the book I shall adopt the standard position as presented in Chomsky 1965, that the grammar of an individual language is set up as a characterisation of the (subconscious) linguistic knowledge that each speaker of a language has, his so-called competence, and that an analysis of the interaction of all the factors which influence communication is not the burden of a theory of competence, but the burden of a theory of performance, a theory which accounts for behaviour in general. This is not to say that the delimitation of what should be accounted for by a competence theory and what by a performance theory is not without its problems. Indeed, as we shall see, it is particularly in disputes within the domain of semantics that linguists disagree about the exact delimitation of the two fields of study. But I shall be assuming both that the distinction between competence and performance is a valid one at least in principle (cf. however 4.2 and 5.4 below), and also that using a

---

[1] The term *utterance* is standardly used in contrast with *sentence*. A sentence, S_n, is what is characterised by the grammar as an abstract structured string with a semantic interpretation. An utterance of S_n is one instance (or token) of that sentence. Since utterances are instances of the use of sentences, it is utterances that lie within the domain of a theory of performance.

speaker's intuitions as the data which a linguistic theory is set up to account for is a methodological necessity.

In conclusion, we have seen that a linguist is concerned with the construction of a general theory as to the nature of language, and in conjunction with this with the construction of grammars of individual languages which both capture the knowledge which a speaker of that language has which enables him to use his language as a means of communication, and which provide the testing-ground for postulated universal constraints on grammars of natural languages. In connection with semantics, I put forward three conditions which a semantic component of such a linguistic theory would have to meet: (i) it must characterise the nature of word meaning and sentence meaning for any language, and explain the nature of the relation between them; (ii) it must give an account of ambiguity, synonymy, entailment, contradiction, logical inclusion, etc., and for any given language make the correct predictions; (iii) it must give these characterisations in the form of a finite set of rules capturing the regularities contained in some specific infinite set of sentences. We must now turn to consider in some detail the basic assumption on which any formalisation of semantic generalisations must rest – the nature of meaning itself. And this, as we shall see, has always been the traditional controversy of semantics.

RECOMMENDED READING

An understanding of what is said to constitute a theory that is scientific is an essential prerequisite for an appreciation of the way in which linguistics has developed since the 1940s. An excellent introduction to the philosophy of science in general is Hempel *Philosophy of Natural Science*. On the requirement of falsifiability on theories, see Popper 'Conjectures and refutations', an article in the book of the same name, and also Magee *Popper*, which gives an informal introduction to Popper's work. Popper's ideas have since been developed, in particular by Lakatos: see Lakatos 'Falsification and the methodology of scientific research programmes' in Lakatos and Musgrave (eds.) *Criticism and the Growth of Knowledge*. Methodology has been a neglected subject in linguistics, but see for example Labov 'Methodology' and Botha *The Justification of Linguistic Hypotheses*. On the infiniteness of natural language, see Chomsky *Syntactic Structures*, and *Aspects of the Theory of Syntax*. This property of natural languages has been disputed by Reich 'The finiteness of natural language' (reprinted in Householder (ed.) *Syntactic Theory*), and by Ziff 'The number of English sentences'. For a discussion of linguistic universals, students cannot do better than to read Chomsky

Aspects of the Theory of Syntax ch. 1, but see also Chomsky *Language and Mind* (enlarged edition), and Bach *Syntactic Theory* ch. 11. The problem of the nature of linguistic evidence has not been given much detailed attention by transformational linguists but see Sampson *The Form of Language* ch. 4, Labov 'Methodology', Fillmore 'On generativity' and Householder 'On arguments from asterisks'. The distinction between competence and performance is discussed in Chomsky's *Aspects of the Theory of Syntax*, and in more detail in Lyons and Wales (eds.) *Psycholinguistic Papers* (see in particular Fodor and Garrett 'Some reflections on competence and performance'). Chomsky's account of this division has been attacked by Hymes 'On communicative competence', and more recently by G. Lakoff and others (see the recommended reading for chapter 4).

2

Explanations of word meaning

In the first chapter I suggested some preliminary conditions of adequacy for semantic theories by which particular theories could be tested, and it might seem that we are now in a position to consider the detailed mechanism of some proposed theory. But there was one large and unwarranted assumption in the way that these conditions were specified; it was assumed that the relationship between a word and what it is used to imply and that between a sentence and what it is used to imply presented no problems, and were not a matter for debate. But, quite to the contrary, an explanation of these relationships – i.e. the problem of what we mean when we refer to the meaning that a word or sentence has – is the classical problem of semantics, the problem indeed on which semantics has traditionally foundered. Since any formal representation of semantics will implicitly present one particular solution to this problem, we cannot usefully consider the details of such a theory except in the light of a coherent account of meaning.

There are three main ways in which linguists and philosophers have attempted to construct explanations of meaning in natural language: (*a*) by defining the nature of word meaning, (*b*) by defining the nature of sentence meaning, and (*c*) by explaining the process of communication. In the first way, word meaning is taken as the construct in terms of which sentence meaning and communication can be explained; in the second, it is sentence meaning which is taken as basic, with words characterised in terms of the systematic contribution they make to sentence meaning; and in the third, both sentence and word meaning are explained in terms of the ways in which sentences and words are used in the act of communication. It is no coincidence that there are these three types of explanation. In the first place, there clearly is a relation between words and objects. We use words to refer to objects, and to actions (consider such words as *cup, horse, woman, graduate, cooking, sweeping, thinking*), and the explanation of this relation is indubitably the task of semantics. Similarly sentences are used to describe events, beliefs, opinions, and it is unquestionably the task of semantics to explain the nature of the relation between sentences and the states of affairs those sentences describe. Finally, since language is the vehicle by means of which we effect communication, it is arguable that the interpretation of language should be explained in terms of its role in communication. Moreover these three aspects of meaning, word meaning, sentence meaning, and communication, are reflected in different uses of the word *mean*. Corresponding to explanation (*a*) is:

(1) *Supererogatory* means 'superfluous'.
(2) *Spinster* means 'unmarried woman'.

Corresponding to (*b*) is:

(3) The sentence *James murdered Max* means that someone called James deliberately killed someone called Max.

In these two uses, the word *mean* has a meaning approximating to *indicate*. But the word *mean* is used in a different sense in the following conversation between two speakers, A and B, a sense which corresponds to explanation (*c*):

(4) A: Are you going to bed soon?
B: What d'you mean?
A: I mean that I'm tired, and the sooner you go to bed, the sooner I can.

In this case, *mean* is attributable to speakers and has the same meaning as the expression *intend to indicate*. Thus we have at least three possible starting points from which to construct an explanation of meaning – the signification of words, the interpretation of sentences, or what a speaker is intending to convey in acts of communication. Of these three uses, most traditional explanations of meaning constitute an attempt to explain meaning in terms of the naming relation which holds between a word and its object, and it is this that we shall be concerned with in this chapter.

2.1 Meaning and reference

The naming relation between a word and its object is most transparent with proper names, the paradigm case of naming. Here there is a one-to-one correspondence between name and object: for example the name *The Parthenon* refers to the object the Parthenon in Athens, the name *Ruth Kempson* refers to the individual who wrote this book. This relationship between word and object is called the relationship of reference, and there is a long tradition of equating the problem of meaning with the problem of reference. According to this view, known as extensionalism because of its treatment of meaning in terms of the objects, called extensions, to which the items of the language refer,[1] the meaning of a word can be explained in terms of the relation between that word and object or objects to which it refers. Just as proper names refer to individuals, it has been said, common nouns refer to sets of individuals, verbs refer to actions, adjectives refer to properties of individuals, and adverbs refer to properties of actions. Thus, for example, it would be said that the relation between the expression *Ruth Kempson* and the individual Ruth Kempson is directly comparable with the relation between the word *mice* and the sets of objects which can be referred to by the use of that word; and moreover both of these relations are said to be similarly comparable to the relation which holds between, say, the word *red* and the sets of objects which have the property of redness, and too to the relation which holds between the word *quickly* and the sets of actions which have the appropriate property of speed.

However, assuming for the moment that we can accept the claim of homogeneity in connection with these different relations, there are a number of reasons to believe that any theory of meaning which attempts to explain all aspects of word meaning in terms of reference is mistaken. In the first place, there are a number of embarrassing counter-examples: even if the relationship of reference can be said to hold between a word such as *imagination* and some class of abstract objects which constitute acts of imagination, there is no sense in which words such as *and*, *not*, *whether* refer to anything. And all prepositions present a similar problem. What does *of* refer to? What, in this very sentence, does the preposition *in* refer to – or indeed *very* or *what*? Not only is there a large and non-homogeneous class of exceptions, but there are a number of anomalies in explaining more straightforward cases. The relationship of reference which holds between expressions and non-existent objects will be the same: it is therefore hard for a theory which explains meaning in

---

[1] The most well-known exposition is Russell 1902, but this view has recently been expounded again by Davidson (cf. Davidson 1967a) within a truth-based theory of meaning (cf. 3.1 below).

terms of reference to avoid predicting synonymy between all of the following: *the pterodactyl, the unicorn, the first woman to land on the moon.* And, for the same reason, an expression such as *the first man to land on the moon* will be predicted to be quite different in kind from the expression *the first woman to land on the moon*, because only in the former case is there a referent to which the expression can stand in a referring relationship. Problems arise even in an analysis of common nouns which refer to a set of objects. For in what sense can there be said to be a consistent identifiable relationship of reference between the word *iguana* and a set of objects to which it refers in (5) – (7)?

(5) Iguanas are not very common.
(6) Are iguanas extinct?
(7) Professor Branestawm is looking for iguanas.

In (5), the word might be said to refer to a class of objects, viz. iguanas; but in (6), the word either refers to a class of objects or a null class, apparently depending on the answer to the question.[1] And in (7), the problem is no less acute: for on one interpretation there may be, say, two specific iguanas that Professor Branestawm is looking for, but on another interpretation he may just be looking without there necessarily being any such object. On this interpretation, it makes no sense to question which objects does the word *iguana* refer to? This problem arises in a large number of cases (called 'opaque contexts'), following verbs such as *believe, want* and *hope*; and these present a notorious problem to anyone attempting to provide an analysis of reference. Furthermore, if we return to the paradigm case of referring, proper names, we find an important difference between these and any other syntactic category. Though in proper names there is a one-to-one correspondence between word and object, it is not obvious that proper names have any meaning at all, for it makes no sense to ask 'What is the meaning of the expression *Noam Chomsky*?': one can only ask 'Who does the expression *Noam Chomsky* refer to?' This suggests at the very least that a semantic account of proper names should not be like that of other words. But if this is so, then the original assumption of homogeneity in the semantic properties of proper nouns and the other categories, common nouns, verbs, adjectives, adverbs, and so on, was a mistake.

---

[1] Sentences such as these pose considerable problems for a theory of reference, as witness the large amount of philosophical literature on the subject.

This is not to deny that there are problems in the analysis of reference. On the contrary, the solution to the problem of opacity in particular remains an open one, and something of an issue for philosophers. But it does cast doubt on the assumption that any solution to the problems of reference automatically provides a solution to the problem of meaning.

2.2 The image theory of meaning

Another solution to the problem of explaining the nature of word meaning, which has an equally long tradition, is to explain the meaning of a word in terms of the image in the speaker's (or hearer's) brain. The problem here is to know what form the images take. The most obvious point is that these images cannot be visual. For suppose my image of a triangle is an equilateral:

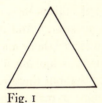

Fig. 1

If this is said to constitute for me the meaning of the word *triangle*, then either *triangle* has to mean equilateral triangles only, or *triangle* has to be said to be ambiguous according as the image is equilateral, isosceles, or scalene. For each of these is mutually exclusive. In a similar vein, an owner of an alsatian may have a radically different image of dogs from an owner of a miniature poodle, but it is not obvious that they thereby speak a different language. There is no image corresponding to what is shared between dogs, and none either which has just those features shared by all triangles. And this is just one of the many problems facing a simple image theory of meaning. Further problems are presented by the fact that (*a*) one may have more than one image for a single expression, and (*b*) two expressions may have the same image. Thus the expression *a tired child* may evoke either an image of a child (notice that there is no visual image neutral as between a boy or a girl) curled up and nearly asleep, or an image of a child stamping its foot and screaming. According to an account of meaning which equates the meaning a word has with an image, any word which relates to more than one image is predicted to be ambiguous. But despite the prediction, the expression *a tired child* is not ambiguous. On the other hand, should two expressions bear the same image, the image theory of meaning predicts that they will be synonymous. But many expressions have the same image: *a tired child, an unhappy child, an angry child, a future tyrant* may all evoke the identical image of a child stamping its foot and screaming. Yet these expressions are by no means synonymous. As I have already partly indicated, an image theory of meaning faces the additional problem of speaker variation. The images we have of what might be referred to by any word may not only vary from occasion to occasion, but since they are dependent on our experience are certain to differ in many details, if not radically in substance from those of other people. Take the word *lecture* for example. To those who give lectures, the word might call up an image of an audience of between, say, twenty and one hundred people staring up at one wretched individual who, perhaps self-consciously, walks up and down in front of them. But for those who have never lectured, the image is more likely to be that of one person droning on, often boring, sometimes incomprehensible, with the accompanying sensation of having to fight feelings of drowsiness. Such different images should, if they correspond to the meaning associated with the word *lecture* guarantee that communication between two such groups of people using the word *lecture* would be impossible because each group has radically different images of lecturing and hence different conceptions of the meaning of the word *lecture*. Worst of all, there are many words with which it is impossible to associate any image at all – *and, or, because, therefore*, etc. Yet they are by no means meaningless.

2.3 **Meaning and concepts**

The standard retreat from the extreme form of the image view of meaning is to say that the images are not visual; but, if so, it is not obvious what claim is being made. Consider for example the suggestion that 'the speech element 'house' is the symbol, first and foremost, not of a single perception, nor even of the notion of a particular object, but of a 'concept', in other words, of a convenient capsule of thought that embraces thousands of distinct experiences and that is ready to take in thousands more' (Sapir 1921: 13). What is involved in this claim that a word has as its meaning a 'convenient capsule of thought'? If this is a retraction from an image theory of meaning, as it is, then it is a retraction from a specific, false claim to one that is entirely untestable and hence vacuous. It does no more than substitute for the problem term *meaning* the equally opaque term *concept*. It does not provide an explanation of the required kind (cf. p. 1 above). If meaning is to be explained in terms of concepts, it is essential that the term *concept* itself be given a rigorous definition.

Sapir's Swiss contemporary, de Saussure, goes some way towards providing such a characterisation. For though, like Sapir, de Saussure talks freely of concepts, he stresses that the concept (the word he uses is *signifié*) an element stands for is solely due to its value in the system: 'Language is a system of interdependent terms in which the value of each term results solely from the simultaneous presence of others'. On this basis he would have said that the word *bachelor*, for example, has the meaning it does solely by virtue of the other items in the system to which it is related – *spinster, woman, husband, boy*. Similarly, right across the vocabulary. Thus each of the members of the following sets of words stands in a certain relation one to another (labelled *valeur*), which is itself a determinant of the interpretation of the word:

have	criticise	angry	mother
give	praise	happy	uncle
lend	accuse	calm	aunt
borrow	assess	pleased	grandparent
rent	blame	annoyed	nephew
hire	reprimand	upset	cousin

It is not of course obvious that this observation saves the problem of defining *concept* from vacuity, for it is not clear how the inter-relationship of value (valeur) and meaning (signifié) can itself be tested. In any case, de Saussure's account is open to objections similar to those raised against both a reference theory of meaning and an image theory of meaning. In particular, words such as *and, because, or*, etc., are counterexamples to this view, for it is not clear whether their interpretation can be analysed in terms of concepts. It will not do to suggest that the meaning of *and* is the concept of co-ordination, for what is co-ordination other than by joining by *and*? Similarly with *or*: it is meaningless to explain *or* as having the concept of disjunction for its meaning, when in order to explain disjunction one needs to refer to *or*. And the general problem remains: to explain meaning in terms only of concepts is unempirical.

2.3.1   *Componential analysis*

The assumption of systematic relationships of meaning between words is however independent of the problem of explaining the basis of these relationships; and a considerable amount of detailed work on the structure of the vocabulary has been done in recent years. Many linguists have turned to what has been called componential analysis to give an explicit representation of the systematic relations between words. On this view the meanings of words are analysed not as unitary concepts but as complexes made up of components of meaning which are themselves semantic primitives.[1] In this vein, *spinster* might be analysed as a semantic complex made up of the features (equivalently called components,[2] or markers) [FEMALE], [NEVER MARRIED], [ADULT], [HUMAN]. This form of analysis was used in particular by anthropologists seeking to give an account of kinship terminology in various cultures. For example, the distinction between *mother* and *aunt* in English might be made explicit if the terms were analysed as contrasting complexes of the components [FEMALE], [PARENT OF], [CHILD OF].[3] Such componential analysis is not of course restricted to kinship terms: it can be applied in many areas of the vocabulary. For example, the distinction between *murder* and *kill* can be stated explicitly and economically if *murder* is analysed as having a meaning which is a complex of components representing intention, causation, and death, and *kill* as having a complex of only the components representing causation and death. In a similar way, *give* and *take* can be shown to be distinct by virtue of their contrasting complexes of components representing causation and change of ownership. By this means, de Saussure's concept of valeur characterising the relationship which a word holds to other words in the system can be stated explicitly in terms of related but distinct component complexes, and indeed the main value of componential analysis lies in the economy of statement of these relationships which it allows.

However in so stating the inter-relationships between words in terms

[1] For a more detailed discussion of the status of these components, cf. 6.2 below.

[2] I shall use the term *semantic component* with systematic ambiguity, both to mean the section of the over-all grammar in which the semantic generalisations are stated, and to mean the elementary semantic units isolated by componential analysis.

[3] Cf. Lehrer 1974 and Leech 1975 for detailed analyses of English and other kinship terminologies.

of more primitive semantic components, one is transferring the burden of semantic explanation from word meaning onto the components which together, in different combinations, constitute word meanings. Indeed what remains to be explained in such componential analyses, as we shall see below (6.3.2), is the relationship between the words of a given language and the apparently independent components. We may glibly say that the word *spinster* has a meaning which is a complex of the semantic components [FEMALE], [HUMAN], [ADULT], [NEVER MARRIED], but the central problem is the relationship between the word *human* and the component [HUMAN], and so on for the remainder of the vocabulary. Unfortunately the account of the semantic components themselves given by linguists using the methodology of componential analysis is often no more substantial than de Saussure's or Sapir's characterisation of word meaning. For example, it has been claimed that semantic features are not defined in terms of 'physical properties and relations outside the human organism' but are symbols 'for the internal mechanisms by means of which such phenomena are conceived and conceptualised' (Bierwisch 1970: 181). Katz, one of the central exponents of semantics within transformational grammar, gives a much more detailed account, but with little more substance:

A semantic marker is a theoretical construct which is intended to represent a concept that is part of the sense of morphemes and other constituents of natural languages. By a concept in this connection we do not mean images or mental ideas or particular thoughts. Concepts . . . are abstract entities. They do not belong to the conscious experience of anyone, though they may be thought about, as in our thinking about the concept of a circle. They are not individuated by persons: you and I may think about the same concept. (Katz 1972: 38)

Neither characterisation does more than say that the meaning of a word is a (complex) concept, and this we rejected as vacuous. Yet Katz roundly dismisses this rejection, maintaining that 'it is quite unreasonable to insist at the outset . . . on a clarification of the ontological underpinnings of the notions of concept and proposition as a precondition for accepting the explanations of semantic properties and relations given by a theory employing 'semantic marker' . . .' (Katz 1972: 39). However Katz' mere dismissal of the attack is not warranted. In the first place, as we have already seen in part, differing accounts of the nature of meaning make different claims about what constitutes the proper domain of semantics. And the setting up of a formal semantic theory as one component of a general linguistic theory, presupposes a solution to this question: thus any such theory, as indeed the one Katz provides, must be implicitly presenting some claim as to the nature of meaning – and if this claim is unfalsifiable, then the theory itself becomes unempirical. Secondly, in defining meaning in terms of mental constructs, Katz' theory has no apparent place for an explanation of the relation between a word and some object that it may be used to refer to, or of the relation between a sentence and the state of affairs it describes. Each of these relations has been merely reduced to an untestable relation between an expression and a mental construct. And in the case of English words such as *human* where there is a one-to-one correspondence between the word and a semantic component, we are given no explanation at all other than the bald statement that the meaning of *human* is the concept represented by [HUMAN]. This is not only not explanatory as an account of meaning, but it is also quite unfalsifiable. So, while the method employed in componential analysis may be useful (and I shall indeed be making use of it in later chapters of this book), the theoretical underpinnings provided by an account which incorporates a definition of semantic components in conceptual terms are not those of a falsifiable theory. If semantics is to be part of an empirical science, such an account must be made more substantial.

In attempting to unravel the concept of meaning in natural languages by considering the nature of meaning, we seem to be in a paradoxical position: characterising meaning merely in terms of concepts is unexplanatory, and characterising meaning in terms of reference seems to enter into too many problems to be a convincing solution. This is not of course to suggest that problems in the analysis of reference can be dismissed, but merely that the relationship of reference does not provide an adequate basis for an explanation of word meaning. We must now turn to the second of the three main possibilities that I outlined earlier – an account of sentence meaning.

RECOMMENDED READING

2.1 The problem of identifying properties of meaning with properties of reference is almost invariably included in introductions to philosophy of language: see for example the introduction to Parkinson (ed.) *The Theory of Meaning*, and Alston *Philosophy of Language* ch. 1 (which also gives a critical exposition of both behaviouristic theories of meaning and ideational theories). The most famous attempt to analyse meaning in such terms is Russell's

'On denoting' (reprinted in Olshewsky (ed.) *Problems in the Philosophy of Language*); but this view was until recently thought to be untenable for reasons brought forward by Frege: see Frege 'Über Sinn und Bedeutung' (translated as 'On sense and reference'), and Dummett's detailed account of Frege in *Frege: Philosophy of Language*. Russell's analysis has also been attacked for independent reasons by Strawson: in this connection see the recommended reading for chapter 9. However the reduction of the problem of meaning to the problem of reference has been re-introduced, both by Davidson (see Davidson 'Truth and meaning') and within possible-world semantics (see Hintikka 'Semantics for propositional attitudes' (reprinted in Linsky (ed.) *Reference and Modality*)). On the problems of analysing sentences such as *Are iguanas extinct?*, students should refer to the literature on existence: see for example Moore 'Is existence a predicate?', Pears' and Thomson's articles of the same name (reprinted in Strawson (ed.) *Philosophical Logic*), Quine 'On what there is' (in *From a Logical Point of View*). On the problems presented to theories of reference by opaque contexts see Linsky (ed.) *Reference and Modality*. For a linguistic approach to the problem of opacity, see Hall-Partee 'Opacity, coreference and pronouns' and 'Opacity and scope'. There is considerable disagreement over the semantic properties of proper names: for a representative set of views see Searle *Speech Acts* ch. 7, Kripke 'Naming and necessity', Dummett's reply to Kripke in *Frege: Philosophy of Language*, and Mates 'On the semantics of proper names'.

2.2   The classic statement of an ideational theory of meaning is given by Locke, whose exposition is reprinted in Lehrer and Lehrer (eds.) *Theory of Meaning*. The twentieth-century linguistic representative of this view is Sapir: see Sapir's *Language*.

2.3   De Saussure's account of semantics, given in *Cours de Linguistique Générale*, is now mainly remembered for the emphasis he gave to structural relationships between lexical items. Two forms of semantic description can be associated with his work: description in terms of so-called lexical fields, and, much later, description in terms of componential analysis. An excellent account of work done on lexical fields and of componential analysis is given in Lehrer *Semantic Fields and Lexical Structure*, and she summarises the work of Trier who was the most well-known early exponent of analyses in terms of lexical fields. For a useful survey of work on semantic fields, see Vassilyev 'The theory of semantic fields: a survey'.

2.3.1   A detailed introduction to the analysis of kinship terms is given in Burling's *Man's Many Voices*, which includes an analysis of the set of English kinship terms. This book is incidentally an excellent account of componential analysis and the problems in its application. Other references include Lounsbury 'The structural analysis of kinship semantics', Goodenough 'Componential analysis and the study of meaning', and Conklin 'Lexicographical treatment of folk taxonomies'. For an account of items such as *give* and *take* and other related items see Bendix *Componential Analysis of General Vocabu-*

lary. For general problems in the methodology of componential analysis see Nida *Componential Analysis of Meaning*. The first application of the methods of componential analysis within the framework of transformational grammar was Katz and Fodor 'The structure of a semantic theory' (reprinted in Rosenberg and Travis (eds.) *Readings in the Philosophy of Language*). The most complete discussion of problems in semantics by Katz is arguably *Semantic Theory*, but for a further detailed defence of his position that a semantic marker (equivalent to a primitive component of meaning) needs no characterisation other than a conceptual one see Katz 'Logic and language: an examination of recent criticisms of intensionalism' s. 6. This position is also defended, against a truth-based theory of meaning, by Harman in 'Meaning and semantics'. For further references on componential analysis, see the recommended reading for chapter 6.

3
Meaning and truth

3.1 Tarski's truth definition and sentence meaning

The attempt to explain the basis of meaning in terms of the relationship between a word and the object it may be used to refer to has a long tradition in philosophy. Recently however a rather different starting point for a theory of meaning has been advocated. In line with work in logic by Tarski, a logician whose theory of truth put forward in 1933 is now widely held by philosophers, it has been suggested that it is the characterisation of what we mean by talking of the meaning of a sentence that is the basis for a semantic theory, and not the characterisation of word meaning. Tarski proposed for formal languages constructed by logicians, that a definition of truth could be given for a language if for each sentence of the language[1] a rule schema can predict correctly the formula

S is true if and only if p

where S is the name of the sentence (i.e. a mere spelling out of the sequence of symbols making up the sentence) and p the conditions which guarantee the truth of that sentence. The significance of this suggestion for logic is of course not our concern here. However it has been claimed (Davidson 1967a) that Tarski's formula for a theory of truth can also provide the basis of a theory of meaning for natural languages. The suggestion is that to know the meaning of a sentence is to know under what conditions that sentence would be true. To take Tarski's classic example, to know the meaning of the string of words making up the sentence *Snow is white* is to know what conditions have

---

[1] In fact he was referring not to sentences of natural language but to statements of a formal logic. Cf. 3.4.1 below for a discussion of the distinction between *sentence* and *statement*.

to pertain in order for the sentence *Snow is white* to be true. This is standardly expressed by the formula

Snow is white is true if and only if snow is white

and it is claimed that we have a complete theory of meaning for a language if we have a rule formulation which can provide a sentence analogous to the formula just given for each sentence of the language. In other words a complete theory of meaning for a language involves a matching procedure between sentences and sets of conditions which when applied to each of the infinite sentences of a language automatically yields a sentence of the form

S is true if and only if p

where, as with the Tarskian formula for a theory of truth, S is the name of the sentence and *p* is the set of conditions under which that sentence is true.

The initial reaction of linguists when they are first introduced to this theory of meaning is almost invariably either one of impatience or one of bewilderment. On the one hand, it is often seen as trivial and uninformative to require of a semantic theory that it generate an infinite set of sentences of the form

S is true if and only if p

where the one example given as illustration is

Snow is white is true if and only if snow is white

On the other hand, the connection between an explanation of sentence meaning and an account of conditions for the truth of sentences does not seem as transparent as, say, the connection between an explanation of word meaning and an account in terms of concepts. The reaction of bewilderment is perhaps justified, since expositions of this view tend to presuppose an understanding of Tarski's theory of truth and are therefore often opaque to linguists. The reaction of impatient dismissal however is not. The formula

Snow is white is true if and only if snow is white

is quite misleading if it is taken at face value as a simple pairing of a sequence of strings which make up the sentence with the sentence itself. The pairing which a theory of meaning of this kind presents as an explanation of meaning is between the name of the sentence, i.e. the sequence of items of that sentence *without* any account of their interpretation (on the left hand side of the formula) with a set of conditions minimally guaranteeing the truth of that sentence (on the right hand side of the formula). Since, it is claimed, these conditions constitute the meaning of the sentence, a convenient way of referring to them is by using the sentence itself. Hence the formula containing the name of the sentence and the sentence itself. Furthermore this pairing between an uninterpreted string and a set of truth conditions must be by a general formulation simply by virtue of the infiniteness of natural languages. So on this view of semantics, semantic interpretation involves a set of rules automatically pairing each sentence of the language with the appropriate set of conditions.

That rules of semantic interpretation involve a pairing of an uninterpreted string and something else corresponding to the interpretation of that string is uncontentious. That this interpretation is in fact to be equated with a set of conditions for the truth of that sentence is more controversial. In order to grasp the basic insight which such a theory of meaning purports to capture, consider a sentence such as *A boy hurried to his home*. If we try to explain the meaning of this sentence, we would presumably say, at least, that it meant that some individual who had the qualities which we standardly attribute to boys (such as being male and not adult) went to the place where he lived with a particular fast kind of movement which we characterise as hurrying. Suppose on the other hand, we attempt to specify the conditions under which we would agree that the same sentence was true. We would presumably say that the sentence would be true if some individual who had the qualities which we standardly attribute to boys went to the place where he lived with a particular fast kind of movement which we call hurrying. That is to say, at least for a straightforward declarative sentence such as *A boy hurried to his home*, in specifying the conditions that have to hold for a sentence to be true, we are in effect characterising what we take to be the meaning of that sentence.

So far then I have put forward as the basis of a theory of meaning the characterisation of sentence meaning in terms of conditions necessary for a sentence to be true, and I have equated this with the formula

$$S \text{ means that p} \equiv S \text{ is true if and only if p}$$

There are many problems with this equation. Perhaps chief of these is
that the schema given by the formula

S is true if and only if p

cannot in fact be equated as it stands with the claim that to give the
meaning of a sentence is to state (all and only) the conditions necessary
for its truth, for there is no guarantee written into the formula that some
sentence S will be paired only with the condition or conditions necessary
for its truth. Consider the formula again. What it states is that some
condition p will constitute the meaning of S if and only if p is true when
S is true. But this lets in too many cases. Take the pair of sentences
The sun is shining, *The sky is blue*. It may well be the case that when the
sun is shining, the sky is blue, but we certainly would not wish to
deduce from this either that the sky's being blue is the unique condition
which guarantees the truth of the string *The sun is shining* or, worse, that
the sky's being blue is a specification of the meaning of the string *The
sun is shining*. Yet the formula allows this as a possible pairing. Furthermore, the schema does not differentiate between the substitution of S
and p to yield

Snow is white is true if and only if grass is green

on the one hand and on the other the substitution of S and p to yield
such formulae as

> *A boy hurried to his home* is true if and only if a male child
> quickly went to the place where he lived
> *John killed Bill* is true if and only if John caused Bill to die
> *Christ is immortal* is true if and only if Christ lives for ever

Yet it is only if we can guarantee the matching of synonymous pairs
such as represented in this latter group of formulae[1] that we can fulfil
the conditions of adequacy listed in chapter 1 and give an account of
word meaning and its relation to sentence meaning. What the formula
allows is a matching between sentences which happen both to share the
same truth value, with no distinction between sentence pairs which
coincidentally share the same truth value and sentence pairs which
necessarily share the same truth value; but what we require is a much
more restrictive matching between only those sentences which must

---

[1] I am assuming here that the pairs in question are synonymous, since any
disagreement over particular pairs does not affect the principle.

have the same truth value. In order then to exclude pairings of a sentence name such as *Snow is white* and a sentence such as *Grass is green*, we have to strengthen the formula so that the contingent coincidence of two sentences happening to be true is not sufficient to meet the condition of the schema. More specifically, in order to generate just the right pairings, the relationship between an uninterpreted sequence of words making up a sentence and truth conditions constituting the interpretation of that sequence must be a necessary dependence, independent of how the circumstances which determine whether the sentence is true or false might alter. Thus our formula

$$S \text{ means that p} \equiv S \text{ is true if and only if p}$$

has to be strengthened to

$$S \text{ means that p} \equiv \text{Necessarily } S \text{ is true if and only if p}$$

This more restrictive formula is now equatable with a characterisation of sentence meaning as the set of conditions minimally guaranteeing the truth of that sentence. In other words our formula now captures the insight that to give the meaning of a sentence is to give the set of conditions which are both necessary and sufficient for the truth of that sentence. This additional qualification of *necessary and sufficient* is essential, for notice first that John's having brutally murdered Bill is a sufficient condition for the truth of the sentence *John caused Bill's death*, and secondly that Bill's dying is a necessary condition for the truth of the same sentence. Yet neither correspond to the meaning of that sentence: the first condition though sufficient for its truth is not a necessary one; and the second though necessary for the truth of the sentence is not a sufficient one. More generally, the set of the conditions required in the specification of what a sentence means is the set of conditions which is both necessary *and* sufficient for the truth of the sentence.

It must be pointed out immediately that this revision of the Tarskian formula to become

$$S \text{ means that p} \equiv \text{Necessarily } S \text{ is true if and only if p}$$

is extremely controversial, and would in fact be disputed by almost all logicians and philosophers. For by invoking the concept of necessity, we leave the straight and narrow path represented by a theory of meaning based on the relative security of a Tarskian theory of truth and enter a veritable hornet's nest of philosophical problems.[1]

[1] Some philosophers currently prefer an account of natural languages in

3.2 **Truth conditions and word meaning**

Before entering into any consideration of the difficulties posed by characterising sentence meaning in terms of necessary truth, we need to make clear the relationship between word meaning and sentence meaning which such an account assumes, for this relationship plays a central part in the dispute about necessity. I pointed out in chapter 2 (p. 11) that, of these two concepts, only one stands in need of independent explanation: if word meaning is given the independent characterisation, then sentence meaning could be given a derivative characterisation in terms of word meaning; and if sentence meaning is given the independent characterisation then the meaning of words could be explained in terms of their contribution to sentence meaning. It is this latter course which a truth-based account of meaning assumes.

What is the precise nature of the relation between the meaning a word has and the meaning a sentence has? It is an assumption standard in linguistic semantics that semantic theory must give an account of the compositional nature of sentence meaning, of the way in which the interpretation of a sentence is dependent on the interpretation of the words[1] of that sentence and the structural relations which hold between those words. If on the basis of the previous section of this chapter, we now assume that a specification of the interpretation that a sentence has is a specification of the conditions necessary and sufficient for the truth of that sentence, then our account of word meaning must be in terms of the systematic contribution a word makes to the truth conditions of sentences in which it occurs. This view is arguably not counter-intuitive. For consider the sentences (1)–(4).

(1) The cat chased the dog.
(2) The little boy chased his sister.
(3) Bill chased the rolling stone.
(4) The cat followed the dog.

terms of truth simpliciter, but this option is not open to linguists since, as these philosophers themselves admit (cf. the introduction to Evans and McDowell 1976), though such an account may give insight into problems of reference and truth (which are of prime interest to philosophers), it does not provide a theory of meaning.

[1] I am assuming here and throughout this chapter that there is no indeterminacy in the term *word* itself and that each word has but one interpretation. Cf. 6.1 below for a discussion of the term *word* and the problem of multiple interpretations of words, and chapter 8 for a general discussion of ambiguity.

Each of (1)–(3) share a certain set of truth conditions, that the object referred to by the expression in the position of grammatical subject is moving in a particular fast way after the object, which is also moving, which is referred to by the expression in position of grammatical object. Furthermore the conditions necessary for the truth of (1) differ from those necessary for the truth of (4) solely in respect of the meaning difference between *chase* and *follow*, one specific difference being that *follow* carries no suggestion of speed.[1] Thus it seems clear that the interpretations assigned to words contribute in a systematic way to the truth conditions of sentences in which they occur. On this view then, a dictionary entry characterising the meaning of a word is in fact a schematic representation of its contribution to sets of truth conditions which comprise the meaning of sentences. In other words, we are dealing with a two-way dependence: the interpretation a sentence is given depends on the interpretation of the words in that sentence, but an explanation of the interpretation of those words is an account of how they contribute to the interpretation of sentences in which they occur. There is no vicious circularity in this, for one of the terms, *sentence meaning*, is given an independent characterisation. This inter-relation between word meaning and sentence meaning has been most clearly explained by Quine (1967: 306).

The unit of communication is the sentence and not the word. This point of semantical theory was long obscured by the undeniable primacy, in one respect, of words. Sentences being limitless in number and words limited, we necessarily understand most sentences by construction from antecedently familiar words. Actually there is no conflict here. We can allow the sentences a full monopoly of 'meaning' in some sense, without denying that the meaning must be worked out. Then we can say that knowing words is knowing how to work out the meanings of sentences containing them. Dictionary definitions are mere clauses in a recursive definition of the meanings of sentences.

As Quine points out, the interpretation of the sentences of a language must be explained compositionally in terms of the combination of the words making up those sentences, for it is the set of words in a language which is finite, and listable, not the set of sentences.

How, one might ask, does the characterisation of word meaning and the consequent requirement that the account of sentence meaning for any language be compositional, relate to the revised formula for a truth-conditional semantics:

[1] I am ignoring here the interpretation in which *follow* is understood temporally. Cf. p. 28 n. 1 above.

$$S \text{ means that } p \equiv \text{Necessarily } S \text{ is true if and only if } p$$

Recall that this formula is a mere schema. What it represents is the commitment of such a theory to providing for any language an infinite set of such sentences, corresponding to the sentences of a language. And the set of sentences which this formula schematises is a pairing between the uninterpreted sentences of the language (characterised as *S*) and their interpretations, sets of truth conditions (characterised as *p*). The burden of the theoretical account, which we have not yet touched upon, is to state the general principles (semantic rules) which underlie the pairing of a sentence with its truth conditions. And this is where the compositional nature of sentence meaning arises. For the specification of such a semantic theory will involve a precise statement of the regularities whereby for each and every sentence of the language, the meanings of words as specified in the dictionary combine to form the meanings of sentences. We shall consider in some detail one account of how this might be done in chapters 6 and 7. For the moment suffice it to say that the program for a truth-based theory of meaning is to devise a set of semantic rules which provide a principled way of mapping an uninterpreted string of symbols constituting a sentence onto an interpretation of that string (the interpretation in each case being a set of conditions) via an interpretation of its constituent parts.

3.3 **Meaning and necessary truth**

Why is the concept of necessary truth such a thorny one? A detailed account of necessary truth is beyond the bounds of this book, but, briefly, there are two reasons why the concept of necessity particular to natural language (called *analytic truth*) is held in such wide disrepute. In the first place it has been argued most convincingly, by Quine (Quine 1953c: 20–46), that the terms *analytic truth*, *meaning*, *definition* and *synonymy*, are interdefinable and that in consequence any proposed explanation of one term by means of the others is circular, and an essentially empty exercise. So if we propose to explain synonymy in terms of meaning, and meaning in terms of analytic truth, then it is essential that analytic truth be explained in terms of some independent construct if the explanation of meaning is to have any content at all. However the standard move in explaining analytic truth *is* to refer to meaning. In the second place, Quine has also argued (Quine 1953c) that a clear distinction cannot be drawn between sentences which are analytically true and sentences which are contingently true, and that in consequence the distinction should be abandoned entirely.

Let us look at the problem a little more closely and retrace the steps which led to this impasse. The suggestion that sentence meaning be characterised in terms of conditions for the truth of sentences is an attempt to explain the concept of meaning in terms of some other concept which is better understood and hence open to more rigorous testing. In particular the explanation of meaning in terms of truth seems promising initially since theories of truth are, though by no means universally agreed on, very much more articulated than theories of meaning. However the move from the Tarskian formula for a truth definition to a formula invoking the concept of necessity has to be made in order to guarantee that an uninterpreted string, the name of a sentence, be mapped only onto a set of conditions corresponding to its meaning and not onto a set of conditions which by coincidence happen to share the same truth value. Yet, in so doing, we confront all the problems which face analyticity, for the concept of necessity being invoked is precisely that of analytic truth. Analytically true sentences are sentences such as (5)–(8), which are standardly characterised as being true in virtue of their meaning.

(5) If John is a bachelor, then John has never been married.
(6) If John ran home, then he did go home.
(7) If John chased Bill to the station, then he followed Bill to the station.
(8) Spinsters are unmarried women.

Just as in our revised truth definition, these sentences are necessarily true, quite independent of contingent circumstances, by virtue of the relations between the words of which the sentences are made up. Hence the characterisation of analytic truth as truth in virtue of meaning, or equivalently as truth in virtue of the semantic rules of the language. But to explain the semantic rules of the language in terms of a particular kind of necessity (analytic truth), and then to explain that same necessity in terms of the semantic rules of the language is of course no explanation at all. If moreover the concept of necessity in terms of which the so-called explanation is given is itself cast in doubt, then the explanation is not merely circular, but entirely misconceived.[1]

---

[1] Quine's charge of circularity would of course be side-stepped if an independent account of analytic truth could be given, and one such move

The attack that the concept of analytic truth is an empty one, non-distinct from contingent truths, is based on the claim that no clear-cut distinction can be drawn between statements which are true in virtue of their structure and those which are true in virtue of external circumstances, and Quine's mode of attack at least in part was to take particular examples and demonstrate how for these sentences it is hard to determine the point at which the distinction should be made. Now this move is not a particularly convincing one. For to admit that some cases may be hard to determine is not sufficient cause for denying the concept of analytic truth altogether. As Fodor, Bever and Garrett have pointed out (Fodor, Bever and Garrett 1974: 178–9), there are cases which are indubitably true solely in virtue of properties of language. Not only do we have (9)–(11):

(9) If John is a bachelor, then he is not a married man.
(10) If Edmund ran to the station, then he went to the station.
(11) If that woman is married to that man, then that man is her husband.

but also such uncontentious examples as (12)–(13):

(12) If Sue hit Lucy, then Lucy was hit by Sue.
(13) If it is possible that Jethro will be at the party, then that Jethro will be at the party is possible.

On the basis even of these, one has grounds for doubting the force of Quine's suggestion that the concept of analytic truth simply does not exist.

The charge of circularity is more substantial. It is much harder to escape and, if justified, threatens to render the whole exercise of explaining meaning in terms of truth conditions vacuous and no improvement on an explanation of meaning in terms of concepts. There is however reason to think that the attack of circularity is not as convincing as it

is to characterise analytic truth as truth in all possible worlds. This program however provides no solution to the problem of meaning, for the delimitation of the relevant set of possible worlds necessary for a characterisation of the term *possible world* returns full circle to the term *semantic rule*: the set of possible worlds relevant to explicating the concept of analytic truth would be the set of worlds in which the semantic rules hold (cf. Lewis 1973: 4–8). The increasing body of work done by logicians within the domain of possible-world semantics thus seems to offer little consolation to linguists searching for a solution to the characterisation of meaning in natural languages.

first appears, and the reason is an indirect one. Consider the parallel case of logic. Logic is the study of a necessary truth generally agreed to be distinct from analytic truth[1] – logical truth – as exemplified by the arguments listed below as (14) and (15).

(14) If Socrates is mortal, Socrates is a man.
Socrates is mortal.
Therefore Socrates is a man.

(15) All men are liars.
The President is a man.
Therefore the President is a liar.

In order to explain the concept of logical truth, logics are set up, with rules of logic articulated precisely in order to preserve logical truth. So if we ask for an explanation of logical truth, the only answer is truth in virtue of the laws of logic. If however we go on to ask for an explanation of the laws of logic, the only answer is in terms of logical truth. The point is this. Quine's attack of circularity on theories of meaning and on the concept of analytic truth has caused widespread scepticism as to the value of explanations of meaning in terms of necessity, and indeed as to the possibility of giving any substantial account of meaning at all. Yet logicians do not in general extend their scepticism to their own field where a parallel argument pertains. Even Quine himself fluctuates between embracing this position of extreme scepticism in which no statement, even those of logic, is necessarily true and immune from revision, and the rather weaker position in which at least the logical truths are said to be necessary.[2] It is certainly a radical move for philosophers to adhere to the view that the entire tradition of explaining logical truth by constructing logics is an empty exercise beset by circularity, and not many join Quine in such a rejection of their subject. But if it is not generally thought by logicians that constructing logics is an exercise without explanatory power, then as a linguist one has reason, *pace* Quine, to remain optimistic at least in principle[3] not only about the program of explaining meaning, but more specifically about explaining meaning in terms of truth conditions.

[1] In 3.4.2 below I present arguments to suggest that there is in any case no distinction in principle between logical truth and analytic truth.

[2] Compare Quine's position in 'Two dogmas of empiricism' with the less extreme position adopted in Quine 1960 (cf. pp. 57–61).

[3] We shall consider the criticism of truth-conditional semantics that it is insufficient as a theory of meaning in 3.4.3 and 5.3 below.

3.4 **Truth conditions and logical form**

The characterisation of meaning in terms of truth conditions is often said to be equivalent to equating meaning with the logical form of a sentence. In order to assess this equivalence, we must first consider what is normally meant by the term *logical form*. Let us recall first the general purpose in constructing a logic. The logician sets out to characterise patterns of valid inference such as (14) and (15) (cf. p. 33 above), (16) and (17),

> (16) Either Socrates is a man or Socrates is not mortal.
> Socrates is mortal.
> Therefore Socrates is a man.
> (17) Socrates is a man and all men are mortal.
> Therefore Socrates is mortal.

and corresponding necessary truths such as (18),

> (18) If Socrates is a man and all men are mortal, then Socrates is mortal.

Part of this program is to reconstruct the logical form of arguments (or such necessarily true statements as (18)), and then to show how the validity of the argument or statement in question follows by general rule. Accordingly the logical form of an argument is a statement of the properties of an argument from which the relevant valid inferences can be shown to follow by an automatic procedure. For example, since we can deduce the validity of argument (14) without any interpretation of the words in the sentence other than *if* (symbolised by ' $\supset$ '), the logical form assigned to this argument is

> $P \supset Q$
> P
> Therefore Q

(A similar point holds for the argument listed as (16).) However we cannot deduce the validity of the argument listed as (17) without access to the interpretation of the sentence-parts, for (17) contains three different sentences (the same point holds for (15) and (18)). There is no valid inference:

> P & Q
> Therefore R

If however we isolate the interpretation of the quantifier *all*, we are in a position to show the validity of the argument. Accordingly the logical form assigned to (17) is

> Ma & (x) (Mx ⊃ Nx)[1]
> Therefore Na

As these two arguments demonstrate, according to the central sense of *logical form* (attributed to arguments), the logical form of a statement varies according to the structure of the argument: the statement *Socrates is a man* is assigned a different logical form in each of these two arguments. However a standard extension from the use of *logical form* in connection with the form of arguments is in connection with statements. Just as an argument has a logical form from which the inferences can be derived by general rule, the logical form of a statement may be said to be a specification from which all inferences relevant to the role of that statement in arguments can be deduced by general rule.[2] According to this extended sense of *logical form*, the logical form of *All men are mortal* is not merely 'P' as required for the argument listed as (14) but the more detailed specification

> (x) (Mx ⊃ Nx)

as required for (17).

How is this concept of logical form, which is predicated, in logic, of statements, comparable to a specification of truth conditions for a sentence? There are three apparent points of difference between these two formulae. First the concept of logical form is attributed to statements, but the concept of having a truth condition we have attributed to sentences. Secondly, the type of truth which logical forms are set up to characterise is logical truth, the so-called 'truth of reason', whereas it is analytic truth which we invoked in discussing truth conditions on sentences. Finally, the characterisation of logical form is in terms of inferences, whereas the characterisation of meaning is in terms of truth conditions. Each of these distinctions is more apparent than real.

---

[1] *M* stands for the predicate *is a man*, *a* stands for a proper name (in this case *Socrates*), *N* for the predicate *is mortal*, and (*x*)(...) stands for *for all x such that* . . . So the formula reads informally as ' 'a' is a man and for all individuals x, if x is a man then x is mortal. Therefore 'a' is mortal.'

[2] Strawson refers to the logical power of a statement. Cf. Strawson 1952: 50.

35

3.4.1   Sentence *v.* statement

The distinction between *sentence* and *statement*, though real enough, is one which currently tends to be glossed over, both by philosophers and linguists. The term *statement*[1] is used in logic to refer to the content of what a sentence is used to assert on any particular occasion. For example, in saying the sentence *I am very hot* on this day, 11 May 1977, the statement I am making is that Ruth Kempson is very hot on the eleventh day of May 1977, but that same sentence would be being used to make a different statement if uttered by someone else. Now it has been argued that it is only statements which can be said to have a truth value, true or false, and not sentences (Strawson 1950). On this view then, only statements play a part in arguments, and accordingly only statements can be said to have a logical form. Indeed, in general, it is statements that logicians consider as their domain of study, and not sentences. So it seems that there is a radical difference between the terms *statement* and *sentence* and hence between talking about logical form (which can be attributed to statements) and truth conditions (which we have attributed to sentences). However on this traditional view of the sentence–statement distinction, it is not possible to talk of truth conditions on sentences either, since this involves predicting truth of sentences, which is said not to be legitimate. In thus characterising sentence meaning in terms of truth conditions we have already flown in the face of this view, and if this move is justified, then there is no further conflict in talking of the logical form of sentences. While there are considerable problems of detail in assigning truth values to sentences (cf. Wiggins 1971: 21–3, Davidson 1967a), the view that sentences can be said to have a truth value relative to a context is not thought to be as controversial a view as it was once thought to be, and indeed it is a view which is now commonly assumed by philosophers without argument. In accordance with this view, I have already assumed that it is not illegitimate to assign truth conditions to sentences, and if this assumption is justified, there is no conflict in extending the concept of logical form from that of statements to sentences. Since the logical form of a statement is a specification from which all inferences (relevant to logical truth) can be drawn, I shall therefore refer to the logical form of a sentence as a specification from which all inferences can be deduced by general rule.

[1]   The term *proposition* is often used with this sense, but not invariably. Cf. Lemmon 1966 for a discussion of the distinctions between the terms.

3.4.2   *Logical truth v. analytic truth*

The second distinction between the characterisation of the logical form of a statement and the specification of truth conditions on sentences related to the distinction between logical truth and analytic truth. The representation of logical form given to a statement (or sentence) is decided on the basis of the inferences relating to logical truth, whereas an assignment of truth conditions to sentences relates to analytic truth, as we have already seen. The distinction between logical truth and analytic truth is however not clear-cut and not of obvious relevance to linguists. For in analysing the logical form of an argument in a given language, the logician chooses to isolate the words on which the structure of the argument depends. Thus in the case of the arguments in (14)–(18) (pp. 34–3), the logicians' interest centres on the inferences contributed by the presence of the words *or*, *if*, *and* and *all*, and not such words as *Socrates* and *man*. The reasons for this distinction is said to be that whatever proper name is submitted for *Socrates*, and whatever class term is substituted for *man*, the argument remains valid. In characterising the nature of a valid argument, a logician is in effect giving a characterisation of the contribution to the logical form of an argument made by a section, albeit a small one, of a natural language, namely by items such as *and*, *or*, *not*, *if*, *all*, *some*. But to a linguist, there is no difference in principle between the inferences of (14)–(18) and the inferences between the sentences in (19) and (20).

> (19) Bill is a younger son.
>   Bill either has or had a brother.
> (20) Bill is a bachelor.
>   Bill has never been married.

The argument in (14) depends on the interpretation of *if*, the argument in (15) on *all*, the argument in (16) on *or* and *not*, the argument in (17) and (18) on *and* and *all*, the argument in (19) on *son* and *brother*, the argument in (20) on *bachelor* and *married*. Each argument is dependent on inferences which can be drawn by virtue of the meaning of the words of which the argument is made up. A linguist therefore has no motive for isolating (14)–(18) from (19) and (20): in characterising the nature of meaning in natural languages, he is committed to characterising the basis of each of these inferences.

In any case, as an increasing number of so-called non-standard logics are being devised, and the sub-section of natural language analysed by logicians is steadily increasing, the distinction between logical truth and analytic truth becomes harder to maintain. There are now logics of knowledge (epistemic logic), logics of belief (doxastic logic), tense logics, modal logics (characterising the concepts of necessity and possibility), to mention but a few. Thus an increasing number of valid inferences in natural language are now characterised under the domain of logic, and there seems no reason to distinguish between inferences such as (14) and (16) (characterised by Aristotelian logic), (15), (17) and (18) (characterised by predicate calculus), (21) (characterised by epistemic logic), and (19) and (20) which are not characterised by any logic.

> (21) Bill knows that he has cancer.
> Bill has cancer.

One might indeed say that it is simply that logicians are gradually extending their interests to larger and larger sub-sections of natural language. But if this is so, then the distinction between the inferences pertaining to logical truth and the inferences pertaining to analytic truth is not one of great importance to linguists. In line with this position, I shall assume that it should be ignored.[1]

3.4.3 *Truth conditions and entailment*

Granted that sentences can be assigned a logical form, and that no non-arbitrary distinction can be drawn between logical truth and analytic truth, it is now possible to see why characterising the meaning of a sentence in terms of truth conditions on that sentence is said to be equivalent to characterising the meaning of a sentence in terms of its logical form. For the logical form of a sentence is a specification from which all inferences (whether pertaining to analytic truth or logical truth) can be drawn by general rule. So for example, in giving the logical form of a sentence such as *Bill is a bachelor*, we must provide a specification from which the following inferences, among others, can be derived: *Bill has never been married*,[2] *Bill is a man, Bill is an adult, Bill is human*. But these inferences are conditions necessary for the truth of

---

[1] Cf. however Fodor, Fodor and Garrett 1975 who, on the basis of psycho-logical-reality evidence, argue against a level of semantic representation, but in favour of a level of logical form, where logical form remains for them the level from which inferences relevant to logical truth can be drawn.

[2] I am assuming that *bachelor* has one meaning. Cf. 6.1 below for a discussion of the term *word* and the problem of homonymy.

the sentence *Bill is a bachelor*. How is it that this is so? Recall that the meaning to be assigned to a sentence was characterised as the set of conditions necessary and sufficient for the truth of a sentence. So, in the case of our example, in order for it to be true of someone that he is a bachelor, it must be true that he has never been married (not having been married is a necessary condition of bachelorhood). But this being so, it follows automatically that if it is true of someone that he is a bachelor it will also be true of him that he has never been married. And so on for every sentence: any condition necessary for the truth of a sentence will by definition simultaneously be an inference of that sentence.

It may seem that in demonstrating that a specification of conditions necessary for the truth of a sentence is simultaneously a specification of inferences of a sentence, I have equated the two, demonstrating that a specification of the conditions both necessary and sufficient for the truth of a sentence is itself a specification of *the* inferences of a sentence. If this were so, we would have reached a paradox, for there is an infinite number of inferences which can be drawn from a single sentence and we would thus be unable to state the meaning of any single sentence. However this is not so. The identification is between the set of conditions which are both necessary and sufficient for the truth of a sentence and the logical form of the sentence, for the concept of logical form (whether of sentences or statements) is not itself a specification of inferences, but a specification from which inferences can be drawn by general rule. Another term which has been used in place of *inference* is *entailment*. The relation of entailment is said to hold between two sentences,[1] S_1 and S_2, if when S_1 is true S_2 must be true: in other words S_2 is a necessary condition for the truth of S_1. Given this definition of entailment, and the characterisation of logical form just outlined, we can say that to give the meaning of a sentence in terms of the necessary and sufficient conditions for the truth of that sentence is to provide a specification from which the entailments of a sentence can be derived by an automatic procedure.

This formulation now allows us to see why a truth-based semantics is a forceful contender for the semantics of natural language. For by its very definition, it fulfils the basic conditions of adequacy that we placed on semantic theories in chapter 1: it provides the basis for a systematic account of the relation of sentence meaning and word meaning (cf. 3.2 above), and it allows for the automatic prediction of the entailments of

[1] Being a logical relation, it is in fact defined to hold between statements.

every sentence of the language. Moreover since the semantic relations of entailment, synonymy and contradiction are all interdependent, the successful characterisation of one of these terms will guarantee that the other relations can be accounted for. Synonymy for example is defined by logicians as mutual entailment, so by definition a characterisation of meaning in terms of truth conditions will guarantee that when two sentences have identical truth conditions, they will mean the same. This procedure will – if the semantic rules are specified correctly – equate such pairs as *Bill is a bachelor, Bill has always been unmarried*, and *Bill is Sue's husband, Bill is married to Sue*, etc.[1] Contradiction, being the converse of entailment, presents no more of a problem. If we have predicted for any sentence S_1 its set of entailments, $S_2, S_3, S_4 \ldots$, we can predict by general rule that S_1 will stand in a relation of contradiction with the set of sentences not-S_2, not-S_3, not-$S_4 \ldots$ So for example *John murdered Mary* stands in a relation of contradiction to *John did not kill Mary, John did not cause Mary to die, Mary did not die*, each of which is a negation of an entailment of *John murdered Mary*. The one further requirement, that a theory of meaning provide a characterisation of ambiguity, is also straightforwardly met in principle, for a theory of truth conditions will assign to any sentence with more than one meaning, more than one set of truth conditions; and this corresponds precisely to intuitions about sentences having more than one meaning. Consider for example *The helicopter landed on the bank*, which is ambiguous according as *bank* is interpreted as the bank of a river or a financial institution. The conditions for the truth of one interpretation of this sentence are clearly independent of the conditions for the truth of the sentence under the other interpretation. Thus though this characterisation by no means solves all problems of ambiguity (cf. chapter 8 below), it does provide a means of correctly isolating the set of ambiguous sentences. So it appears that in relating the concept of meaning to the concepts of logical form and truth condition, we are able to fulfil the minimal conditions of adequacy that were specified in chapter 1, given of course that the semantic rules for any language are specified correctly (cf. chapters 6 and 7 below).

[1] I am assuming that sentences such as these are synonymous, though it has sometimes been doubted whether two sentences are ever truly synonymous. This latter view depends on a wider delimitation of semantics than that proposed here. Cf. chapter 5 below for a discussion of the distinction between semantics and pragmatics as part of an over-all linguistic theory.

3.5 **Sentence meaning and the non-declaratives**

In this chapter we have seen how the interdependence between meaning and truth can provide the basis for a theory of meaning, provided that the concept of truth invoked is that of analytic truth rather than simply of truth itself. Furthermore, this foundation for a semantic theory seems promising in so far as it allows for the fulfilment of all the initial requirements of adequacy that I outlined for semantic theories in chapter 1. However because this account of meaning is founded on the concept of analyticity, the need for a solution to Quine's charge of circularity remains of paramount importance, a need which is at present quite unfulfilled (though cf. p. 31 n. 1 above). Moreover, we have glossed over distinctions such as the *sentence–statement* distinction and the distinction between logical truth and analytic truth which many would feel are of considerably greater importance than I have suggested.

Even if we ignore these problems and assume that a truth-based account of meaning does at least have some content, it can be criticised on the basis of its insufficiency. There are a number of areas of meaning which undoubtedly must be characterised in some way by an over-all theory of language, and which many have claimed cannot be incorporated within a truth-conditional account of meaning. Such an account will therefore either have been falsified, since it will make the wrong predictions with respect to these problems, or at least it will be insufficient as an account of meaning in natural languages. Chief among these areas[1] which fall outside the domain of a truth-based theory of meaning are non-indicative sentences – questions and commands – and sentences which are used for performative utterances (see below). Many people have pointed out that only declarative sentences can be used to make statements (cf. 3.4.1 above), and so only these can be true or false. There is no sense in which questions or imperatives can be said to be either. It seems therefore, at the very least, that a truth-conditional semantics only accounts for one type of sentence – declarative indicative sentences: it has no means of characterising what we mean by using interrogative or imperative sentences. However it has been argued further that it is not only interrogatives and imperatives which a truth-conditional semantics cannot account for. There are many sentences in a

---

[1]   A small and unhomogeneous group of lexical items also seems to resist analysis in terms of truth conditions. These include *even, but, deplore*, and some uses of *if*. Cf. Cohen 1971, Wilson 1975, and Walker 1975.

declarative form which are no more descriptions of events than are questions or commands. Consider for example (22)–(24).

(22) I promise that I will be there.
(23) I hereby agree that I was wrong.
(24) I suggest that he is innocent.

Sentences such as these were first noticed by the philosopher J. L. Austin, who drew attention to the fallaciousness of assuming even that declarative sentences were invariably descriptions of events, which would be said to be true or false depending on the correspondence or lack of it between the sentence and the non-linguistic event which the sentence described. Sentences of this second type were said by Austin to be used for performative utterances, so-called because they are not used for describing anything but on the contrary constitute actions. For example the very utterance of a sentence such as (22) itself constitutes the performance of the action of promising, the utterance of (23) is itself an action of agreement, and the utterance of (24) the action of suggesting. This is in dramatic contrast to most declarative sentences: the utterance of *I enter the stage from the back* does not itself constitute the act of entering, nor is the utterance of *I can hear you now* itself the action of hearing. Now these performative utterances are particularly important for linguists because not only do they seem to resist a truth-based account of their meaning (though cf. 5.3.1 below), but they play an important part in an alternative account of semantics which stems from Austin's work on performative utterances – speech act semantics. This account of semantics has been developed since Austin's original exposition in 1962 and has become one of the strongest influences on linguists currently working in semantics.

The central task for semantics, according to those linguists who turn to theories about the speech act for the solution to the problem of meaning, is to explain the meaning of a sentence, not in terms of some relation between sentences and the non-linguistic states of affairs those sentences are used to represent and according to which they will be either true or false, but in terms of what a speaker does with a sentence, what act he carries out, and what assumptions he has (called *presuppositions*) in carrying out the act. If the problem of sentence meaning is approached in this way, there is no need to distinguish between sentences which can be characterised in terms of truth conditions and those which cannot. The importance of speech act semantics is accordingly that it is by no means restricted to explaining (a sub-set of) declarative sentences. On the contrary, it is intended to capture the full range of linguistic actions that speakers carry out with language – statements,[1] questions, commands, promises, suggestions, agreements, denials, and so on. So it appears that speech act semantics can explain not only the properties of declarative sentences, as can a truth-conditional semantics, but also many of the areas which prove problematic for truth-conditional semantics. Furthermore, since such an account of meaning does not invoke the concept of a (necessary) truth condition, the problems of analyticity do not arise. For these reasons, speech act theories of semantics provide the most substantial alternatives to truth-based theories of meaning, and so might be considered to give a more general and hence more explanatory characterisation of the nature of meaning in natural languages. It is therefore time to turn to the final alternative that I listed in chapter 2 – the possibility of explaining meaning in terms of the communication process.

RECOMMENDED READING

3.1 Tarski's exposition of his theory of truth was first published in 1933 as 'Projecie prawdy w językach nauk dedukcyjncych' ('The concept of truth in the languages of the deductive sciences') which is translated into English in Tarski *Logic, Semantics, and Metamathematics*. There is also the shorter article 'The semantic conception of truth and the foundations of semantics'. For its application to language, see Davidson, whose best known paper is 'Truth and meaning' (reprinted in Rosenberg and Travis (eds.) *Readings in the Philosophy of Language*). See also his 'Semantics for natural languages' (reprinted in Harman (ed.) *On Noam Chomsky*). The best introduction to Davidsonian semantics to my knowledge is given by Hacker *Why Does Language Matter to Philosophy?* (ch. 12); and this approach to semantics is developed in the papers in Evans and McDowell (eds.) *Meaning and Truth*. Their own introduction to this book gives a clear if technical account of Davidsonian semantics and its problems. Criticisms of the Davidsonian approach to meaning have been made by Katz 'Logic and language: an examination of recent criticisms of intensionalism' s. 3, Dummett 'What is a theory of meaning? (II)', and Chihara 'Davidson's extensional theory of meaning'.

1 The ambiguity in this term is unfortunately often ignored. The content of a speaker's utterance, the logical interpretation of *statement*, is not identical to the act of stating that utterance, the speech act interpretation of *statement*. It is the former which is true or false: it is the latter which only a speech act semantics will characterise.

3.2   An excellent discussion of truth-conditional semantics in general, the need to build in a reference to necessary truth, other problems facing truth-conditional semantics, including the problem of ambiguity, is given by Wiggins 'On sentence-sense, word-sense and difference of word-sense. Towards a philosophical theory of dictionaries'. For a detailed account of Frege's approach to semantics, from which the entire development of twentieth-century semantics by logicians might be said to have stemmed, see Dummett *Frege: Philosophy of Language*, particularly chs. 1, 5, and 6.

3.3   The literature on analyticity is never-ending, but books of readings almost invariably have a sub-section on analytic truth (see Rosenberg and Travis (eds.) *Readings in the Philosophy of Language* and Olshewsky (ed.) *Problems in the Philosophy of Language*, and references cited there). Perhaps the most helpful collection of articles is Sumner and Woods (eds.) *Necessary Truth*. Of all the articles in these collections, Quine's seminal article 'Two dogmas of empiricism' which is reprinted in all these books is the most essential reading, but students should also read the Grice and Strawson reply 'In defence of a dogma'. On the defence of analyticity that the same charge of circularity can be brought against logical truth, see Katz 'Logic and language: an examination of recent criticisms of intensionalism' s. 4, and also Katz and Nagel 'Meaning postulates and semantic theory' s. 8, where it is pointed out that Quine's own position on the necessity of logical truth is not at all clear. Possible-world semantics is associated with what has been called model-theoretic semantics. See Lewis 'General semantics', *Counterfactuals*; Hintikka 'Semantics for propositional attitudes' (reprinted in Linsky (ed.) *Reference and Modality*), 'The semantics of modal notions and the indeterminacy of ontology'; Stalnaker 'A theory of conditionals' (reprinted in Sosa (ed.) *Causation and Conditionals*), 'Pragmatics' s. 1; and Taylor 'States of affairs'. The literature on possible-world semantics does tend to presuppose knowledge of intensional logic and so is often hard for linguistics students to grasp: students may find helpful Martin's short account of model-theoretic semantics in s. 5 of 'Some thoughts on the formal approach to the philosophy of language'. Like almost all other theoretical constructs of semantic theory, the concept of a possible world has been attacked by Quine: see Quine 'On what there is' (*From a Logical Point of View* ch. 1). For a penetrating criticism of Lewis' use of possible worlds, see Richards 'The worlds of David Lewis'. For a critical approach to model-theoretic semantics, see Jardine 'Model-theoretic semantics and natural language' and Potts 'Model theory and linguistics'. See also in this connection Harman 'Logical form'.

3.4   For a representative discussion of the logicians' use of the term *logical form*, students should consult Quine 'Methodological reflections on current linguistic theory', where he makes clear that logical form is a property not of a sentence or a statement but of an argument. This point is also emphasised in J. D. Fodor's excellent introductory article 'Formal linguistics and formal logic'.

3.4.1   The various positions which philosophers have taken about the sentence–statement distinction and its importance is excellently summarised in Lemmon 'Sentences, statements and propositions' (reprinted in Rosenberg and Travis (eds.) *Readings in the Philosophy of Language*), and students should also read Strawson 'On referring' s. 2, and Cartwright 'Propositions'. Both Wiggins in 'Sentence-sense, word-sense and difference of word-sense. Towards a philosophical theory of dictionaries' and Davidson in 'Truth and meaning' also discuss ways in which sentences can be said to have a truth value.

3.4.2   The distinction between logical truth and analytic truth is outlined in Quine *Philosophy of Logic* pp. 47–51. However students should also read Katz 'Logic and language: an examination of recent criticisms of intensionalism' s. 4, where he discusses in detail the concept of logical truth and its non-distinctness from analytic truth. Non-standard logics include logics of knowledge and logics of belief – cf. Hintikka *Knowledge and Belief*, Rescher *Topics in Philosophical Logic* ch. 5; logics of tense – cf. Prior *Past, Present and Future, Time and Tense*, Clifford 'Tense logic and the logic of change', Von Wright *Norm and Action: A Logical Inquiry*; the logic of command – cf. Rescher *The Logic of Commands*, Lemmon 'Deontic logic and the logic of imperatives', Rescher (ed.) *The Logic of Decision and Action*; modal logics – cf. Hughes and Cresswell *An Introduction to Modal Logic* and references cited there; erotetic logic (the logic of questions) – cf. Åqvist *A New Approach to the Logical Theory of Interrogatives, Part I: Analysis*, 'Revised foundations for imperative-epistemic and interrogative logic', Harrah 'A logic of questions and answers', Hintikka 'Questions about questions' and references cited there. Useful collections of papers in these fields are in Rescher *Topics in Philosophical Logic* and Hintikka *Models for Modalities*.

3.4.3   Fodor, Bever and Garrett *The Psychology of Language* ch. 6 pp. 175–88 emphasise the relation between a specification of logical form for a sentence and a specification of the inferences of a sentence. This chapter is also an excellent general introduction to semantics, both to the problem of meaning itself and to the problem of the specification of a semantic component within transformational grammar. Harman 'Deep structure as logical form' identifies logical form as a syntactic level. See also Harman 'Logical form'. See chapter 10 below for an assessment of linguistic arguments suggesting this same conclusion, and chapter 11 for a discussion of logicians' identification of logical form and syntactic structure.

3.5   The adequacy of a truth-conditional semantics rests not only on its internal coherence but also on the extent to which all sentences can be assigned a truth value. White's short introduction, *Truth*, gives an easily assimilatable account of the assignment of truth values to future statements (ch. 3), and this problem is gone into in much greater depth in Dummett 'What is a theory of meaning? II'. Counterfactual conditionals form another set of sentences which threaten to pose problems for a truth-based semantics. See Wilson *Presuppositions and Non-Truth-Conditional Semantics* pp. 120–2 for an argument that their implications cannot be characterised as entailments: but see also Stalnaker 'A theory of conditionals' (reprinted in Sosa (ed.) *Causation and Conditionals*) and Lewis *Counterfactuals* for two proposals within a possible-world semantics. On the question of whether performative utterances can or can not be assigned a truth value, see references to this problem listed in the recommended reading for chapter 5. For general reading on speech act semantics, see the recommended reading for chapter 4. For other examples about which there is disagreement over whether or not they can be handled within a truth-based semantics see Cohen 'Some remarks on Grice's views about the logical particles of natural language', Walker 'Conversational implicatures', Kempson *Presupposition and the Delimitation of Semantics* ch. 8, 8.7 and 8.8, Wilson *Presuppositions and Non-Truth-Conditional Semantics* ch. 6–7. Truth-conditional semantics has been criticised in a more general way by Strawson, in 'Meaning and truth', who favours a Gricean approach to meaning (see the recommended reading for chapter 5), and by Harman, in 'Meaning and semantics', who favours a conceptual approach to meaning.

4

Meaning and language use

4.1 Bloomfield and behaviorism

Since the central function of language is as a vehicle of communication, many people have looked to the process of communication for an explanation of meaning in natural languages. In recent linguistic history this was first suggested in the 1940s when, in rejection of the meaning–concept equation, two linguists independently advocated the specification of meaning in terms of the situation in which sentences are uttered. In England such a suggestion was made by Firth and in America it was made by Bloomfield. Since similar criticisms can be levelled at both accounts and since Bloomfield's account is both more detailed and is also within a more articulated theoretical framework, I shall only consider the latter.

In assessing Bloomfield's, and indeed Firth's, account of semantics, it is important to bear in mind the attitude to scientific theory then prevalent. In contrast to the deductive view of science outlined in chapter 1, the prevailing belief was in a rigid form of inductivism. The job of the scientist, it was believed, was to accumulate facts without any preconceived theory and to expect that a careful sifting of the facts would in the course of time lead to the correct theory. With this emphasis on data collection, the defining property of science was thought to be its method – objective and not swayed by such subjective factors as opinion, guess, or intuition. A consequence of this concern for objectivity was that abstract theoretical constructs were only tolerated as scientific if they could be defined in terms of observable events.

As a committed empiricist, who moreover sought to re-establish linguistics as a science, Bloomfield suggested accordingly that the meaning of a linguistic form has to be analysed in terms of the important elements of the situation in which the speaker utters it. He analysed the situation into three constituent parts:

A speaker's stimulus
B utterance (= speaker's response and hearer's stimulus)
C hearer's response

and his specific suggestion was that the meaning of an utterance consists of the speaker's stimulus and (secondarily) the hearer's response (cf. Bloomfield 1933: 24–6). But the practical event, A, consists not of ideas but of the actual concrete elements of the situation. His stock example consisted of a heroine, Jill, who seeing an apple felt hungry (= A), which stimulated her to respond with an utterance (= B), which in turn acted as a stimulus to the hearer, Jack, whose response is C. Thus if an item such as an apple were part of the meaning of Jill's utterance, it would follow from such a characterisation that the utterance of the item *apple* has as its meaning the object apple. Worse, the contraction of the muscles and the formation of saliva which caused the hunger which caused Jill to utter, say, *I'm hungry – please get me that apple* would also be part of that utterance's meaning. This approach was extended to all aspects of meaning, not merely utterance meaning. So the meaning of the word *hungry* would on this view be the contraction of the stomach muscles and the formation of saliva. But this is nonsensical. There is no sense in which the interpretation of a word is, literally, a contraction of muscles.

To avoid such a naïve identification of word meaning and object, Bloomfield suggested that word meaning could be characterised in terms of the distinctive features of the situation, the meaning of a word being the features common to all situations in which the word is uttered. But such a retraction does not help to save the theory, if the concept of meaning is still expressed in terms of stimuli on the speaker (and hearer). For a given word can be uttered without the object in question being present. Consider for example whether there is necessarily anything common to the situations in which the following set of sentences might be uttered:

(1) Bring me my shirt.
(2) This shirt is frayed.
(3) I need a new shirt.
(4) Shirts were rarely worn before the fourteenth century.
(5) Does your husband wear a size fifteen shirt?

The answer is, bluntly, "No". (1) could be uttered with no shirt in the speech situation: on the contrary the speaker might have only a pair of pants on and the stimulus which causes him to utter (1) is not the sight of the shirt, but the cold which is causing his skin to goose-pimple. An utterance of (2) could be caused by a sensation of tickling on the back of the speaker's neck. (3) similarly; or perhaps by the speaker's finding no shirts in his drawer. (Notice that this same situation could cause the speaker to utter the sentence *Why haven't you washed my shirts?*, yet no theory would want to predict the synonymy of either (2) and (3), or of (3) and the question *Why haven't you washed my shirts?*, even at the level of utterance meaning.) (4) could not characteristically be uttered in anything like the domestic situations so far outlined (where one might attempt to modify the position by referring to an expectation of the presence of the object in question), but in a classroom situation, where the speaker's stimulus might be anything from a desire to prevent the students from asking unanswerable questions, to a desire to pass on knowledge about the domestic setting in former times. Finally the utterance of (5) might be stimulated by nothing more related to the object of a shirt than a poster displayed in the street informing passers-by 'It's only ten days to Christmas'. What these anecdotal speech settings suggest is that the attempt to explain the meaning of words or sentences in terms of the features 'which are common to all the situations that call forth the utterance of the linguistic form' (Bloomfield 1933: 141) was entirely misguided, for there is no such common element.

Bloomfield was by no means the only expounder of a behavioristic theory of meaning, and after Bloomfield a group of psychologists further investigated the possibility of a behavioristic theory of meaning. Quine too has suggested a stimulus–response view of meaning (in accordance with his attack on analyses of meaning in terms of other semantic terms such as necessity, definition, etc.). However, despite the sophistication of a bahavioristic account of meaning such as Quine's, all accounts of meaning in terms of a stimulus–response account of behaviour seem doomed to failure. In order to overcome the obvious fallacy of equating the meaning of the forms of a language with actual speaker stimuli or responses, the standard retreat of behavioristic accounts of meaning is to analyse the meaning of word forms in terms of predispositions to respond on the part of a speaker. But the concept of a predisposition to respond is entirely opaque, with no obvious relation to actual speech situations, and with no more observable content than the term *concept* itself. It is thus no more empirical than a conceptual account of meaning. Indeed behavioristic theories of meaning seem rather anachronistic: they are set up as part of a general endeavour to use theoretical constructs which are testable in the sense of being observable and yet they make crucial use of quite unanalysed concepts such as *dispositions to respond*. The importance of stimulus–response theories of meaning is largely historical since the theory of behaviorism on which they are based is now very generally thought to be mistaken (perhaps the most well-known critique is Chomsky's review of Skinner's *Verbal Behavior*). They do however serve to show how the interpretation of a language cannot be reduced to the non-linguistic elements of the communication situation.

4.2 Speech act semantics

Not all theories of meaning in terms of the process of communication are subject to this form of criticism. In particular, speech act semantics is not open to such a charge of reductionism, since it purports to characterise the nature of language not in terms of the observable elements of the situation but in terms of an abstract concept of speech act.

The central insight of speech act semantics is that we use language to do things, that describing is only one of the things we do: we also use language to promise, to insult, to agree, to criticise, etc. Austin himself suggested that in uttering a sentence, a speaker is generally involved in three different acts (Austin 1962: lecture VIII). First there is the locutionary act: the act of uttering a sentence with a certain meaning. In addition, the speaker may have intended his utterance to constitute an act of praise, criticism, agreement, etc.: this is the so-called illocutionary act. Finally he may have uttered the sentence he did utter to achieve a certain consequent response from his hearer – for example to frighten him, to amuse him, to get him to do something: this is the perlocutionary act. Suppose for example my child is refusing to lie down and go to sleep and I say to him, "I'll turn your light off". Now the locutionary act is the utterance of the sentence *I'll turn your light off*. But I may be intending that utterance to be interpreted as a threat, and this is my illocutionary act. Quite separate from either of these is the consequent behaviour by my child that I intend to follow from my utterance, namely that he be frightened into silence and sleep. The distinction between the illocutionary act and the perlocutionary act is important: the perlocutionary act is the consequent effect on the hearer which the speaker intends should follow from his utterance (cf. Austin 1962: 101). Such acts are not normally thought to be relevant to a linguistic account of meaning.[1] But illocutionary acts are not consequences of locutionary acts. It is not a consequence of my uttering "I'll turn the light off"[2] that it constitutes a threat – it is an integral part of my utterance: it is what I intend my utterance *as*. The illocutionary act carried out by the use of some sentence is said to invest the utterance of that sentence with a particular illocutionary force. The three-fold distinction can then be referred to in the following way: a speaker utters sentences with a particular meaning (locutionary act), and with a particular force (illocutionary act), in order to achieve a certain effect on the hearer (perlocutionary act).

Now in the case we have just considered, the illocutionary force was merely implicit in the utterance – it was not expressed as part of the locutionary act. But this isn't always so. In some cases the illocutionary force is made plain. These are the so-called explicitly performative utterances:

(6) I promise you that I'll be there.
(7) I bet you she'll fall over.
(8) I agree that I was wrong.

It was this type of utterance of which Austin said it made no sense to talk of its being true or false because such utterances are not descriptions but actions (cf. Austin 1962: 70). These are distinct from other utterances using the same verbs:

(9) He promised her that he would be there.
(10) She bet you that she would fall over.
(11) They agree that I was wrong.

Sentences (9)–(11) can none of them be used as performative utterances for they would all be used as descriptions, not as actions, of promising, betting or agreeing.

Austin suggested that performative utterances, instead of being assessed as true or false, could only be assessed as appropriate or not, and that they could be characterised accordingly in terms of the differing

---

1 Though cf. Grice 1957, 1968, 1969 for a contrary view.
2 The use of double quotation marks as opposed to italics is to distinguish utterances from sentences. Cf. p. 8 n. 1.

sets of conditions necessary for their appropriate use.[1] For example, among the main appropriacy conditions of an utterance of *I promise you that I will be at the station* are that the speaker intends that his utterance will place him under an obligation to be at the station, that he intends to be at the station, that the hearer would prefer his being at the station, and that it is not obvious that he would otherwise be at the station in the normal way of things. In addition there are standard conditions for successful communication such as that both speaker and hearer speak the same language, that if they are in a speech situation the hearer is not stone deaf, etc., etc. All these conditions must be fulfilled if the utterance is to count as a successful and appropriate promise (cf. Searle 1969 ch. 3 for a detailed analysis).

Now just as we saw that all utterances and not merely performative utterances could be seen as simultaneously comprising three different acts, locutionary, illocutionary and perlocutionary, so the concept of appropriacy condition can be extended from performative utterances to all utterances. A sentence may be uttered appropriately as a promise if the speaker–hearer relations match the appropriacy conditions on promising. That same sentence may on another occasion be appropriate as a warning if the speaker–hearer relations match the appropriacy conditions on warning.

It is no coincidence that so far I have referred to utterances in talking of illocutionary acts. The analysis of speech acts given by Austin, and extended by other philosophers after him, is an account of acts of speech, of utterances: it was not intended as an account of sentences (cf. p. 8 n. 1 above). However recently linguists have turned to the account of speech acts as the solution to the problem of meaning. It has been suggested that rather than talk of word meanings or sentence meanings in vacuo, one can more usefully talk about conditions for appropriate use for both sentences and words (cf. Fillmore 1971: 273–5). So, for example, it has been suggested that the word *criticise* has as conditions for its appropriate use that the criticiser assume or presuppose that the one criticised is responsible, and states that the action criticised is bad (cf. Fillmore 1971: 282–4), whereas the word *accuse* conversely has as conditions for its appropriate use the conditions that the accuser say that the one accused is responsible and that the accuser assume that the action in question is bad.

---

[1] These conditions have been called variously *appropriacy conditions, felicity conditions, happiness conditions.* I shall use the first of these terms.

Part and parcel of this recent speech act approach to meaning by linguists is the use of the term *speaker-presupposition*.[1] This term is said to contrast with *assertion*, and the meaning of a sentence is said to be divided between the part that a speaker asserts and the part that he presupposes, or assumes, to be true. This distinction has been used for example to explain the difference between sentence pairs such as (12)–(13), (14)–(15), and (16)–(17):

(12) Bill is addicted to morphine.
(13) It is morphine that Bill is addicted to.
(14) Bill is addicted to morphine.
(15) What Bill is addicted to is morphine.
(16) My sister is at the party and my brother's in bed with 'flu.
(17) My sister is at the party but my brother's in bed with 'flu.

In the first two pairs of cases, it is said that in the second sentence the speaker is presupposing that Bill is addicted to something and asserting that that something is morphine; in the final pair the speaker is said by using *but* to presuppose that there is some element of contrast between the two sentences joined by *but*, the specific contrast in this case being carried by the presupposition that my brother is not at the party (this standing in the requisite contrast to *My sister is at the party*). These statements in terms of speaker-presupposition can be straightforwardly translated into statements about appropriacy conditions. For example, instead of talking of what a speaker presupposes in saying (17), one might equivalently say that a speaker will only be using this sentence appropriately if he presupposes some requisite element of contrast between the two conjuncts on either side of *but*. Now in principle such an account might expect to be particularly successful in dealing with different sentence types, since, one might anticipate that questions and imperatives would each have a set of appropriacy conditions different from the set of appropriacy conditions associated with statements. Thus we might for example say (cf. Searle 1969: 66–7) that an imperative form is appropriate if (*a*) the hearer is believed to be able to carry out the action that is proposed, (*b*) it is not obvious that he would do so in the normal course of events, and (*c*) the speaker wants the hearer to carry out this action (or, equivalently, that in using an imperative form a speaker presupposes these three conditions).

---

[1] In fact the term *presupposition* is generally used to cover both speaker-presupposition and logical presupposition, but in order to avoid this indeterminacy, I shall always use the more specific term.

Before we consider such a speech act semantics in more detail, it is important to make plain the theoretical position that such a semantics implies if it is adopted as a basis for characterising sentence meaning. Sentence meaning and word meaning will be thought of in terms of conditions for appropriate use, and thus implications of sentences will be characterised not as a property of the sentence itself but as a presupposition on the part of a speaker using that sentence, a requisite set of beliefs if the speaker is to use the sentence appropriately. The fit between this kind of semantics and the rest of the grammar is not an obvious one. Transformational grammar has in general assumed a competence–performance distinction and in so doing makes a difference of logical priority between the description of a speaker's knowledge of his language, his competence, and the description of his use of that knowledge, his performance. A theory which characterises the regularities of language is a competence theory; a theory which characterises the interaction between that linguistic characterisation and all the other factors which determine the full gamut of regularities of communication is a theory of performance. In particular a grammar of a language as part of a theory of competence predicts the grammaticality of a certain (infinite) set of sentences. Yet if the semantics of a natural language is to be expressed in terms of conditions for use, it would seem prima facie to be a semantics for a theory of performance: such a semantics makes no distinction between grammatical and ungrammatical sentences (cf. p. 7 n. 1), only between appropriate and inappropriate uses of sentences. Furthermore a semantic theory which explains meaning in terms of use is assuming that an explanation of use is logically prior to an explanation of meaning: appropriate use is the primitive notion, in terms of which the concept of meaning is to be explained. Thus if we maintain the competence–performance distinction as outlined in Chomsky 1965, we have arrived at an impasse – we are explaining performance in terms of a competence grammar (among other things) which generates sentences and their meanings, yet we are explaining those meanings in terms of conditions for their use – i.e. their performance. If we maintain a speech act view of semantics then we must at the very least reconsider the assumptions made in the competence–performance distinction.

One way in which it has been suggested that this distinction be revised is to demand of a linguistic theory that it characterise not simply the regularities of the language which a speaker must command as his competence but rather the regularities implicit in his use of the language in communication – called communicative competence. According to proponents of this view the account of competence proposed by Chomsky in 1965 (cf. p. 8 above) has to be abandoned in favour of an account of communicative competence, and such an account is consistent with a speech act theory of meaning. However this suggested revision is entirely terminological: there is no discrepancy between a theory of communicative competence and Chomsky's exposition of competence. For a theory characterising a speaker's ability to use his language appropriately in context, a theory of communicative competence, is, simply, a performance theory. There is therefore no conflict between a truth-conditional account of semantics as part of a theory of linguistic competence and a speech act theory of utterance meaning as part of a theory of communicative competence, or performance. It is only if an account of speech acts is used as a means of characterising sentence meaning that the conflict arises and the Chomskian dichotomy between competence and performance has to be abandoned.

At this point there are then two main alternatives open to us: it appears that either we maintain the competence–performance distinction together with a truth-conditional account of sentence meaning, invoking concepts such as speech acts only in an account of performance regularities, or we adopt a speech act account of sentence meaning and revise the fundamental assumption of classical transformational grammar, the assumption of a competence–performance distinction. A comparison of these two options will be the burden of the following chapter.

RECOMMENDED READING

4.1 For Firth's approach to meaning, readers should consult the collection of his papers in *Papers in Linguistics 1934–51*, and for a criticism of this approach Lyons 'Firth's theory of "meaning"'. Bloomfield's account of semantics is outlined in his *Language*. A summary and criticism of it and other behavioristic theories of meaning is given in Alston *Philosophy of Language* ch. 1. The most sophisticated account of semantics along behavioristic lines is that of Quine in *Word and Object*. Behaviorist psychology itself has as its central representative Skinner – see his *Verbal Behavior*; and of those behaviorist psychologists who modified his views, Osgood is perhaps the most well known: see for example his 'A behavioristic analysis of perception and language as cognitive phenomena'. See also Morris *Signs, Language and Behavior*. A detailed account of the inadequacy of theories of meaning based on causation, and in particular of Osgood's, is given in Fodor, Bever and

Garrett *The Psychology of Language* ch. 6. For an exchange of views by Chomsky and Quine over the use of the term *disposition* in semantics, see Chomsky 'Quine's empirical assumptions' and *Reflections on Language* pp. 190–5, and Quine 'Reply to Chomsky' and 'Methodological reflections on current linguistic theory' (reprinted in Harman (ed.) *On Noam Chomsky*).

4.2 The originator of speech act semantics was Austin with his series of lectures published as *How to Do Things With Words*, and it is instructive to compare these lectures with later speech act accounts. See also Austin 'Performative-constative' (reprinted in Searle (ed.) *The Philosophy of Language* and in Olshewsky (ed.) *Problems in the Philosophy of Language*). The distinction between locutionary, illocutionary and perlocutionary acts is one of the central concerns of *How to Do Things With Words*. This tripartite division has been criticised by Searle 'Austin on locutionary and illocutionary acts' and by Cohen 'Do illocutionary forces exist?' (both of which are reprinted in Rosenberg and Travis (eds.) *Readings in the Philosophy of Language*). The most well-known development of Austin's ideas is the work of Searle: see *Speech Acts*, 'What is a speech act?' (reprinted in Searle (ed.) *The Philosophy of Language* and in Rosenberg and Travis (eds.) *Readings in the Philosophy of Language*), 'Indirect speech acts', and 'A taxonomy of illocutionary acts'. See also the work of Alston, who takes the strongest position of speech act semantics among speech act philosophers that even word meaning can be explained in terms of illocutionary acts: Alston *Philosophy of Language* chs. 2–3, 'Meaning and use' (reprinted in Parkinson (ed.) *The Theory of Meaning* and Rosenberg and Travis (eds.) *Readings in the Philosophy of Language*), and 'Semantic rules'; and too that of Strawson, in particular his 'Intention and convention in speech acts' (reprinted in Strawson *Logico-linguistic Papers*, Olshewsky (ed.) *Problems in the Philosophy of Language* and Rosenberg and Travis (eds.) *Readings in the Philosophy of Language*). For criticisms of speech act theory, see a review of *Speech Acts* by Fraser (*Foundations of Language* 1974), Stampe 'Meaning and truth in the theory of speech acts', and Holdcroft 'Meaning and illocutionary acts' (reprinted in Parkinson (ed.) *The Theory of Meaning*). On the concept of appropriacy condition, see Austin *How to Do Things With Words* lectures II–III (called by him *felicity conditions*), and Searle *Speech Acts* ch. 3. On the extension of appropriacy conditions to lexical and other linguistic analyses, see, for example, Fillmore 'Verbs of judging: an exercise in semantic description', and Green 'How to get people to do things with words'. On speaker-presuppositions, see Keenan 'Two kinds of presupposition in natural language' and Stalnaker 'Pragmatic presuppositions'. Fillmore and Langendoen (eds.) *Studies in Linguistic Semantics* is a collection of articles almost all of which make use of speaker-presuppositions. Green *Semantics and Syntactic Regularity* invokes speaker-assumptions in a more general way for analyses of certain syntactic problems. On the characterisation of sentence types in terms of speech act concepts, see Searle *Speech Acts* p. 69, Sadock *Towards a Linguistic Theory of Speech Acts*, Hudson 'The meaning of questions'. The attempt to incorporate into syntactic analysis the insights of Austin on performative verbs was made by Ross in 'On declarative sentences' and 'Act'. This position has been adopted by several linguists: see Sadock *Towards a Linguistic Theory of Speech Acts*, Schreiber 'Style disjuncts and the performative analysis', G. Lakoff 'Linguistics and natural logic', Ross 'Where to do things with words'. For a detailed analysis of word meaning in terms of speaker-presupposition with explicit reference to speech act theories, see Fillmore 'Verbs of judging: an exercise in semantic description'. The item *but* has been analysed in terms of speaker-presupposition by R. Lakoff in 'If's, and's, and but's about conjunction'. On the conflict between the standard competence–performance distinction and a semantics which incorporates concepts such as appropriacy condition and speaker-presupposition, see G. Lakoff 'Presupposition and relative well-formedness', 'The role of deduction in grammar', and R. Lakoff 'Language in context'. *Communicative competence* is a term that was introduced by Dell Hymes in 'On communicative competence'. Non-transformational linguists whose view of language is closer to this than to the 1965 division between competence and performance include Halliday (see his 'Language structure and language function'), and Campbell and Wales (see their 'The study of language acquisition').

5

Speech act semantics v. truth-conditional semantics

5.1 Speech act semantics and sentence relations

In the opening chapter of this book, I isolated certain conditions which a semantic theory should be expected to fulfil. These were that it must give some account of word meaning and sentence meaning, explaining the nature of the relation between them, and that it must be able to predict correctly for any language entailment, synonymy, contradiction and ambiguity. In chapter 3 we saw that a truth-based semantics, despite its problems, was able to fulfil these conditions at least in principle. Yet a truth-based semantics appeared to be too restricted. It has nothing to say about any type of sentence other than a declarative sentence, and indeed it appears to have nothing to say about even some declarative sentences – namely sentences which could be used in performative utterances, those whose illocutionary force is made explicit. By contrast, speech act semantics seems to offer an account which is neutral as to type of sentence and which is therefore not open to some of the objections facing a truth-based semantics. Moreover if a speech act semantics could provide the basis for an account of sentence meaning it would be independent of the meaning–analyticity circle and in this respect in particular speech act semantics presents a real competitor to a truth-based semantics. If therefore such a theory is also able to meet the required standards of adequacy, it is certainly to be preferred over the more restricted truth-based approach.

The problem in assessing a speech act semantics as the basis of an account of the interpretation of the elements of language, sentences and words, lies in the extension of the terms *speech act*, *illocutionary force*, and *appropriacy condition* from the utterance to the sentence. As we shall see immediately, this extension raises serious problems. Let us take the prediction of ambiguity first. Recall that the concept of appropriacy conditions was first introduced in Austin's analysis of those utterances which were explicitly linguistic actions – i.e. performative utterances. He himself then pointed out that all utterances were actions in this sense whether the type of act performed was made explicit with a performative verb or not. The concept of appropriacy conditions must therefore in any case be generalisable to all utterances. The problem that we face in the prediction of ambiguity is that those sentences which do not have any explicit illocutionary force indicator can be used in a variety of ways. For example the sentence *There are four large bulls in that field* may be used as a warning (to a walker who is about to cross the fence), a statement (to a new assistant on the farm), a boast (to a fellow farmer), or a threat (to a boy who is misbehaving), to name but a few possible linguistic actions for which this sentence could be used. But conditions for appropriate use are defined on utterances, not or not solely on the sentence being used, for they depend on what act is being carried out. So the conditions for the appropriate use of the above sentence as a warning will differ from those for its appropriate use for any other action: the appropriacy conditions for warning, stating, boasting and threatening, for example, are all distinct. If therefore we attempt to explain the meaning of a sentence in terms of conditions for its use in performing speech acts, we find that there are many different sets of conditions for each sentence of the language – indeed as many sets as there are distinct linguistic actions that we can perform with sentences (Austin suggested that there were more than one thousand – Austin 1962: 149). And if, having called the meaning of a sentence the set of conditions for its appropriate use we attempt also to explain ambiguity along these lines, it follows that a sentence which has, say, two distinct sets of conditions for its appropriate use will be predicted to be two-ways ambiguous. But unfortunately we have just seen that every sentence of the language can be used in a large number of different ways. So it seems that a speech act semantics – if it is intended as a semantic characterisation of the sentences of a language – is committed to predicting that all sentences of the language are multiply ambiguous. But this does not accord with our intuition as speakers of the language that a sentence such as *The chicken is ready to eat* differs from a sentence such as *We are ready to eat the chicken* precisely in that only the former is ambiguous.

What has gone wrong here? Why has the reduction of meaning to conditions of use led to this result? Recall that originally speech act analysis was an analysis of utterances, individual tokens of sentences.

Any one such utterance was then said to be analysable into three acts, the locutionary act, the illocutionary act, and the perlocutionary act. Now the illocutionary act is the act which the speaker intends his utterance to be taken as. In particular it is not necessarily made explicit by the elements of the sentence with which the speaker has made that utterance. Thus there is no need for there to be any direct relationship between the words uttered and the intended illocutionary act. Suppose I say the sentence *James will be at the party tonight*. If I, the speaker, know that the hearer has recently been turned out of James' flat having lived with him for five years, then I may know that my utterance of this sentence will be taken as a warning. In contrast to this, if I, the speaker know that James is a famous author who moreover the hearer tried to get to a party of hers and failed, I may know that my utterance of this same sentence will be taken as a boast. Now in both cases, it was the assumptions shared by the participants in the speech act which determined whether this sentence was to be taken as a warning or a boast. There was no relationship between the conditions which guaranteed its varying illocutionary force and the meaning of the sentence itself. There is thus no reason to expect that explaining word or sentence meaning in terms of the speech acts we can use our sentences to perform will give us any insight into the meaning of the words and sentences of the language.

Perhaps we have reached this conclusion too swiftly to be convincing. What about the predictions of entailment and synonymy in terms of appropriacy conditions? We have already seen that entailment is logically defined as a relationship between two sentences[1] such that if one is true the other must be. So if the entailments of sentences are to be successfully predicted in terms of the conditions appropriate for effecting speech acts, then we must be able to predict for example that *James will be at the party tonight* has among its entailments the sentences *There is an individual called James*, *There will be a party tonight*,[2] but how can we do this when the appropriacy conditions differ according to the act performed? If for example a speaker utters the sentence *James will be at the party tonight* intending his utterance as a warning, then among the appropriacy conditions will be the condition that the speaker believes that James' coming to the party is not in the

---

[1] In fact the logical definition concerns a relationship between two statements. Cf. 3.4.1 above.

[2] For a discussion of the assignment of truth values to future statements, cf. White 1970 and references cited there, and Dummett 1976.

hearer's best interest (cf. Searle 1969: 67). Or, if the same sentence is uttered as a boast, then one of the appropriacy conditions will be (approximately) that the speaker believe that the utterance of his sentence will place him in some advantage over his hearer. But neither of these conditions has any bearing on the entailments of the sentence uttered: they are not entailments of that sentence. So unless we have some means of isolating the relevant appropriacy conditions (for example that the speaker believes that there will be a party tonight and that there is an individual called James, and that James will be at the party), the concept of appropriacy condition will not lead us to a prediction of the entailments of every sentence of the language. Clearly the required sub-set of the appropriacy conditions on the utterances of a sentence are those conditions which have a bearing on the meaning of the sentence. But this means of isolating the required appropriacy conditions is not open to a linguist who intends to explain meaning in terms of appropriacy conditions: meaning is what he is seeking to explain – it cannot therefore be referred to as an essential term of the explanation. Synonymy is open to the same problems as entailment, for synonymous sentences are mutually entailing sentences.

5.2 Speech act semantics and non-declaratives

It is beginning to seem as though a speech act account of sentence meaning cannot meet the conditions of adequacy put forward in chapter 1. At this point let us look at the area where such a semantics looked most promising: the non-declaratives – interrogative and imperative sentence forms. This seemed promising on the assumption that the characterisation of what it means to use an interrogative and of what it means to use an imperative will both correspond to a different range of speech acts from the characterisation of what it means to use a declarative form. Thus we might anticipate, while declaratives are typically used for giving information, interrogatives are typically used for requesting information, and imperatives for requesting action. Since there would be different appropriacy conditions in each of these three cases, the isolating of such appropriacy conditions will correspond to what we might otherwise call the meaning of the declarative, the interrogative and the imperative forms. But is this so? Can we say that declarative sentences such as (1) and (2) give information, that interrogatives such as (3) and (4) are requests for information, and that imperatives such as (5) and (6) are requests for action?

(1) I would be grateful if you could tell me the time.
(2) I insist that you stay here.
(3) Did you know they've just announced on the news that the Prime Minister has resigned?
(4) How many times have I told you not to do that?
(5) Consider the fact that Rubenstein was a Zionist.
(6) Tell me whether I'm right or not.

It seems clear that we cannot. A child accused of misbehaving in the following way would be, rightly, outraged.

(7) A: How big is the moon?
B: Not as big as the earth.
A: How big is the earth?
B: Big enough.
A: How big is big enough?
B: Stop asking questions and eat your cereal.
A: Could you pass the milk and sugar?
B: I told you not to ask questions: now get on with your breakfast.

The point is this. While declaratives are often used for giving information, this is by no means their only use, as Austin himself pointed out so convincingly: an utterance of the sentence *I entreat you to give me a pound* would not characteristically be used as a descriptive statement. But the problem is not restricted to the declarative: interrogatives are not necessarily requests for information, and imperatives are not necessarily requests for action. Moreover, the three sentence types do not even delimit different ranges of illocutionary force: we can use an interrogative form to give information (cf. (3) above) or to make a request for action (cf. (4) above), and we can also use an imperative both to give information and to request information (cf. (5) and (6) above). Since this is so, the original hope that speech act semantics could provide a natural means of characterising the difference between the three types of sentence seems misplaced.

It might be suggested that this conclusion does not follow against speech act semantics because, while a declarative form may be used for other purposes than informing, it remains an informative statement, and similarly for interrogative and imperative forms. Thus, it would be said (cf. Gordon and Lakoff 1975, Searle 1975b) that, though *Could you pass the milk and sugar?* is a request for action, it is also a question. But the conversation between speakers A and B above (p. 62) provides an example where this isn't so (if we take *question* to mean 'a request for information'). Of course it remains an interrogative form,[1] but it is the interpretation of that form that we are concerned with, not the form itself. Moreover there would be no disagreement between linguists that sentences which are used to make performative utterances are not, in general, statements of information. Whether they are not depends solely on the verb used: *I inform you that* . . ., *I say that* . . ., *I tell you that* . . . are of course means of informing the hearer but *I beseech you to* . . ., *I beg of you to* . . ., *I entreat you to* . . . are not characteristically used as informative statements. So the advantage of a speech act semantics, that it can provide a characterisation of the different sentence forms, seems after all to be a spurious one. It does not apparently provide an analysis which distinguishes the different sentence types.

5.3 A re-appraisal of the problems

What compromise position is there between the two theories? Truth-conditional semantics appears neatly to characterise at least a certain part of language, and the analysis of speech acts provides insights into our use of language. What we seem to need is a theory of language which enables us to combine the insights of both. Linguists currently differ as to how this combination can best be formulated. Before adopting any particular position, let us recapitulate the advantages and drawbacks of both truth-conditional semantics and speech act semantics. A theory of semantics based on truth provides a natural means of capturing the required predictions of an interpretation for each sentence of the language, of synonymy, ambiguity, entailment, etc. However on the one hand it appears to have nothing to say about non-declarative sentence forms or about sentences used to make performative utterances, and on the other it takes truth, indeed necessary truth, as a primitive in terms of which meaning is to be explained. It therefore depends on an independent characterisation of necessary truth, a task which has beset philosophers for centuries. A theory of semantics based on an analysis of how sentences are used in speech acts faces quite different problems. The analysis of the utterance into three different kinds of act, locutionary, illocutionary and perlocutionary, provides some means of accounting for the way in which we use language, but in

[1] Even this has been doubted. Cf. Sadock 1970.

order to account for those aspects of utterance meaning which are intrinsic to the sentence used (rather than due to some other factor of communication: cf. 5.4 below), there must be some meaning-independent way of distinguishing those appropriacy conditions relevant to the analysis of words and sentences from those which are a part of a theory of communication in general, and there are no obvious ways of doing so. In particular, the appropriacy conditions for illocutionary acts seem to be independent of the conditions appropriate for the locutionary acts in question (except in the case of performative utterances: cf. Searle 1968), and hence there is no necessary relation even between sentence type and range of illocutionary act. So it appears that the characterisation of non-declarative sentences is a stumbling block for both truth-conditional semantics and speech act semantics.

5.3.1 *Performative utterances and truth-value assignment*

Having seen the considerable difficulties involved in extending speech act concepts from utterance meaning to sentence meaning, we must now return to truth-conditional semantics and re-consider the criticism that it allows for no account of precisely those utterances which are central to speech act theories – performative utterances. To recapitulate, it was utterances of this type of which Austin said they could only be assessed as appropriate or inappropriate (in fact, felicitous or infelicitous – cf. Austin 1962: lecture II), not as true or false, this being a serious fault in truth-conditional semantics and one major reason for the adoption of a speech act analysis. First let us look in more detail at the data. The class of verbs which can be used in explicitly performative utterances have two properties: (i) they are used to describe an act which can only be carried out by speaking (or some other form of communication), (ii) in the first person present tense, the action depicted by the speaker is not so much described by his statement as carried out by that statement. Thus *I promise to go* is not a description of a promise but, subject to the satisfaction of the appropriacy conditions, will itself constitute a promise when it is uttered. Other examples are *acknowledge, assert, promise, warn, accuse, testify, announce, condemn*. There are two main tests which distinguish these verbs from others:[1] the performative use of these verbs, the simple present, can be accompanied by *hereby*, as

---

[1] Austin discusses a range of tests (Austin 1962: 56–66), of which these are the strongest.

in *I hereby name this ship Elizabeth*. This is not the case with any other tense, nor with any non-performative verb. Thus while (8) is a normal sentence, neither (9) and (10) are, nor (11) and (12):

(8) I hereby warn you that you are being duped.

(9) ?They hereby warn her that she is being duped.

(10) ?They hereby warned her that she was being duped.

(11) ?I hereby run to the station.

(12) ?I hereby give you your supper.

Another argument in support of the isolation of the performatives as non-statements is the difference between these verbs and other verbs in their interpretation of the present tense form. While non-performative verbs can not generally be used in the simple present form to indicate a present time interpretation, the present tense use of performative verbs characteristically *does* have a present time interpretation. Thus *She sings* does not mean that she is at the present time singing, but *I promise to sing* does mean that I am at the present time promising to sing. The relation between the present tense form and the so-called progressive tense form therefore appears to be quite different for performative and non-performative verbs. For non-performative verbs, there is no relation at all between the two forms. The present tense form is generally used for habitual action, whereas it is the progressive tense form which has the present time interpretation. Hence the distinction between *She sings* and *She is singing*, and between *She paints* and *She is painting*. The relation between the present tense of performative verbs and their progressive tense is much closer and more subtle. While the utterance of *I warn you that your tenants will take action against you* will under all normal circumstances constitute an action of warning, the utterance of *I am warning you that your tenants will take action against you* is said not to (cf. Austin 1962: 64): it is a description of an act of warning – something that one might say to describe and make explicit the act of warning which is simultaneously being given.

So much for the data. Now it is precisely the relation between the present and progressive tense uses of performative verbs which a speech act supporter would say cannot be captured by a truth-based account. For on this view the values true and false can only be assigned to utterances which constitute a description of some event. Since performative utterances are actions, and not descriptions, these cannot be said to be true or false. It is only the descriptions of those actions and other non-performative uses of the verb such as the progressive tense form which can be characterised by a truth-conditional semantics. Now the question is whether this particular contrast between progressive tense and present tense both used to convey a present time interpretation is specific to verbs which can be used performatively. If it is, then a speech act account may be justified in explaining it in terms of the contrast between an action and a description, assigning only the latter the values true or false. But if this contrast is not specific to those verbs which can constitute linguistic actions, then it is not obvious that the contrast should be explained in terms of the action–description contrast. And it is not. There are some verbs which have a similar relation between the interpretation of the simple present and progressive forms, but are clearly not performative. Take for example the verb *consider*. *I consider that she is wrong* does not contain a performative use of the verb; for the utterance of such a sentence would not itself constitute an act of considering. It is as odd to say *I hereby consider that she is wrong* as it is to say *I hereby dislike you*. Yet such a verb has the related pairs *I consider that she is wrong, I am considering whether she is wrong; Mike considers that Elaine should sell her house, Mike is considering whether Elaine should sell her house*. In particular the use of the present tense *does* indicate a present time consideration, not a habitual repeated action of considering. Similarly the verb *wonder*. Like *consider* it is a verb of judgement or opinion, not a verb the very utterance of which can ever constitute a linguistic action. Yet equally possible are both *I wonder whether we should go home* and *I am wondering whether we should go home*. Since there is no distinction between action and description for the two uses of these verbs, there is no reason to doubt that the contrast between simple present and progressive forms of these verbs can be captured by a truth-conditional account. On the contrary, it will capture the contrast by means of some distinction between a completed action and an ongoing action: *I consider that she is right* and *I wonder whether she is right* are both descriptions of a completed action (of considering and wondering respectively) but *I am considering whether she is wrong* implies that the act of consideration is not yet complete, and so too does *I am wondering whether we should go home*. But this is precisely the contrast between *I warn you that your tenants will take action against you* and *I am warning you that your tenants will take action against you*. Thus if the contrast can be captured within a truth-conditional semantics for verbs such as *wonder* and *consider*, the same contrast can be captured for verbs such as *promise, warn, threaten,* etc. Thus there seems to be no justification for invoking at this point the distinction between actions and descriptions, and excluding an interpretation of the first person present tense use of verbs of saying from a truth-based account. It therefore seems that it was misleading to consider the contrast between verbs of saying which have a natural simple present interpretation, and verbs of action (such as *knit*) which do not. Furthermore, it is not only the verbs *consider* and *wonder* which use the present tense form to indicate present time. All verbs of belief share with verbs of saying the natural interpretation of the present tense form as referring to the simple present. Thus though *Enid knits a cardigan, Sammy teases his little brother,* and *Michael signs his name* do not have the interpretation of describing actions taking place at the time of utterance, *I think she's right, I suspect that Margo will fail* and *I believe that capitalism is an unavoidable evil* all *do* describe opinions held at the time of utterance. The only natural conclusion from this evidence, I suggest, is that sentences such as *I say that he's right* and *I warn you that the bull is about to charge* are true or false according to circumstances, just like any other declarative sentence. So under this analysis, performative utterances can and do carry a truth value; what is odd about them is that the mere fact of their utterance guarantees the fulfilment of at least part of the conditions for the truth of the proposition conveyed. The idiosyncratic feature of performative statements is therefore not that they cannot be either true or false but rather that their truth value is at least partially determined by the very fact of their being uttered. If this is correct, then this class of verbs is not excluded from a truth-based semantics, and so one motivation for seeking an alternative to such a semantics disappears.

At the beginning of this chapter, I isolated as three advantages of a speech act theory of semantics that it purports to offer an account which is neutral as to the different sentence forms, indicative, imperative, and interrogative, that it offers an account of performative utterances, and that it avoids the meaning–analyticity circle. These three advantages were said to be conditional upon such a theory meeting the conditions of adequacy on semantic theories that I outlined in chapter 1. We have however considered evidence which suggests that these conditions are not met if the speech act concepts are extended to provide the basis of an account of sentence meaning. Furthermore the apparent advantage of a speech act theory of semantics over a truth-based theory of semantics, that it provides a basis for distinguishing between the interpretation of indicative, interrogative and imperative sentence forms, appears to be unfounded. On the other hand, the charge against a truth-based semantics that it can in principle give no account of the performative, present time interpretation of first person present tense sentences containing verbs of saying is, I have argued, mistaken and should not be upheld. So it appears that a truth-based semantics is like a speech act theory of semantics both in that it can give an account of performative utterances (though not the same account) and in that it cannot give a satisfactory account of the three sentence forms imperative, indicative, and interrogative. Given that, unlike a speech act account of sentence meaning, a truth-based account in principle naturally fulfils the listed conditions of adequacy, it seems that it provides a more satisfactory basis for a semantic theory.

5.4 A theory of language use: pragmatics

That an account of the nature of the speech act does not provide a solution to the problem of meaning should come as no surprise to a speech act theorist, for such a theory was not originally intended (by Austin) to provide an analysis of sentences or words but solely of utterances, uses to which words and sentences are put.[1] The question we now have to pose is what is the precise nature of the relation between a semantic interpretation of the words and sentences of a language given, say, by a truth-conditional semantics, and a theory of language use? Where do Austin's insights into the nature of the speech act fit in? One solution which is currently being discussed is the setting up of a theory of communication separate from but dependent on a previously stated account of semantics – a theory of pragmatics.[2] The main aim of such a theory is expected to be the explanation of how it is that speakers of any language can use the sentences of that language to convey messages which do not bear any necessary relation to the linguistic content of the sentence used. This type of theory would also have to explain the

---

[1] Austin indeed accepted without discussion a traditional account of sentence meaning in terms of sense and reference (cf. Austin 1962: 100). It is only more recently, and largely by linguists, that speech act concepts have been used in the explanation of sentence meaning.

[2] The trichotomy between syntax, semantics and pragmatics was suggested by Morris 1938. The three-fold distinction was brought back into recent philosophical discussion by Bar-Hillel 1954.

relation between the use of a sentence and the linguistic act (illocution-ary act) which that sentence is used to perform.

One such account has been made by Grice (Grice 1975), who has suggested the following explanation. In all communication there is a general agreement of co-operation between a speaker and a hearer, to be called the Co-operative Principle. Under this general heading, a number of general maxims can be isolated which specify the conventions which participants in a conversation should and normally do obey. These are as follows:

Quantity
(1) Make your contribution as informative as is required (for the current purposes of the exchange.).
(2) Do not make your contribution more informative than is required.

Quality
(1) Do not say what you believe to be false.
(2) Do not say that for which you lack adequate evidence.

Relation
Be relevant.

Manner
This maxim has an over-all instruction 'Be perspicuous'. Grice sub-divides this general instruction into four further maxims:

(1) Avoid obscurity.
(2) Avoid ambiguity.
(3) Be brief.
(4) Be orderly.

Each of these constitutes a convention that is normally obeyed. In an exchange of conversation, one generally expects for example that the people one is talking to are telling the truth. Conversations would not follow the pattern they do if every statement made was assumed to be false. Now it is the flouting of these conventions which Grice suggests is the basis for the flexibility of the message that can be conveyed by the means of a single sentence. Of course these conventions, or norms, are

unlike linguistic rules since they are in any case often broken: there are
many lies told and there are many conversations which change their
subject abruptly as someone makes a statement quite irrelevant to what
was said before. But these norms may also be deliberately and flagrantly
broken, in such a way that the speaker knows and intends that the
hearer shall recognise that a maxim has been broken. The hearer then
has two alternatives: one is to say "You're a liar" or "That's irrelevant"
or whatever, in which case, the Co-operative Principle has broken down.
But he may – and characteristically does – choose a second alternative.
He assumes that the speaker is in general observing the Co-operative
Principle and reasons in the following way: 'If he is observing the Co-
operative Principle and if he is flouting a maxim in such a way that I
shall notice the breakage, then he is doing so in order to convey some
extra information which *is* in accordance with the Co-operative Principle,
and moreover he must know that I can work out that information'. Let
us take for example Grice's own case of a Philosophy don who is asked
to give a reference for a past student who is applying for a lectureship in
Philosophy. He writes: 'Dear Sir, Jones' command of English is
excellent, and his attendance at tutorials has been regular. Yours faith-
fully'. The writer of the letter is clearly and openly violating the maxim
of Quantity (if not that of Relation too): he is offering absurdly little
information. The receiver of the letter, faced with this blatant violation,
will not however throw the letter away: he will assume that its sender is
trying to convey information other than what his letter strictly says –
namely that Jones is no good at Philosophy. Since if the recipient makes
this assumption the man's letter no longer violates the Co-operative
Principle, and since the man clearly intends that the recipient of the
letter will deduce precisely this information, this is therefore what his
letter implies: or as Grice labels it, this is the implicature of what he has
written. These 'conversational implicatures' of an utterance are, by
definition, assumptions over and above the meaning of the sentence used
which the speaker knows and intends that the hearer will make, in the
face of an apparently open violation of the Co-operative Principle, in
order to interpret the speaker's sentence in accordance with the Co-
operative Principle. Other examples are provided by (13), which flouts
the maxim of Relation and (14), which flouts the maxim of Quality:

(13) The police came in and everyone swallowed their cigarettes.
(14) You're the cream in my coffee.

Someone hearing an utterance of (13) and not knowing about the illegality of marijuana might think that swallowing cigarettes is a stupid pastime and what did it have to do with the police anyway. However, anyone using such a sentence in the current political climate (1976) would assume that the hearer was able to work out that the second part is relevant if one assumes that the people would only swallow their cigarettes when the police came in if those cigarettes were illegal. Since people smoking illegal cigarettes are generally smoking marijuana (not opium, cocaine or other drugs) one interprets the sentence as implicating that everyone was smoking marijuana. The problem involved in understanding (14) is rather different. Since (14) is a sentence which is necessarily false,[1] in order to interpret an utterance of (14) as not breaking the maxim of Quality, the hearer must assume that the speaker is trying to convey something other than the literal meaning of the sentence. Since cream is something which is not only a natural accompaniment to coffee, but a perfect accompaniment, the speaker is perhaps saying that the hearer possesses similar attributes. He is therefore paying the hearer a great compliment. Now the significance of this interpretation of (14) is that it is metaphorical, and it therefore seems as though Grice's outline of pragmatics provides a natural basis for explaining how and why metaphorical interpretations involve the super-imposition of one interpretation (which commonly involves non-linguistic assumptions about the world) upon the other, literal, interpretation.[2]

Five characteristics of conversational implicature stand out:

(i) They are dependent on the recognition of the Co-operative Principle and its maxims.

(ii) They will not be part of the meaning of the lexical items in the sentence since their interpretation depends on a prior understanding of the conventional meaning of the sentence.

(iii) The implicature of an utterance will characteristically not be the sole possible interpretation of that utterance. There may well be more than one possible assumption which will reinstate the Co-operative Principle in the face of an apparent breakage. Since these assumptions

---

[1] Cf. 7.2 below on the distinction between anomaly and contradiction.

[2] Metaphor has traditionally presented a problem for semantic analysis, and linguists differ over the extent to which they think it can be handled within a purely semantic account of language: cf. Weinreich 1966, Bickerton 1969, Matthews 1971.

are not explicit, they are often indeterminate (for example, the inter-pretation of (14)).

(iv) The working out of an implicature will depend on assumptions about the world which the speaker and the hearer share (for example the interpretation of (13)). They will therefore not in general be predictable independently of the shared assumptions particular to individual speakers and hearers.

(v) They are cancellable. That is, an interpretation which is not part of the conventional meaning of the utterance can be explicitly denied without contradiction. Thus for example our referee might have written a letter such as 'Dear Sir, Jones' command of English is excellent, and his attendance at tutorials has been regular. Moreover his ability at and enthusiasm for Philosophy are quite adequate for the job. Yours faith-fully'. Similarly I might say 'The police came in and everyone swallowed their cigarettes though they were doing nothing illegal', or 'You're the cream in my coffee but since I don't like cream, that's a dubious compli-ment'. It is thus predicted that in actual use sentences will not be restricted to an interpretation determined by the form and meaning of the sentence itself and that furthermore these interpretations vary according as the assumptions made by the speaker and hearer vary. As a bonus, we seem to have an account of metaphor which accords closely with the characteristic indeterminacy of metaphorical interpreta-tion.[1]

Moreover Austin's account of speech acts naturally meshes in with Grice's account of communication; for both the determination of the illocutionary force of an utterance and any implicated message it may be intended to convey depend on shared assumptions by the speaker and hearer (strictly on a set of assumptions which the speaker believes he and the hearer share). Thus it seems that the illocutionary force of an utter-ance can be seen as one part of the total message implicated. So, for example, someone who utters the sentence *James will be at the party tonight*, knowing that the hearer has recently stopped living with James, at his instigation, will know that, on the basis of working out the rele-vance for herself of such an utterance, the hearer will understand the speaker to be implicating to her the warning that she should not go to

---

[1] It seems clear that stylistic effects could naturally be handled along similar lines with a specification of a set of style maxims, perhaps under the general maxim of Manner. This possibility has not however yet been investigated in any detail (though cf. R. Lakoff 1974).

the party (like all other cases this is not the only possible illocutionary force nor the only possible content of the warning).

5.5 Summary

We embarked on this chapter in the hope of assessing together the respective claims of a truth-based semantics and a speech act semantics. During the course of it, I have suggested that we make a separation between a semantic account of a language (which assigns interpretations to the words and sentences of that language) and an account of communication (pragmatics) which assumes the prior existence of such a semantic account. Making this distinction enables us to explain a wider range of phenomena than either a truth-based semantics or a speech act semantics could explain alone. Yet in so arguing, it has become apparent, I suggest, that an account of speech acts is, as the philosophers who originally devised it, assumed, part of an account of communication and not part of (nor a basis for) an account of any individual language. Furthermore, if such a separation of semantics and pragmatics is indeed valid, then it is arguable that this distinction accords reasonably well with the Chomskian distinction between competence and performance. An account of how we use sentences to convey a wide variety of messages and to effect linguistic actions such as warnings, threats, etc., is on this view one aspect of a theory of performance.[1]

At this point, let us look back to see to what extent the theoretical basis suggested matches any pretheoretical expectations we may have had about a semantic theory. According to the position I have argued for here a semantic theory (as part of a competence model) will assign interpretations to sentences where these interpretations are for each sentence a set of conditions necessary and sufficient for the truth of that sentence. It will not assign metaphorical interpretations to sentences;[2] it will not characterise stylistic distinctions between sentences. So it will characterise as contradictory the sentence *Her eyes danced with pleasure*,[3]

---

[1] For an account of a theory of performance which accords with this view, cf. Fodor and Garrett 1966, Fodor, Bever and Garrett 1974.

[2] Words involving so-called dead metaphor will be entered in the lexicon as having a separate meaning. For example the word *run* will have two separate entries corresponding to its different meanings in the sentences *She ran home, The road runs from Manchester to Birmingham.* This is not of course to dispute the problem that there are large numbers of unclear cases.

[3] Cf. 7.2 below for a discussion of the distinction between contradiction and anomaly.

and it will characterise as synonymous the pair of sentences *The reports you send in must be as simple as possible, It is obligatory that the reports to be sent in by you be maximally simple.* Such metaphorical and stylistic interpretations will be characterised within a theory of pragmatics. This theoretical stance represents a claim that the analysis of metaphor demands two separate levels of interpretation, one of which demands reference to general principles of co-operative behaviour and to the assumptions speakers make in using their language according to these principles (cf. p. 71). Now while it may at first seem strange that semantics should have nothing to say about metaphor, it is arguably not counter-intuitive that metaphor can only be characterised by two levels of interpretation. Though there are undoubtedly many problems in accounting for metaphor adequately along these lines, I shall assume for the rest of this book that there are principled reasons of this type why a semantic theory should not itself contain an analysis of the problems presented by either metaphorical or stylistic interpretations.

What is currently more controversial among linguists is the dichotomy between semantics and pragmatics (and accordingly between competence and performance) that I have presented. Many people consider the distinction less clear cut than Chomsky's initial separation of competence and performance allows for, and would, presumably, dispute my arguments against speech act semantics. However, despite this area of controversy, there is one point which is not in dispute. Whether or not in years to come linguists continue to analyse the semantics of natural language in terms of a primitive notion of truth, with the consequent narrow delimitation of the domain of semantics, all linguists continue to agree that the central task of any semantic theorist must be to make the correct predictions of relations such as synonymy, entailment, etc. And since this is naturally predicted by a truth-based semantics, it seems certain that, whatever form semantic theories eventually take, they will incorporate the insights gained by adopting a truth-based approach. For this reason, I shall only consider problems raised by truth-based implications in the remaining chapters of this book.

RECOMMENDED READING

For reading on speech acts, see the recommended reading list for chapter 4.

5.4   The term *pragmatics* is used in several different senses. For a distinction between these various senses, see Kempson *Presupposition and the Delimitation of Semantics* ch. 7. Grice's work falls into two separate categories – his theory of meaning$_{nn}$, so-called, and his theory of conversation. His theory of meaning, which has not been generally discussed by linguists, is presented in his articles 'Meaning' (reprinted in Strawson (ed.) *Philosophical Logic*, Rosenberg and Travis (eds.) *Readings in the Philosophy of Language*, Olshewsky (ed.) *Problems in the Philosophy of Language*, and Steinberg and Jakobovits (eds.) *Semantics*), 'Utterer's meaning, sentence-meaning and word-meaning' (reprinted in Searle (ed.) *The Philosophy of Language*), and 'Utterer's meaning and intentions'. This theory has been criticised by Ziff 'On H. P. Grice's theory of meaning' (reprinted in Steinberg and Jakobovits (eds.) *Semantics*), and extended by Schiffer in *Meaning*. But it is his theory of conversation outlined in Grice 'Logic and conversation' which has attracted the attention of linguists. See Wilson *Presuppositions and Non-Truth-Conditional Semantics*, Kempson *Presupposition and the Delimitation of Semantics* ch. 7–8, the collection of articles in Cole and Morgan (eds.) *Syntax and Semantics 3: Speech Acts*, Geiss and Zwicky 'On invited inferences'. A more formal approach to pragmatics has been made by Kasher 'Mood implicatures: a logical way of doing generative pragmatics'. For an independent account of pragmatics, see Lewis *Convention: A Philosophical Study*, a book which is critically evaluated together with Grice's work in Schiffer *Meaning*. Linguists have disagreed as to whether an analysis of metaphor should be part of a semantic account of language. See in this connection: Brooke-Rose *A Grammar of Metaphor*, Weinreich 'Explorations in semantic theory', Bickerton 'Prolegomena to a linguistic theory of metaphor', Matthews 'Concerning a "linguistic theory" of metaphor', Cohen and Margalit 'The role of inductive reasoning in the interpretation of metaphor'. For a bibliography of work on metaphor, see Shibles *Metaphor: An Annotated Bibliography and History*. See also Loewenberg 'Identifying metaphors', and Black 'Metaphor' in Black *Models and Metaphors*. On problems of style, see Ullmann *Meaning and Style* (and references cited there), Jacobs and Rosenbaum *Transformations, Style and Meaning*, Jakobson 'On the verbal art of William Blake and other poet-painters', Ohmann 'Generative grammars and the concept of literary style', Thorne 'Generative grammar and stylistic analysis' (and references cited there), and Katz *Semantic Theory* ch. 8. For reading on the disagreement over the competence–performance distinction, see the recommended reading list for chapter 4. On the related problem of the status of pragmatics within linguistic theory, see Schmerling 'Asymmetric conjunction and rules of conversation', Morgan 'Some interactions of syntax and pragmatics' and other articles in Cole and Morgan (eds.) *Syntax and Semantics 3: Speech Acts*, Kempson *Presupposition and the Delimitation of Semantics* ch. 9, and R. Lakoff 'Language in context'. For an account of performance which is in agreement with the position adopted in this book, see Fodor and Garrett 'Some reflections on competence and performance', Bever 'The cognitive basis for linguistic structures', and Fodor, Bever and Garrett *The Psychology of Language*.

6

The formalisation of word meaning

In chapter 3 I argued that to give the meaning of a sentence was to specify the necessary and sufficient truth conditions of that sentence, and I argued further that this was equivalent to specifying the logical form of that sentence (the level from which all entailments can be derived by general rule). Two of the conditions of adequacy that I outlined in chapter 1 have however so far been completely ignored: that a semantic theory, whatever its basis, characterise formally the relation between word meaning and sentence meaning for every sentence of the language; and since this set of sentences is infinite, that it do so in the form of a finite set of rules (or general principles). We have now to face this problem of formalising a semantic theory on the assumption that what is required is a set of general rules characterising the logical forms of the sentences of a language.

In so doing we are immediately confronted by a dilemma. The extent of the disagreement over the basis of meaning may have seemed fairly extreme, but the disagreement over the formalisation is much worse: almost every linguist and almost every logician working within semantics has his own terminological suggestions. Yet despite these idiosyncrasies, there are two main controversies over which linguists and logicians are currently arguing. These are (i) the nature of semantic rules, (ii) the relationship between the semantic properties of a language and the syntactic properties of a language. I shall be taking up both of these problems in more detail in due course (chapters 10 and 11), but it is important to have some idea of the issues before embarking on the details of any one proposed solution. The first problem concerns the status of semantic rules based on semantic components of the kind isolated by componential analysis (cf. 2.3 above). Until very recently, many linguists, particularly within transformational grammar, assumed that the task in semantics was merely to state the generalisations about relations between word meanings and to characterise the relationship between word meaning and sentence meaning; and they furthermore assumed that these generalisations could be most economically captured by means of semantic components (or features) combined in various ways to reflect relations and contrasts of meaning. Linguists have not generally provided an account of how these abstract components are themselves interpreted (cf. Katz' claim, discussed on pp. 19–20, that there was no need to define the term *semantic marker*). Accordingly, a representation of the meaning of a sentence given by linguists has commonly been an abstract componential representation. This view of the interpretation of sentences is very widely rejected by philosophers. The basis of their attack seems to be that a matching between the syntactic structure of a sentence and some representation of what is said to be the semantic structure of that sentence cannot be an explanation of the meaning of a sentence, for to explain the meaning of a sentence is to explain how the string of elements which make up a sentence are used to talk about non-linguistic entities such as individuals, properties, events, etc. Accordingly for them, a sentence[1] is only interpreted (i.e. given a meaning) if rules, called *functions*, are given for relating that sentence to non-linguistic entities such as individuals, properties, and the values true and false. So the first issue is whether semantics can legitimately involve abstract representations of meaning, based on components, at all. The second issue, which overlaps with the first (cf. 11.1 below), is whether syntactic generalisations are distinct from semantic ones. To those who are used to thinking of grammar (syntax) as obviously different from meaning, this may seem an unreal issue. But it is not. For if every generalisation we wish to make about the syntactic structure of the sentences of a language turns out to have an explanation in terms of the meaning of those sentences, then there is a real sense in which the syntactic generalisations we make are in fact semantic generalisations. The details of these positions we shall consider in due course: with these two independent problems outlined however, we can now envisage four possible solutions.

1 To explicate the meaning of a sentence is to give an abstract representation of the semantic structure of that sentence, but since there is no necessary relation between semantic generalisations about a

---

[1] In general all the relevant discussions within philosophy are about statements rather than sentences (cf. 3.4.1 above).

language and syntactic generalisations, this representation of semantic structure is separate from (though related to) the representation of syntactic structure of the sentence. (This was the position of Chomsky in 1965.)

II To explicate the meaning of a sentence is to give an abstract representation of the semantic structure of that sentence; and moreover for any sentence in a language its semantic representation is all that is required to capture syntactic generalisations about that sentence. (This is what has become known as generative semantics.)

III To explicate the meaning of a sentence is to do not one, but two things: (i) to give an abstract representation of the semantic structure of that sentence, just as in the first solution, (ii) to state functions between that semantic representation and the non-linguistic entities of truth values, as is schematically presented by the Tarskian formula discussed in chapter 3. The abstract semantic representation listed under (i) is said to be necessary because the relations to be stated under (ii) do not bear any direct relation to the generalisations characterised by the representation of syntactic structure (in this respect this position is identical to solution I).

IV To explicate the meaning of a sentence is to state the relation between the abstract system which constitutes the language and the values true and false (exactly as in III); but this relation can be stated directly from the constructs set up to capture generalisations about the syntactic structure of that language. There is thus no need for a level of semantic representation in addition to the representation of syntactic structure.[1] (This is a view which is widespread among logicians.)

I shall not be adopting either of the first two positions but shall instead be arguing for the third of these positions. For reasons which will emerge in the chapters which follow, in my view the evidence at present confirms what is the traditional view that the generalisations about the semantic properties of any given language do not correspond in anything like a one-to-one fashion to the generalisations about syntactic properties of that language. So in order to state semantic generalisations about a language, we need to set up semantic structures of some sort to capture the generalisations about meaning for any language. Since I have already argued that to give the meaning of a

---

[1] There is a misunderstanding between logicians and linguists as to the domain and function of syntax. Cf. 11.1 below for a discussion of their different conceptions of the term *syntax*.

sentence is to give the conditions for the truth of that sentence, and that a specification of these truth conditions is a specification of the logical form of a sentence, it follows that the semantic representations of sentence meaning that we set up in the following chapters will be specifications of logical form.[1] But in order for these semantic representations to be characterised as truth conditions within the theory, we need to have rules stating explicitly the relation between these abstract structures and the values true and false. In other words, the alternative listed as III which I shall be adopting is a conflation of the traditional linguist's view of semantics (listed as I) and the philosophers' view of semantics. With this conception of semantic representation in mind, we must now turn to the problem of the specification of such semantic representations.

Our main task in this chapter is to provide a means of capturing the meanings of words and their relationships one to another – in other words we shall be concerned here with what has been called lexical structure. I pointed out earlier (cf. p. 11 and 3.2 above) that if sentence meaning were given a meaning-independent characterisation, the meaning of words could legitimately be explained in terms of sentence meaning, the meaning a word has being the systematic contribution a word makes to the meaning of all the sentences in which it occurs.[2] Accordingly in a truth-conditional account of meaning, the meaning of a word will be the contribution it makes to the truth conditions of all the sentences in which it occurs.

6.1 *Word, lexical item* **and the problem of homonymy**

Before entering into the details of providing a formal characterisation of word meaning, we must clear up an ambiguity in the use of the term *word*. On the one hand, one might say that there is one word *tap* having various different meanings, as in the expressions *to give someone a tap on the shoulder*, and *a water tap*; but on the other hand, one might say that these expressions contain two different words *tap*. Words, in this latter sense of *word*, are often referred to by the term *lexical item*,

---

[1] The extent to which these specifications differ from a logician's concept of how logical forms are specified, I shall take up in due course: cf. 6.2.3 and 11.1 below.

[2] We shall shortly see (6.2.2) that though this is correct in so far as it goes, we still require an independent characterisation of the components in terms of which word meaning is characterised.

and from now on I shall use this separate term, and shall, in general, restrict the term *word* to the phonological complex. Isolating the construct of *lexical item*, or *lexeme* as it is sometimes called, enables us to characterise the paradigm *run*, *runs*, *running*, *ran* as different forms of one lexical item on the one hand and, on the other hand, to characterise the form *runs* in the two sentences *He runs the motorshow* and *He runs for Hampshire* as two separate lexical items, each with a separate entry in the dictionary. So for example, I shall say that though there is one word *bank*, there are two lexical items *bank*, one describing a side of a river, the other describing the financial institution referred to by the same phonological word. This phenomenon of multiple ambiguity of (phonological) words is known as homonymy, a term traditionally reserved for unrelated meaning of words. What are listed in the lexicon (theoretical dictionary) then, are lexical items, not words. And what we require of the theoretical account of lexical meaning is that this lexicon includes a specification for each lexical item of the contribution which that lexical item makes to the truth conditions of all the sentences in which it occurs.

This requirement is not as uncontroversial as it might seem. Are we entitled to say that a single lexical item has a consistent meaning which is common to all the occurrences of that item? Take for example the word *man*. Can one say that *man* represents two quite different lexical items in the sentences *Man is mortal* and *A man hit me*? Should one not rather say that even using the construct of lexical item, one has to allow for vacillation of meaning from context to context, a phenomenon traditionally distinguished from homonymy by the term polysemy? It seems that we are faced with two alternatives: one is to say that the meaning of a lexical item is not constant but varies from context to context; the other is to say on the contrary that the meaning a lexical item has is constant, but that sentences such as the two just mentioned contain two different lexical items, man_1 and man_2. If we adopt the former approach, we appear to be avoiding setting up numbers of lexical items for each distinct phonological word, but we have to be able to specify in a systematic way the interaction between context and lexical item. If we adopt the second approach, the lexicon in which each lexical item is characterised will be very much larger than might have been anticipated, for the phenomenon of related or extended senses of lexical items is a common one. To what extent are these apparently opposed viewpoints really alternatives? Let us consider another example of a word which involves multiple meanings, to assess the difference between these formulations. Consider the word *run* in the following sentences.

(1) He ran onto the field.
(2) He ran the race for Hampshire.
(3) The ball ran onto the field.
(4) The car is running well.
(5) The road runs from Manchester to Birmingham.
(6) He ran the motorshow.

None of these examples seems to be a case of metaphor,[1] which we have already argued should not in any case be captured at this level (cf. pp. 73–4), so each of them provides a potentially distinct lexical item. If we say that *run* in these sentences is the same lexical item, then our lexical entry for *run* will have to characterise *run* as having a disjunct specification of meaning: either it has a meaning corresponding to its use in (1) and (2) (when the referent of its subject is animate and has legs), or it has a meaning corresponding to its use in (3), where presumably the implication of fast directional motion is retained but not any of the precise physical characteristics of running, or it has a meaning corresponding to its use in (4) where only the implication of motion is retained, without any implication of direction, or it has a meaning corresponding to its use in (5) where only the implication of direction is retained without any implication of motion, or it has a meaning corresponding to (6) where the implication of motion is generalised as in (4), and in addition transferred to an event in time, the resultant implication being a general causative corresponding to 'cause to function'. We shall thus have a five-part disjunction to characterise the meaning of *run*. If on the other hand we take the alternative of specifying *run* as five-ways ambiguous, we shall have distinct lexical items, each with a distinct semantic representation. Characterised in this informal way, it might seem that despite the conflict in claims as to what constitutes a lexical item, there is little to choose between these alternatives, since both allow the (phonological) word *run* to have more than one interpretation. However, they lead to rather different predictions about sentence

---

[1] Each of the examples (3)–(6) could of course be argued to be metaphorical, but the strength of these arguments would depend on the extent to which these examples demand a double interpretation, a literal contradictory one as well as a re-interpreted metaphorical one (cf. p. 71 above). None of these, I think, has this dual property.

ambiguity.[1] The latter formulation implies that in environments where more than one of these interpretations is possible, the resulting sentence will be ambiguous with clearly distinct interpretations. If the first formulation of lexical meaning is correct, in which lexical meaning is characterised as vacillating for each lexical item over a listed set of possible interpretations, then, without any additional restriction, one would expect that in environments where more than one of these interpretations is possible, they should be simultaneously present as implications of the sentence. Let us consider an example. We have already seen that *run* can be used transitively either with its central sense to imply a specific kind of swift motion, or with a transferred causative sense to imply an action of organising on the part of the subject. The range of subjects with which these two senses of the verb can co-occur is very similar; the verb phrase *to run a race* can be predicated of animate subjects, the verb phrase *to run an organisation* can be predicated of human subjects. A sentence such as (2), *He ran the race for Hampshire*, therefore provides us with an example of the required type. It can certainly be used to imply that he was a competitor in the race, and it can also be used to imply that he organised the race. But can it be used to convey these two implications simultaneously? Surely not. Anyone who so attempted to use such a sentence would be accused of punning, and a pun depends for its effect at least in part on breaking the convention that where a sentence or word is ambiguous, only one interpretation may be conveyed at any one time. The prediction that (2) has two possible interpretations, but not a third in which the two interpretations are simultaneously implied, is an automatic consequence only of the formulation of varying lexical meaning in terms of quite separate lexical items, each of which has a constant semantic value: it is not an automatic consequence of the formulation of lexical meaning in terms of a single lexical item vacillating in its interpretation. For another example, notice the impossibility of using the sentence *Your car is running well down the hill* to imply both that your car is functioning well (corresponding to the sense of *run* in (4)), and that it is going fast down the hill (corresponding to the sense of *run* in (3)). This evidence suggests that our theoretical account of word meaning, which is undoubtedly variable, should in general for cases of multiple meaning be in terms of a number of separate lexical items for each phonological word, each lexical item having a specific semantic value corresponding to its systematic con-

[1] Cf. chapter 8 below for a more detailed discussion of ambiguity.

tribution to the interpretation of all the sentences in which it occurs.[1] Accordingly, in what follows I shall assume that the characterisation of lexical meaning is in general in terms of a single semantic represent-ation for each lexical item.

6.2 Lexical structure

We are now in a position to tackle the main problem of this chapter – the nature of semantic representation of lexical items, and the relations between these representations which any account of lexical structure must provide. We have already seen in chapter 2 that the vo-cabulary of a language is not an unrelated aggregate of words. On the contrary, as de Saussure among others pointed out early in this century, there are systematic relations between words within a language; and one of the burdens of a linguistic account of lexical meaning is to provide a characterisation of these relations.

What then are these inter-lexical relations which de Saussure and other linguists since then have drawn attention to? As a simple example, consider the set of words *man, woman, adult,* and *child.* The lexical item *man* which is used to refer to the human race (cf. p. 80 above) is a more general term than and its meaning includes that of the other lexical item *man,* and also that of the items *woman, adult* and *child.* What they all have in common is that they are used to refer to humans. This relationship between a more and a less general term is called hyponymy,[2] a definition of which we shall consider shortly. A similar example is provided by the set *woman, spinster, wife,* and *mother.* What each of these has in common is an implication of womanhood, human, adult and female; *wife, spinster* and *mother,* the less general terms, being hyponyms of the more general term *woman.* In contrast to this relation of hyponymy, where the meaning of one lexical item is totally included

---

[1] Examples of lexical items which *do* appear to need a disjunct semantic interpretation are words such as *book,* which can simultaneously be interpreted in terms of the physical properties of the object (when it behaves like a concrete noun) and in terms of the contents of the book (when it behaves like an abstract noun): *My book is three hundred pages long and is quite incomprehensible.* Examples such as this are not however generally thought to be the central cases of multiple meaning. Another example of a different sort whose semantic interpretation involves a disjunct specification is *or.* For a discussion of this kind of disjunction, cf. pp. 126–8 below.

[2] This term was first coined in linguistics by Bazell 1955, but its use in this sense was introduced by Lyons 1963.

within the meaning of the other are the relations between lexical items whose meanings are incompatible. Now clearly, in stating relations of lexical structure, we are not concerned with mere difference: we would not wish to say that a lexical item such as *chair* stood in any relation to an item such as *shout*. However we are concerned with the relations between items such as *chair*, *sofa*, *stool*, and between *shout*, *whisper* and *mutter*. The term which is in general use for the relation between lexical items whose meanings conflict is antonymy, oppositeness of meaning. But this is not a very helpful term since there are many ways in which lexical items can stand in opposition to each other. Along one parameter *man* stands in opposition to *woman*, but along another parameter *man* stands in opposition, not to *woman*, but to *boy*. More helpful is the division of incompatibility relations into four types. First there is the case of simple binary opposition, the true antonyms. The meaning of the item *alive* is incompatible with and opposed to the meaning of the item *dead*; the meaning of *married* is incompatible with and opposed to the meaning of (one sense of) *single*. In each case of these cases, there are just two terms in the set of incompatible items, the one the opposite of the other. However there are many cases where there is more than one item in the set of items, whose meanings are incompatible. The most well known is the set of colour terms. The meaning of *blue* is incompatible with the meaning of *red*, but it is also incompatible with the meanings of *yellow*, *brown*, *green*, etc. The set of colour terms is not restricted to two members whose meaning is opposite, but has many members, each of which stands in opposition to the other. Other examples of this type are classes of objects dealing with different types: *dining-room*, *sitting-room*, *bedroom*, *kitchen*, *bathroom*; *iron*, *lead*, *copper*, *zinc*; *saucepan*, *frying pan*, *poacher*; *glass*, *cup*, *mug*. These are the multiple taxonomies, sets of items containing more than two members, each with the same point of similarity, each with its particular distinguishing characteristic. A rather different kind of incompatibility is exemplified by the pairs *hot* and *cold*, *young* and *old*, *large* and *small*, for though these are antonyms in being opposite to each other, they are distinct from what I called the true antonyms. Unlike them, they do not correspond to absolute properties but are gradable. These gradable antonyms do not only stand in binary opposition. There may be a set of items, all mutually exclusive, all gradable, representing different points along the scale according to which they differ. For example, *hot* and *cold* are not the sole members of the set of words used for describing temperature. There are also *warm, tepid* and *cool,* whose respective meanings represent different temperature scales. The most striking aspect of the interpretation of these gradable antonyms is that they are not only gradable but that they are graded against different norms according to the items being discussed. For example, the temperature required to describe a swimming pool as hot is not the same as the temperature required to describe a drink as hot; the temperature of a cold ice-cream is not the same temperature as a cold shower. And to take another graded term, *old,* an old man is much older than an old dog, which is in its turn very much older than an old piece of cake. Moreover, even with a single expression, the interpretation is not constant, but may vary according as the norm in question varies. So for example there is no fixed range of years for which a book may be described as old. If one is referring to a standard set by history, a book has to be, say, one hundred years old to be described by the term *old,* but in order to be an old book of four-year-old Johnny, it need only be, say, two years old. The essential property of these gradable antonyms is that they are implicitly comparative terms, *hot* being higher on the temperature scale than the norm, *cold* being lower, whatever that norm may be – and this varies according to the object under description and according to the norm against which the object is being assessed. Similarly *old* is higher on the age scale than the norm for the object in question, *young* is lower on the age scale. It is for this reason that *A small elephant is a large animal* is not a contradiction, even though *A male elephant is a female animal* is contradictory, *male* and *female* not being gradable terms. The final type of incompatibility which can be isolated is the opposition demonstrated by such pairs as *own* and *belong to, buy* and *sell, above* and *below.* These have been called 'converse' pairs (cf. Lyons 1968: 467–9) for they exhibit a converse relation between the objects related. If for example some object A is above some other object B, then B is below A: if some individual A sells to some other individual B, B buys from A: if some individual owns some object B, then B belongs to A. A pair of lexical items form a converse pair if for two items x and y, the following sentence relations hold: *AxB* implies *ByA,* and *AyB* implies *BxA.* This definition includes as converse pairs the gradable items, and there is a parallel here. *Today is hotter than yesterday* implies *Yesterday was cooler than today.* However the terms which have been isolated as converse pairs are not themselves gradable. Many examples of converse pairs can be found among kinship relations. The

85

kinship sense of *child* and the item *parent* form a converse pair for *A is the child of B* implies *B is the parent of A*. So too do *wife* and *husband*.

By isolating these two main types of relation, hyponymy and incompatibility, we can characterise the relations between a large web of items. For lexical items do not just stand in one relationship to one other lexical item, but each stands in relationships to many other items. For example, *wife* simultaneously stands in a converse relation of incompatibility with *husband*, is mutually exclusive with *spinster*, is a hyponym of *woman*. *Woman* itself has as other hyponyms, *sculptress* and *waitress*, but is itself a hyponym of *adult*. *Adult* is incompatible with *child* under one interpretation of *child* (see below), and is itself a hyponym of *person*. If a word is ambiguous and corresponds to more than one lexical item, then the different lexical items will stand in different relationships to other lexical items. *Child* is one such example: it can either be used with a meaning incompatible with *adult* (call it *child₁*), or with a meaning incompatible with *parent* (*child₂*) to which it stands in a converse relation. Only the latter sense is a kinship term. Thus *child₁* is incompatible with *adult* and *parent*, but contains as hyponyms, *toddler*, *boy* and *baby*. *Child₂* is on the contrary not incompatible with *adult*, but is incompatible with *parent*. In a similar way, *man* in the sense of mankind is a hyponym of *man* in the sense of an adult, male, human. All these inter-related items can be said to form networks of relations, or lexical fields, as they have been called.

6.2.1 *Componential analysis and lexical relations*

So far the discussion of hyponymy and antonymy has been extremely informal. A much more explicit, clear and economical way of characterising these relations is to use the method of componential analysis, which assumes as we have already seen (p. 18 above) that words do not have unitary meanings but are complexes of components. On this view, *woman* would be analysed as having for its meaning a complex of components of [FEMALE], [ADULT], [HUMAN],[1] *spinster* as having for its meaning a complex of components of [FEMALE], [ADULT], [HUMAN], [NEVER MARRIED]. Using the method of componential analysis, we can then formally define hyponymy and incompatibility. A lexical item P can be defined as a hyponym of Q if all the features of Q are contained in the feature specification of P; and incompatibility can be defined as a relation between a set of items $P, Q, R, \ldots$ if they share

[1] '[XXX]' will be the notation used for semantic components.

a set of features but differ from each other by one or more contrasting features. On this basis it follows that *spinster* is a hyponym of *woman* because it contains all the features of *woman* as part of its specification; and that *spinster* is incompatible with *bachelor* by virtue of the contrast of sex specification and with *wife* by virtue of the marital specification.

6.2.2 *The relation between lexical items and semantic components*

Three problems present themselves immediately: the relation between the components and the lexical items themselves, the theoretical status of these components, and their formal representation. The second problem we have already touched on in 2.3 above, and we shall be returning to it shortly (6.2.3). However before considering either this problem or the formalisation of lexical items in terms of components in more detail, it is essential to clarify the relation between component and lexical item. The question we have to ask is: what is the relation between [ADULT] and *adult*, between [MARRIED] and *married*, etc.? It is generally claimed by those linguists who postulate the existence of semantic components that the components in terms of which lexical meaning is represented are not themselves lexical items, part of the language being described, but are part of the meta-language, the theoretical vocabulary set up to describe all languages (though cf. 6.2.5 below for a discussion of this view). Components such as [MALE], [ADULT], [NEVER MARRIED] are therefore universal constructs in terms of which such lexical items as *bachelor* in English can be characterised. There is said to be no more significance than mere convenience in using English for the meta-language to describe the lexical items and sentences of the language. It follows that items such as *adult* which happen to correspond to a single semantic component [ADULT] have a unitary semantic characterisation. Now it is particularly clear in these cases that if these semantic components are the basis on which lexical meaning is to be explained there must be some characterisation of [ADULT] independent of the item *adult*, for otherwise we have given no explanation at all. Moreover it will not suffice at this point merely to say that to give the meaning of a lexical item is to specify the contribution which that item makes to the meaning of sentences in which is occurs, though this is correct in so far as it goes. For in explaining the basis of a semantic representation of sentence meaning which includes the component [ADULT] predicated of some argument X (cf. 6.2.3 below) we wish to be able to interpret '[ADULT]X' as a condition for the truth of that sentence that there be an object having the property of being adult. That is to say, in giving a characterisation of sentence meaning in terms of truth conditions, we need to invoke an interpretation of the abstract semantic component [ADULT] which relates it in some way to the non-linguistic property of adulthood. It therefore seems that in addition to the vocabulary of semantic components expressing generalisations between lexical items, we need to have a principled way of relating these abstract components to the properties, individuals, etc., that they describe. This is the sense of interpretation which philosophers demand of the concept *semantic interpretation*. The nature of these rules of interpretation has long been a matter of dispute among philosophers, and I shall have no more to say about it at this point (though cf. 11.1 below), but it is important to bear in mind that unless there is some such interpretation of the semantic components, the characterisation of *adult* as having a meaning specification of [ADULT], or *bachelor* as having a meaning specification [ADULT] [HUMAN] [MALE] [NEVER MARRIED] is an essentially empty exercise. With this caveat in mind, let us now turn to the formalisation of semantic components such as these.

6.2.3 *The formal representation of semantic components*

We have now to consider the details of formally specifying the interpretation of lexical items in terms of semantic components. It has sometimes been suggested that a binary feature format along the lines adopted in phonology is an appropriate formalisation of such semantic components. Accordingly *spinster* might be characterised as having for its meaning

$$-[\text{MALE}] \ +[\text{HUMAN}] \ +[\text{ADULT}] \ -[\text{MARRIED}]$$

bachelor, an item incompatible with *spinster*, as having

$$+[\text{MALE}] \ +[\text{HUMAN}] \ +[\text{ADULT}] \ -[\text{MARRIED}]$$

wife, another incompatible item, as having

$$-[\text{MALE}] \ +[\text{HUMAN}] \ +[\text{ADULT}] \ +[\text{MARRIED}]$$

While this provides the neat characterisation of antonymy that the semantic representation of an incompatible pair differ by the value ('+' or '−') of one feature, this format will not do. We have already seen that sets of incompatible lexical items may not be restricted to being binary sets, and in any case the binary feature notation is quite un-suitable for large areas of the vocabulary. For consider a possible sem-antic representation of a verb like *kill* in terms of binary features:

$$+[CAUSE] \ +[DIE]$$

This is unsatisfactory for there is no representation of what the features are predicated of. Worse, in certain cases of antonymy such as *give* and *take*, where there is a converse relationship, there is no means of dis-tinguishing their semantic representations if no indication is given of what the features apply to. A simple binary feature notation would yield a representation such as

$$+[CAUSE] \ +[CHANGE\ OF\ POSSESSION]$$

for both verbs. The notation used in the standard formulation of predicate calculus avoids this indeterminacy by specifying for every predicate the number of required arguments. For example, *Fa* is a representation of the internal structure of a proposition in which some property *F*, referred to by the term *predicate*, is predicated by some individual *a*, referred to by the term *argument* (in traditional linguistic terms, this is subject and predicate written in the reverse order); and *Fab* is a representation of a proposition in which some relation *F* holds between two individuals *a* and *b* (in traditional linguistic terms, this is subject, verb and object written in the order verb-subject-object). A convenient solution then is to adopt this notation for a componential analysis. Thus instead of

$$+[CAUSE] \ +[DIE]$$

for *kill*, we can specify the meaning of kill as:

$$[CAUSE] \ X \ ([DIE]Y)^1$$

and instead of

$$+[CAUSE] \ +[CHANGE\ OF\ POSSESSION]$$

for *take* and *give*, one might suggest:

> *take*: [CAUSE] X ([HAVE]XY)
> [CAUSE] X (−[HAVE]ZY)

---

[1] Anything enclosed within the round brackets '(' and ')' is a representation of a proposition, which consists of a predicate followed by at least one argument.

give: [CAUSE] X ([HAVE]YZ)
[CAUSE] X (−[HAVE]XZ)

This formulation purports to state as the implications concomitant upon the use of the item *take* that the agent causes a change of possession such that he has the object and the person or object which had the object before does not. Conversely, to give something to someone is to effect a change of possession in the other direction, from agent to some other person.[1] More simple examples such as *wife* would involve just one variable:

[HUMAN] X
[ADULT] X
−[MALE] X
[MARRIED] X

In all these cases, the use of ' − ' is not in contrast to a converse ' + ' feature, but corresponds to logical negation.

In fact this notation is only partly like the notation of predicate calculus. Perhaps the most striking difference is in the use of variables. At this point my use of variables is informal and bears no obvious relation to the variables in logic, which must be bound in all well-formed formulae. The details of this binding however would take us into the characterisation of sentence meaning which is not the concern of this chapter (cf. 7.1.2 below). For the time being, notice only that the representation of what functions as an argument to any predicate is bound to differ from sentence to sentence: it cannot therefore be a lexical matter. There is another point of divergence between the representations given here and predicate calculus: in the representation of meaning for *kill* and *take*, propositions function as the second argument of the main predicate [CAUSE]. There are many more examples that suggest that in natural language, propositions function as arguments, though this is not allowed by the formation rules of predicate calculus. A further complication of the standard so-called first-order predicate calculus is the need to have predicates functioning as arguments. This appears to be necessary when some property is itself modified. Thus for

---

1 This account is extremely approximate, particularly in the use of the component [HAVE] (one can take a book from the table, but one cannot give a book to the table), and also in the lack of time specification relating the two causative complexes in each case. For a more detailed account, cf. Bendix 1969.

example the item *rush* implies a property of motion of some object where this property is of a particular fast kind. This can be captured by describing *rush* as having a semantic representation

[[FAST] MOTION] X

where [MOTION] is a component predicated of some object (represented by the variable X), and this component is itself an argument of which the qualification [FAST] is predicated (for a detailed justification of this particular complication to the notation of predicate calculus, cf. Bierwisch 1969).

In general then we can say that each lexical item is entered in the lexicon with a complex of semantic components[1] which can be represented by a predicate plus argument(s) notation like that of standard logic though with some modifications.[2] It has been further suggested that the semantic specification of lexical items can be stated most economically if the general relations which hold between lexical items are stated by means of so-called redundancy rules,[3] which apply automatically to lexical entries. These rules present an explicit statement of relations of hyponymy and antonymy: for example,

[HUMAN] X	→	[ANIMATE] X
[ADULT] X	→	[ANIMATE] X
[ANIMATE] X	→	[CONCRETE] X
[CONCRETE] X	→	−[ABSTRACT] X
[MOTION] X	→	[ACTIVITY] X[4]
[MARRIED] X	→	[ADULT] X

The specification in the actual entry of a lexical item in the lexicon such as *wife* will then not be

[MARRIED]X [ADULT]X −[MALE]X [HUMAN]X
[ANIMATE]X [CONCRETE]X −[ABSTRACT]X

1   In fact each entry has also its idiosyncratic syntactic and phonological properties.
2   Cf. chapter 9 and 11.1 below for a discussion of the discrepancy between predicate calculus and the logic required for a natural language.
3   These are in some respects comparable to the meaning postulates set up by Carnap: cf. Katz and Nagel 1974 on the distinction between the two formalisations. Cf. also 11.2 below for a discussion of the extent to which meaning postulates provide an alternative to componential analysis.
4   These rules need to be more complicated than this: cf. Bierwisch 1969 for detailed discussion of the problem of formalising such redundancy rules.

but merely

$$[MARRIED]X \quad -[MALE]X$$

Accordingly, within the standard transformational account of grammar, which assumes the correctness of componential analysis, the lexicon is said to contain a set of lexical entries each with a componential specification of its semantic, syntactic and phonological properties; and together with this list of lexical entries are a set of redundancy rules capturing all the general relationships which hold between the semantic components.[1]

6.2.4 *Componential analysis: the nature of the evidence*

Even if we were to accept the theoretical necessity of setting up semantic primitives of this type, it might be argued that such semantic components are entirely arbitrary, set up more or less at the whim of the analyst (cf. Fillmore 1971). However, though the theoretical status of semantic components is highly problematic, this particular accusation is unjust. For consider our characterisation of semantic components so far, keeping in mind the view that the meaning of each lexical item is the contribution that that item makes to the truth conditions of every sentence in which it occurs. On this view, each semantic component will be one part of a lexical item's contribution to sets of truth conditions. It follows from this that in any (positive) declarative sentence[2] a postulated necessary condition for the truth of that sentence cannot be simultaneously denied (i.e. also be not a necessary condition for the truth of that sentence). Take for example the more straightforward cases. Earlier (p. 89) I set up as a semantic representation for *kill*:

$$[CAUSE] \ X \ ([DIE] \ Y)$$

The evidence for this lies in the following sentences, both of which are contradictory:

(7) John killed Bill but Bill didn't die.
(8) John killed Bill but he was not the cause of Bill's death.

---

[1] There are also syntactic and phonological redundancy rules capturing the required generalisations of syntax and phonology. Cf. Chomsky 1970 on syntactic redundancy rules, Chomsky and Halle 1968 on phonological redundancy rules.
[2] There are independent reasons why this test does not work in negative sentences. Cf. 7.3 and 8.3 below for a discussion of negation.

If [CAUSE] is correctly a representation of part of the meaning of *kill*, then any (positive) declarative sentence should not be able to be used both to assert the truth of the action which the item *kill* is being used to describe and to assert the falsehood of the action corresponding to the component [CAUSE]. And so it turns out. Similarly for the component [DIE].[1] That is to say, if we are justified in assuming an interpretation of componential analyses as fully interpreted truth conditions on sentences, as I have argued we must, we can test any purported componential representation by devising a sentence in which both the condition in question and its negation are both necessary to the truth of that sentence. If the component is indeed part of the semantic representation, the resulting sentence is predicted to be necessarily false, a contradiction: if it is not, the sentence is predicted not to be. The importance of this test is that it is based on the assumption that the elements of a componential analysis are not merely abstract constructs of the meta-language but are given interpretations such that for example the relation between *cause*, [CAUSE], and the action corresponding to this component is explicitly stated (cf. 6.2.2). If, and only if, there is such a procedure interpreting the constructs of the meta-language, then we have a systematic procedure for testing proposed analyses. With this test in mind, consider the suggestion that *kill* is an intentional verb, in componential terms that *kill* has as part of its meaning:

$$[\text{INTEND}] \; X \; ([\text{CAUSE}] \; X \; ([\text{DIE}] \; Y))$$

The evidence however is against this since, unlike (7) and (8), (9) is not a contradiction.

(9) John killed Bill without intending to.

That is, if the suggestion that to kill someone always involves the intention to do so was correct, the truth conditions for (9) would include both the condition that John intended to kill Bill and the condition that John did not intend to kill Bill. (9) would therefore be a sentence which would be necessarily false since these two conditions can never simultaneously be fulfilled. That (9) is not a contradiction strongly suggests however that though *kill* can be used to describe actions which are intentional, this implication is not an inherent

---

[1] [DIE] is clearly not a semantic primitive. Cf. McCawley 1968a, Fodor 1970 for more detailed analyses.

property of *kill* (notice that one can equally say *Bill was killed by an avalanche* where there is no question of intention).[1]

For a more detailed example, consider the following sentences.

(10) †John followed Bill but neither of them moved.[2]

(11) †John followed Bill but he went in the opposite direction to Bill.

(12) †John$_i$ followed Bill$_j$ as he$_i$ ran in front of him$_j$.

(13) John followed Bill though he didn't intend to do so.

(14) John followed Bill slowly.

(15) †John chased Bill but neither of them moved.

(16) †John chased Bill but he went in the opposite direction to Bill.

(17) †John$_i$ chased Bill$_j$ as he$_i$ went in front of him$_j$.

(18) †John chased Bill though he didn't intend to go after him.

(19) †John chased Bill slowly.

(20) John chased Bill as Bill walked away.

(21) John chased Bill but he wasn't trying to catch up with him.

Sentences (10)–(12) and (15)–(17) provide evidence that both *follow* and *chase* contain as part of their meaning the implication of movement in a particular direction (or to a particular goal)[3] by both parties, call them for convenience X and Y, X being behind Y,[4] for all of these sentences are contradictory.[5] Sentences (13)–(14) however are not contradictions, indicating that though speed and intention of action are essential properties of the action of chasing, at least on the part of the chaser, they are not in the case of following. Furthermore both (20) and (21) are not contradictory, and they provide evidence against an analysis (Katz 1967, Bierwisch 1969) of the action implied by the use of the item *chase*

---

1 For a more detailed discussion of this sentence in connection with the problem of ambiguity, cf. p. 129 below.

2 '†' is used to indicate a contradiction here and throughout the book from this point. In this connection, cf. 7.2 below.

3 The position is in fact rather more complex than these data suggest. It appears that *follow* either implies both participants moving in the same direction or to the same goal, in that the following sentence is not a contradiction: *John followed Bill to New York but he went via the North Pole instead of the direct route.*

4 On the binding of these variables, cf. 7.1.2 below.

5 It might be objected that (10) and (15) are not contradictory since one can follow something without moving if one is on an escalator, but this is not relevant since one's body has still moved relative to the ground.

as involving speed on the part of both participants or as involving the specific intention on the part of the chaser to catch the one being chased. One can legitimately chase somebody for the fun of running after them. Accordingly, in formalising the semantic properties of *chase*, we have to provide a formal representation of a condition involving a complex intention on the part of the chaser, and in both *chase* and *follow* we have to provide some representation of the directional element (corresponding to an adverbial phrase of direction: compare *to go after John*). At this point we again face a problem: so little work has been done on the formalisation of the semantic properties of adverbials,[1] or indeed of intentions, that a detailed formal specification of items such as *chase* and *follow* cannot yet be given with any confidence of adequacy, even assuming the validity of componential analysis. Suffice it to say that this specification will have to give representations corresponding to the following approximately stated conditions:

> *follow*: [MOTION]X in Z
> [DIRECTION]Z
> [MOTION]Y in Z
> [BEHIND]XY[2]

> *chase*: [[FAST] MOTION]X in Z
> [DIRECTION]Z
> [MOTION]Y in Z
> [BEHIND]XY
> [INTEND] X ([MOTION]X in Z)

Whatever the difficulties of detailed statement, the principle is clear: the componential analyses of lexical items are set up in order to predict the requisite inter-sentence relations of contradiction and entailment; and it is precisely these relations which provide the evidence for the components entered in the lexicon as representations of lexical meaning. Now it may seem as though this method is viciously circular and hence worthless. But this is not so. It is circular of course, but harmlessly so. There is an analogue in the nature of syntactic evidence. For on the basis of the distributional properties of a language, for example that sentences behave like noun phrases, one sets up the grammar to contain rules, for example 'NP→S', which are given their particular form to

---

1 Though cf. Parsons 1972, Thomason and Stalnaker 1973, Lewis 1975.
2 Whether [BEHIND] is a legitimate semantic primitive is extremely doubtful. For an analysis of prepositions such as *behind*, cf. Bennett 1975.

predict the very properties which were evidence for the detailed formulation of the rules. The circle involved is only the circle represented
by data being the evidence for a theory which is set up with a form
precisely geared to predicting (and in this sense explaining) that data
(cf. p. 1 above). Thus if the assumptions on which componential
analysis is based are sound (and this remains debatable – cf. 6.2.2 above
and 11.2 below), then there is a valid method of providing detailed
motivation for individual components.

6.2.5 *Semantic universals?*

So far we have seen the beginnings of a componential
analysis of a vocabulary in terms of components representing the contribution a lexical item brings to the truth conditions of sentences in which
it occurs. The details of how this relation of word meaning and sentence
meaning can be expressed within such a framework remains as a
problem for the following chapter. But before turning to this, we have to
consider one of the most notorious aspects of lexical componential
analysis – the implicit universal status of the components themselves. In
line with the phonological and syntactic features used in transformational
grammar to describe phonological and syntactic properties of lexical
items, semantic components have been said to be part of a universal
language-neutral stock of features, from which each language may choose
a sub-set combined and arranged in varying ways to form the contrasting vocabularies of different languages. Perhaps the most vigorous
attacks on this position have come from anthropology: some anthropologists have argued that as languages reflect the culture of the people
who use them, these languages are no more comparable than the cultures
they reflect, which may be strikingly dissimilar. According to this view,
it is a distorting over-simplification to suggest that languages, as
reflections of their different cultures, use an identical stock of semantic
primitives.

In considering the plausibility of the claim of a universal semantic
vocabulary, it is important to bear in mind the different forms of
universal claims which can be made about semantics. First of all notice
that there is one aspect of semantic theory which is not controversial –
that the relation between lexical meaning and sentence meaning is the
same for all languages; in other words, that the form of rules giving
semantic interpretations of sentences is the same for all languages. In
Chomsky's terminology, these are formal universals, universal properties

of the form of grammars. This amounts to no more than the widespread claim among linguists that the form a grammar of natural languages is given should not vary from language to language. This claim is indeed the essence of theoretical linguistics today (cf. p. 5–7 above). The controversy concerns what Chomsky has labelled substantive universals, the vocabulary of the meta-language used to formulate the specific rules relevant to each language: and in the realm of semantics, this is the set of semantic components in terms of which semantic rules are stated.

The strongest claim of all is that the lexical items of languages stand in a one-to-one correspondence across languages, each item of one language requiring the same complex of features as its corresponding translation equivalent in another language. This claim is very obviously false. Even languages of similar culture as French and English differ at this level: there is no exact translation equivalent of *chair* in French. *Chaise* is used for upright chairs with no arms such as are used for sitting up at a table and eating from, whereas *fauteuil* is used for chairs with arms which are characteristically comfortable, so-called 'easy', chairs. Yet there is no evidence whatever within English that the item *chair* is ambiguous between two senses corresponding to the sense of *chaise* and the sense of *fauteuil*. And for a more striking example, consider Fijian which has six different words corresponding to our one word *we*. The contrasts involved are whether the hearer is implied to be included in the group referred to by the word, whether the group is implied to contain just two people or more than two, if the latter whether in addition the group is implied to contain few people or many. If we represent this diagrammatically in terms of components, we have, corresponding to *we* in English, the following approximate componential representations:

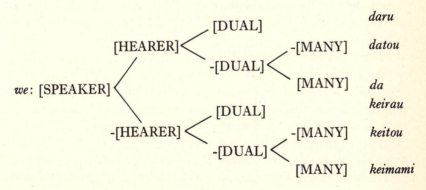

There is no question but that in English we do not have six lexical items $we_1 \ldots we_6$. Though it is sometimes assumed that the semantic universal position can be attacked on this basis (as indeed is implicit in the contrary view expressed by Whorf: cf. Carroll (ed.) 1956), this is not the position held today by those linguists who are committed to a theory using a universal set of semantic components.

There are two main alternative positions which such linguists might hold. The stronger of these is that each language makes use of the same set of semantic components but with differing distributions between languages. Notice that Fijian is not a counter-example to this claim, since in both English and Fijian – and presumably at least the majority of languages – the distinction between speaker and hearer, that between groups of two members and groups with more than two members, and between groups with a few members and groups with many members, are required in the characterisation of the total language, even though not at the same points. If this claim is correct, it would have to follow that all culturally specific items in a language, of which perhaps the most striking are religious terms, could be analysed in terms of semantic components which were universal in the sense of being required at some other point in other languages.

This is the strongest of claims made for the universality of semantic components. It is not however held by many linguists. By far the most widely accepted position with respect to semantic components is a position parallel to the claim made about phonological features. In phonological theory, it is generally claimed, at least within transformational grammar, that there is a universal set of features required in the description of human language, of which each language chooses a sub-set. So in semantics, it is often claimed that there is a universal set of semantic components of which the grammars of individual languages require a sub-set. What is not so often pointed out is that this claim is so weak as to allow the counter-example to its own position. For suppose there is a language which requires in its description a semantic component, apparently not decomposable into other components, which is unique to the description of this language – no other language requires it. There is nothing in this claim about semantic universals to exclude postulating this semantic component as part of the set of universal semantic components: it is just a coincidence that no other language makes use of this particular universal component. It thus appears that this form of the claim about semantic universals is entirely contentless, unless some restriction can be placed on the set of semantic components postulated. Unlike phonology, this has so far not been done (though for a discussion of possible ways of reducing the number of semantic components, cf. Weinreich 1962).

Many linguists who are rightly suspicious of the strong form of universal claim about semantic components suggest that the semantic components required in the description of languages can be divided into two types, those which are universal, required in the description of all human languages, and those which have to be set up for the description of particular languages. Now this claim may seem the most reasonable, but it is important to realise the consequence of adopting such a view. Implicit in some recent formulations of linguistic theory, and in particular in transformational grammar, is the assumption that the goal of a linguistic theory is to specify those features of human language which are both unique to human languages and shared by all of them (cf. pp. 5–7). Moreover it is assumed that it is in the specification of the meta-language – both in terms of the specification of the vocabulary of the meta-language and in terms of the specification of types of rule formulation allowed by that meta-language – that linguists can characterise uniquely what constitutes a human language. Thus intrinsic to the search for linguistic universals is the assumption of a single meta-language for describing the full range of natural languages. If however we adopt the view that a different meta-vocabulary has to be set up for each language, then we are relinquishing this claim, at least with respect to semantics. Implicit in such a view would be the claim that while there are universal constraints on a grammar of natural language with respect to syntactic structure and phonological structure, this claim cannot be fully maintained with respect to semantic structure. Now while this position may turn out to be correct, it is not one for those working in semantics to adopt lightly, for it has as a consequence that only those aspects of semantic structure which can be claimed to be part of a universal linguistic theory will be of interest to those linguists whose concern is to work towards such a unique characterisation of human languages. Other areas, such as lexical meaning, which depend on analyses in terms of components whose universal status is in serious doubt, will simply not be controversial because they will not be part of this over-all linguistic theory.

To sum up, we have considered three alternative views about the universality of semantic components: that all languages require the same set of semantic components; that all languages can be described by a universal set of semantic components of which each language requires a sub-set; that the description of all languages involves a certain set of semantic components, but that in addition a number of semantic components have to be set up for the description of individual languages.[1] The solution to this problem remains an open question. However in assessing the strengths of the alternative positions, it is important to bear in mind those distinctions which seem to be required in linguistic theory for independent reasons. Recall for example the distinction between semantics and pragmatics, which I argued in chapters 4 and 5 were necessary levels in an analysis of communication. It was argued on this view that any message a speaker might convey over and above the strictly defined meaning of the sentence which he uses was best analysed at a second level of pragmatics, an explanation which assumed a prior account of the meaning of sentences. Within the domain of pragmatics, it was further argued, lay an explanation of problems such as metaphor and stylistics. Now much of the debate about semantic universals, which has been going on for many years, centres around the problem of translation. It is often argued on the one hand that the possibility of translation from language to language provides evidence for the universalist semantic position. On the other hand, it is often argued, translation from one language to another is so difficult, and indeed often impossible, that any claim of universal components reflecting this inter-translatability is as crude as the translations from language to language that it reflects. I shall not go into the details of the varying positions. However it must be borne in mind that in translating from one language to another, a translator will be concerned not merely with what the sentences he is translating strictly mean, but with what the author of the sentences is trying to convey. He is in fact attempting to translate from one language to another not merely a set of sentences, but a communication. But we have already seen that in analysing communication, a large number of indeterminacies arise since the content of the communication, may vary according as the assumptions of the particular speaker and particular hearer vary. Allowing for a separation in the explanation of semantic and pragmatic factors in communication thus provides a natural basis for

---

[1] There are in fact a number of additional alternatives. For a much fuller discussion of the problems involved in setting up universal semantic components, cf. Lyons 1977: ch. 9 5.9.9

explaining at least part of the difficulties in translating, as these may often be caused by such indeterminacies. Accepting the separation of a semantic account of language from a pragmatic account of communication has therefore an important consequence for the problem of semantic universals. For many of the difficulties which undoubtedly do arise in translating from language to language, particularly when the cultures involved are widely divergent, will not necessarily affect the universal status of semantic components, since these difficulties may be explained at the level of pragmatics, not by the formal mechanisms of the semantic theory itself. Now it does not follow that problems in translation can all be dismissed as irrelevant to the problem of semantic universals, but it is essential to differentiate between those aspects of translation which are relevant to a truth-conditional, or indeed any account of cognitive, meaning, and those aspects of translation which can be explained at a pragmatic level. For reasons such as these it seems to me that the evidence against the universal status of semantic components is not as overwhelming as some discussions of translation difficulties might lead one to suppose.

6.3 **Summary**

In this chapter we have considered how the phenomenon of widely varying word meaning can be neatly characterised if we assume that for the great majority of cases of multiple meaning, we are dealing with discrete lexical items, each with its own semantic specification. Moreover, having made this idealisation, the methods of componential analysis provide an economical way of characterising the relations between these lexical items. However, as we have seen, even if we accept the idealisation that the phenomenon of multiple meaning in the various uses of a word corresponds in each case to a separate lexical item, the assumptions on which semantic components as part of a general linguistic theory depend, are quite insecure. In the first place, if componential analysis is to provide an explanatory account of lexical meaning, there must be some interpretation of the components themselves relating the components to the properties they are said to correspond to. Yet no linguist has provided such an interpretation as part of a semantic theory,[1] despite the fact that the test for setting up particular

---

1   Until very recently, this has been solely the concern of philosophers and logicians. Cf. 11.1 below for a discussion of the interpretation of semantic representations.

componential representations of lexical meaning assumes the existence of such an interpretation of the components. In addition to this uncertainty about the interpretation of the components themselves, there are very considerable problems in attributing universal status to such components. Yet if universal status is not claimed for these components, it appears that their status within linguistic theory itself is seriously undermined. The accumulation of these problems with the analysis of word meaning has sometimes led to the conclusion that generalisations about word meaning are not something which semantic theory, and hence linguistic theory, can capture. The consequence of so pessimistic a conclusion is that linguistic theory would not characterise the relation between sentences such as *John killed Bill* and *John caused Bill to die*, *Blind men are in danger* and *Men who cannot see are in danger*, and *Those men who have never been married may not join this club* and *Those men who are bachelors may not join this club*. There are few linguists who would accept such a conclusion. In devising a semantic theory as part of a linguistic theory, almost all linguists are committed to explaining relations such as these, and, as we shall see in chapter 10, the disagreement between linguists today as to the relation between syntactic and semantic generalisations, depends to a considerable extent on arguments which assume that relations such as these must be captured by linguistic theory. In line then with the majority of linguists today, I shall assume for the remainder of this book, despite the serious problems involved in componential analysis (though cf. 11.2 below), that an account of lexical meaning in terms of semantic components can be made viable.

In this chapter, we have been concerned solely with lexical meaning and no attempt has been made to capture generalisations about lexical meaning in terms of a system of finite rules generating lexical items. There is good reason for this: despite the fact that a list of lexical items as provided in a lexicon is considerably longer than a list of phonological words, such a lexicon is unquestionably finite. That is to say, the lexical items of a language can indeed be presented as a mere list. The problem of accounting for sentence meaning in any language is rather different, since this involves the description of an infinite set of sentences. It is this problem that is the burden of our next chapter.

RECOMMENDED READING

The amount of terminological variation in linguistic semantics is considerable:
for a representative selection, see Katz *Semantic Theory*, Bierwisch 'On
certain problems of semantic representation', McCawley 'Meaning and the
description of languages', G. Lakoff 'Linguistics and natural logic', Jackendoff
Semantic Interpretation in a Generative Grammar, Leech *Towards a Semantic
Description of English*, Weinreich 'On the semantic structure of language',
Greimas *Sémantique Structurale*, Wierzbicka *Semantic Primitives*, Pottier
Systématique des Éléments de Relation, Bartsch and Vennemann *Semantic
Structures*, Fillmore 'Types of lexical information', Keenan 'On semantically
based grammar'. What these linguists in general share, though Bartsch and
Vennemann, and Keenan, are exceptions, is that an explanation of an inter-
pretation of the sentence takes the form of an abstract representation. Dis-
cussions of the semantic interpretation of natural languages by logicians in-
clude Lewis 'General semantics', Vermazen's review of Katz and Postal
An Integrated Theory of Linguistic Descriptions, Stalnaker 'Pragmatics',
Montague 'English as a formal language', and the collection of articles in
Keenan (ed.) *Formal Semantics of Natural Language*. Alternative I is repre-
sented by Chomsky *Aspects of the Theory of Syntax*, Jackendoff *Semantic
Interpretation in a Generative Grammar*, Katz and Postal *An Integrated
Theory of Linguistic Descriptions* (for more detailed references, see the
recommended reading for chapter 10). Alternative II is represented by G.
Lakoff 'On generative semantics', 'Linguistics and natural logic', McCawley
'The role of semantics in grammar', Seuren 'Autonomous versus semantic
syntax', and the articles in Seuren (ed.) *Semantic Syntax* (more detailed
references are given in chapter 10). Alternative IV is represented by the work
of the logicians listed above. For an account of the nature of word meaning in
a truth-based semantics, see Wiggins 'On sentence-sense, word-sense and
difference of word-sense' s. 2.

6.1   Ambiguity in the term *word* is a traditional problem for linguists: see
for example Robins *General Linguistics: An Introductory Survey* pp. 193–201,
and Lyons *Introduction to Theoretical Linguistics* ch. 5 s. 5.4 for the distinction
between *word* and *lexical item* (the term used by him is *lexeme*). On the distinction between polysemy and homonymy, which I have argued here has no
theoretical significance, see Lyons *Structural Semantics*, pp. 15–18, Lehrer
Semantic Fields and Lexical Structure, Ullmann *Semantics*, Weinreich 'On the
semantic structure of language' p. 142.

6.2   Lyons *Introduction to Theoretical Linguistics* ch. 10 gives an excellent
detailed account of lexical structure; but see also Lehrer *Semantic Fields and
Lexical Structure* ch. 2.

6.2.1   For a characterisation of hyponymy and incompatibility in terms of
componential analysis see for example Leech *Semantics* ch. 6, Katz *Semantic
Theory* ch. 2 s. 6.

6.2.2   Linguists using the method of componential analysis often gloss over the problem of the relation between lexical items and semantic components. See however Wierzbicka *Semantic Primitives*, Weinreich 'Lexicographic definition in descriptive semantics', Lyons *Introduction to Theoretical Linguistics* ch. 10 s. 10.5.5.

6.2.3   The formalisation that I have adopted here is that of Bierwisch: see Bierwisch 'On certain problems of semantic representation', 'On classifying semantic features'. Examples of the use of binary features in semantics are Chomsky *Aspects of the Theory of Syntax*, Leech *Semantics* and *Towards a Semantic Description of English*; and a detailed discussion of their inadequacy is given in Lehrer *Semantic Fields and Lexical Structure* ch. 3. A wide range of vocabulary has now been analysed by means of componential analysis: see for example Lehrer *Semantic Fields and Lexical Structure*, Bendix *Componential Analysis of General Vocabulary*, Bierwisch 'Some semantic universals of German adjectives', Burling *Man's Many Voices*, Wierzbicka *Semantic Primitives*, Wotjak *Untersuchungen zur Struktur der Bedeutung*, Hundsnurscher *Neuere Methoden der Semantik*. A detailed discussion of redundancy rules is given in Bierwisch 'On certain problems of semantic representation', and Katz *The Philosophy of Language* pp. 224–39.

6.2.4   Componential analyses have sometimes been tested by informant tests. See in particular Bendix *Componential Analysis of General Vocabulary* and Leech 'On the theory and practice of semantic testing'. The examples I have used here concern *kill*, and *chase* and *follow*. For an analysis of *chase*, see Katz *Semantic Theory* ch. 3 s. 8, Bierwisch 'On certain problems of semantic representation'. For partial formalisations of the semantic properties of adverbials, see Lewis 'Adverbs of quantification', Davidson 'The logical form of action sentences', Parsons 'Some problems concerning the logic of grammatical modifiers', Fodor 'Troubles about actions', Thomason and Stalnaker 'A semantic theory of adverbs'.

6.2.5   A useful collection of articles on the position adopted by Whorf that languages reflect the culture of the people who speak them and may therefore even be incomparable is in Hook (ed.) *Language and Philosophy* s. 1. For Whorf's own contribution to this area of debate see Carroll (ed.) *Thought and Reality: Selected Writings of Benjamin Lee Whorf*. For general discussions of the problem of semantic universals, see Lyons *Semantics*, Lehrer *Semantic Fields and Lexical Structure*, Weinreich 'On the semantic structure of language'. On the question of semantic universals with respect to specific areas of vocabulary, see Bierwisch 'Some semantic universals of German adjectives', Teller 'Some discussion and extension of Manfred Bierwisch's work on German adjectivals', Berlin and Kay *Basic Color Terms*, McNeill 'Colour and colour terminology'. For Chomsky's distinction of *formal universal* and *substantive universal*, see Chomsky *Aspects of the Theory of Syntax* ch. 1. On the problems of translation see Quine 'The problem of meaning in linguistics' (reprinted in Fodor and Katz (eds.) *The Structure of Language*) and Steiner

After Babel: Aspects of Language and Translation. On the restriction of semantics to exclude lexical relations, see Sampson 'The concept "semantic representation"', and Fodor, Fodor and Garrett 'The psychological unreality of semantic representations'.

7
Sentence meaning

7.1 Deep structure and semantic representations of sentence meaning

The problem of characterising the relation between lexical meaning and sentence meaning and the problem of the extent of the interdependence of syntax and semantics are so closely linked that they are virtually one and the same problem: and it is somewhat artificial to assume that one can be discussed without simultaneously discussing the other. However the relation between syntactic and semantic structure is controversial, and before entering into that particular morass of arguments, we need to consider some general principles of sentence interpretation, and the problems presented by negative sentences and by ambiguity. For purposes of exegesis then, I shall put forward initially a view most closely linked with the standard 1965 theory of syntax.

7.1.1 *The definition of deep structure*

In 1965 Chomsky spelled out and justified in some detail what was entailed in his use of the term *deep structure*. The setting up of this level arose from considering how a grammar must be written if it is to generate (i.e. describe) the infinite set of sentences of which a language is made up together with a structural (syntactic) description of that sentence. As the justification of this level of deep structure becomes important in considering the relation between syntax and semantics, it is worth recalling briefly how the need for such a level arose. It is uncontroversial that all languages involve hierarchical structures, not merely linear strings of words. To capture this hierarchical aspect of language, linguists set up rules, which in accordance with the terminology of transformational grammar, I shall call phrase structure rules.[1] What

---

[1] Alternative theories of grammar to transformational grammar were criticised on this basis by Postal 1964, though it might be argued that they

Chomsky argued in 1957, and in more detail in 1965, was that while grammars containing only such phrase structure rules (a phrase structure grammar) were in principle able to describe an infinite set of sentences making up a language, there were certain generalisations about languages which such grammars could not capture. Chief amongst these were generalisations about structure which are obscured by the actual sequence of lexical items in a sentence. For example, the sentences *John promised Bill to go* and *John persuaded Bill to go* are identical in so far as they contain a subject noun phrase, a main verb, a noun phrase object and a following non-finite verb. What they differ in is the structural relationships between these items – in the second sentence the object noun phrase is understood as the subject of the following non-finite verb, but not in the first. Another generalisation said to be hard to capture in a grammar containing only phrase structure rules is the generalisation about transitivity. Traditionally, transitive verbs have been described as verbs which must have a following noun phrase object, but this is obscured by the sequence of elements in sentences such as (1)–(4) where the object does not follow the verb.

(1) Which book did James buy?
(2) Which book did Sue want James to buy?
(3) Which book did Bill say Sue wanted James to buy?
(4) Which book do you think Bill said Sue wanted James to buy?

What Chomsky suggested was that while phrase structure rules capture one essential aspect of natural languages, they can only capture facts such as these, and many more, at a more abstract level called deep structure, a level at which none of the obscurities in the sentence itself remained, and all the structural properties could be stated explicitly. The consequence of accepting the justification of this more abstract level of description in stating the generalisations about the structure of a sentence, is that such a grammar requires a means of stating the relation between this level, deep structure, and the sentence in question. Now this relation is said to be captured by transformational rules. To take one brief example, consider again *John persuaded Bill to go* and *John promised Bill to go*. If we are to give a structural account of subject–object relations in the sentences of a language, then the distinction between these two sentences requires a level more abstract than the

are not equivalent to phrase-structure grammars as Postal argues and are not therefore open to this form of criticism.

sentences themselves at which the phrase structure configurations actually contain distinguishing structural features, as in figures I and II.

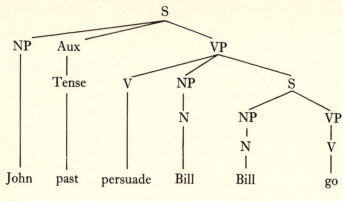

Fig. I

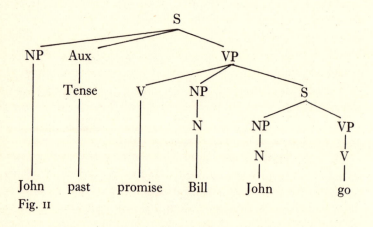

Fig. II

where it is structurally specified that the subject of *go* differs in the two cases. If we now assume that any structural account of these two sentences does indeed require this type of general statement, then our grammar must state the precise relation between this structure and the sentence itself: and it is this which is captured by transformational rules, in these cases deleting the embedded subjects.

In accordance with a considerable body of arguments along these lines, the level of deep structure was generally defined as the level at which subject and object relations are stated, the level at which restrictions such as transitivity v. intransitivity (called strict sub-categorisation restrictions) are stated, the output of the phrase structure rules, the input to the transformational rules, and also the level at which lexical items are inserted from the lexicon (this is a problem I shall return to in chapter 10), and finally a further property of deep structure was said to be that it was the level at which ambiguous sentences were disambiguated.[1] The detailed syntactic justification for this level need not concern us. Suffice it to say that in a Chomsky 1965-type model, it is the deep structure of every sentence which presents an explicit characterisation of relations such as subject and object, with all the information from the lexicon about the idiosyncratic semantic and syntactic properties of each lexical item in the sentence. Thus sentences such as *Kiss David, Shout for Sue's candidate* will have a specified subject at the level of deep structure, and sentences such as *I want Bill to go* and *I want to go* will have their contrasting subjects of *go* specified at that level.

What is of more importance at this juncture is to point out what the level of deep structure does not provide in a Chomskian-style model: it does not give a representation of meaning for the sentence – it merely gives a componential representation of the meaning of each item in the sentence (together with syntactic and phonological features) and a (partial) syntactic analysis of that sentence. In order to obtain a semantic representation of the sentence, we have to combine these two sources of information.

7.1.2 *A projection rule for sentence meaning*

There are several formulations of the way in which lexical meaning in the form of complexes of semantic components systematically combine to form representations of sentence meanings, but all those which linguists have devised so far seem to evade the most interesting problems involved in characterising the interpretation of sentences, and in general they seem crude and simplistic. The formulation which is perhaps least open to this charge is that of Bierwisch (cf. Bierwisch 1969), and it is this formulation that I shall present as a point of departure.

The way in which Bierwisch suggested that the relation between lexical meaning and sentence meaning could be stated concerns the constraining of the variables which form part of the semantic representa-

---

[1] The relation between ambiguity and deep structure is not quite this simple, at least in Chomsky's discussion of deep structure. Cf. pp. 180-1 below.

tion of the lexical items (cf. pp. 89–92 above). Rather than merely being arbitrarily distinguished by the letters X and Y, the semantic representation of a word such as *kill* for example, should state explicitly that (*a*) the (deep structure) subject of *kill* must be interpreted as the individual who is the cause of the killing, (*b*) the (deep structure) object of *kill* must be interpreted as the individual who has undergone the death. The standard way of indexing for subject and object is by the subscripts '[NP,S]' and '[NP,VP]'[1] respectively. Accordingly, Bierwisch suggested that the variables in the lexical entry be indexed with respect to the requisite syntactic functions. The lexical entry for *kill* on this basis would be:

$$[\text{CAUSE}]\ X_{NP,S}\ ([\text{BECOME}]\ (-[\text{ALIVE}]\ X_{NP,VP}))$$

The rule which forms sentence interpretations from a string of lexical items with entries along these lines then merely has to guarantee that the syntactically indexed variables in the lexical representation of the verb

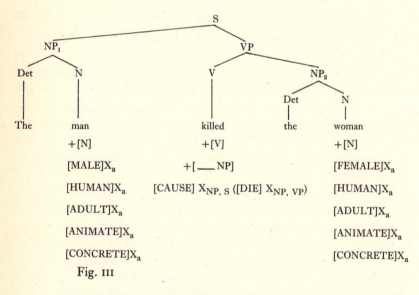

Fig. III

---

[1] A symbol with a subscript of the form [a,b] refers to a node *a* which is immediately dominated by *b*, as in the following configuration:

are in fact interpreted as implying a reference to the same individuals as are implied to possess the properties described in the various noun phrases in the deep structure. Most detailed suggestions of this process depend on an assumption that, as part of its deep structure, each noun phrase has an individual index which guarantees its distinctness from every other individual. Accordingly the deep structure specification of *The man killed the woman* (ignoring the problems of implications of reference and tense) would be as shown in figure III. Bierwisch suggested that a semantic rule of interpretation, a so-called 'projection' rule, then performs two operations: (i) it substitutes the reference index for the syntactic index of the lexical entry (with the constraint that this can only take place for any noun phrase if the syntactic index in question matches the configuration of structure described in that syntactic index);[1] and (ii) it joins all the resulting semantic complexes by '&'[2] to form an unordered set. Thus for example, the phrase marker in figure III is interpreted as:

$$[\text{MALE}]X_1 \ \& \ [\text{HUMAN}]X_1 \ \& \ [\text{ADULT}]X_1 \ \& \ [\text{ANIMATE}]X_1$$
$$\& \ [\text{CONCRETE}]X_1 \ \& \ [\text{FEMALE}]X_2 \ \& \ [\text{HUMAN}]X_2 \ \&$$
$$[\text{ADULT}]X_2 \ \& \ [\text{ANIMATE}]X_2 \ \& \ [\text{CONCRETE}]X_2 \ \&$$
$$[\text{CAUSE}]X_1([\text{DIE}]X_2)$$

One of the main weaknesses in this account of the relation between lexical meaning and sentence meaning, as I have presented it here, is the absence of any specification of the implications of reference or of tense, and these involve numerous problems. There are however two points about this formulation of the relation between lexical meaning and sentence meaning which are worthy of note. First, the use of syntactically indexed variables as arguments for the semantic components provides a neat characterisation of the insight that the meaning of a lexical item is the set of conditions it systematically contributes to the truth conditions of sentences in which it occurs. Secondly, the fact that the output of the rule is stated as a conjunction of semantic components reflects the requirement that our characterisation of sentence meaning should

---

[1] In the case of the lexical entries for nouns, the syntactic index has to reflect the fact that nouns can occur in more than one position in the sentence. Hence in figure III, lexical entries for *man* and *woman* include the syntactic index X_a, where $a \equiv$ [NP,S] v [NP,VP] v [NP,PP]. Here and in all subsequent formulations, 'v' corresponds to the logically inclusive *or*.

[2] '&' represents the logical operator of co-ordination corresponding to *and*.

correspond to a set of truth conditions. To this extent, such a rule formulation seems to represent a tentative step in the right direction. This type of projection rule thus serves as an example of one way of characterising the systematic relation between lexical meaning and sentence meaning where lexical meaning is explicitly characterised as the contribution a lexical item makes to sentence meaning.

What is more important at this point than the details of the formalism is the relation between the semantic representation of a sentence and its syntactic representation which is implicit in this model. On this view, allied to the Chomsky 1965 position, the statement of the semantic properties of a sentence depends on syntactic constructs such as *subject, object, noun phrase, sentence.* That is to say, this model of semantic representations presents the claim that a statement of the semantic properties of a sentence depends on a prior account of syntactic constructs given at the level of deep structure. And this is the sense in which Chomsky's 1965 model of syntax is said to have the generative power, being independent of and logically prior to an account of the semantic structure of the sentence; semantics on the other hand is said to be interpretive, dependent on the constructs defined by the rules describing the syntactic structure. Now the account of the interdependence between syntax and semantics is one of the main current points of controversy, the details of which we shall take up in chapter 10. Indeed this particular view of the syntax–semantics interdependence, in which the representation of the semantic structure of a sentence is said to be dependent solely on information provided by the level of deep structure, is not widely held any longer for reasons which I shall consider in that chapter, but since it is the view from which current disagreements within transformational grammar have stemmed, it forms a necessary starting point for the discussions of the chapters ahead.

7.2 Selectional restrictions: the problem of anomaly

A problem often discussed in connection with the prediction of sentence meaning is the problem of the status to be accorded to sentences such as (5)–(7).

(5) Truth broke the window.
(6) I can see the sounds dancing across the concert hall.
(7) Green ideas slept furiously.

Are these sentences not well formed sentences of the language and as such to be excluded from the competence model as ungrammatical, are they syntactically well-formed but meaningless, or is their oddity due to the impossibility of the event they depict, the oddity in question being a non-linguistic matter? All these alternative solutions have been put forward. The first solution was suggested by Chomsky. In 1965 he suggested that the deviance of this type of sentence would be most economically explained at the level of deep structure, by placing appropriate conditions (called *selectional restrictions*) on the insertion of lexical items into a deep structure representation. So for example *sleep* would be described in the lexicon as only occurring in sentences with a subject noun phrase containing an animate noun. This type of condition guaranteed that no string of the type exemplified by (5)–(7) would be generated by the grammar. There are good reasons however for thinking that an explanation in terms of syntactic structure and individual lexical items cannot be right:

(i) Constraints to block sentences such as (5)–(7) must be stated in terms of the semantic properties of the entire noun phrase, and not in terms merely of the surrounding nouns, because whatever the status of the oddity of *Our brother became pregnant, Our male cousin became pregnant* is just as odd and for the same reasons. The syntax-based explanation cannot account for this for it only has access to the semantic interpretation of the individual nouns, not to the semantic interpretation of phrases such as *male cousin*.

(ii) When embedded as a complement to verbs such as *say*, these so-called selectional restrictions can be violated without giving rise to an oddity of the entire sentence in which they occur:

(8) John said that rocks get diabetes.
(9) Our five-year-old son told Mary that stones have babies.

(iii) In certain negative environments, the same problem arises: a co-occurrence between subject and predicate which would be odd in a positive sentence is entirely well formed in these negative environments:

(10) A rock doesn't get diabetes.
(11) Worms don't worry about money.
(12) You don't kill rocks; you smash them.

In both of these two last cases, special caveats would have to be added to Chomsky's proposal so as to allow the grammar to predict their well-formedness. But there is no way of doing this which is not ad hoc.

(iv) Where a verb or adjective has a particular selectional restriction and the noun it modifies is unmarked for that specification, the resulting phrase is interpreted as having that specification as part of its meaning:

(13) John hit it.
(14) It flew over the buildings.

Thus the object noun phrase of *hit* in (13) is understood as referring to a solid object, the subject noun phrase of *flew* in (14) as referring to something with wings. Again special caveats have to be added to predict the interpretation of these sentences, caveats which would have to specify the environment in which an allegedly syntactic restriction plays a part in the semantic interpretation of sentences.

This evidence suggests fairly unambiguously that Chomsky's proposal is inadequate, and indeed it is not now widely held: whatever else the basis of this type of restriction might be, it is not simply a constraint on the co-occurrence of verbs and their adjacent nouns independent of all other factors.

The suggestion that these sentences are syntactically well formed but meaningless is made by both Katz and Bierwisch, who formulate such selectional specifications as a well-formedness condition, not on syntactic structures as Chomsky did, but on semantic representations. On their view, it would, for example, be a condition of there being an interpretation of a sentence containing the verb *kill* that the (deep structure) object of the verb have a semantic representation containing the semantic component [ANIMATE], thus predicting that where this condition is not met as in *Bill killed the stone*, the semantic projection rule cannot operate, the sentence has no interpretation, and the sentence is, literally, meaningless. According to this view then, the oddity of sentences (5)–(7) is characterised as ungrammatical, but only in the sense that the over-all competence grammar does not include them within the set of well-formed (grammatical) sentences of the language, by virtue of their failing to meet the required conditions stated in the semantic component. The advantage of this view is that it distinguishes between anomalous sentences such as these, which are said to have no semantic interpretation and are hence, in the wide sense, ungrammatical, and sentences such as (15) and (16) which are grammatical and have an interpretation, but this interpretation is contradictory.

(15) † John ran home and yet he didn't run home.
(16) † The student who is working for his exams is not working for his exams.

However there is reason to doubt the validity of any analysis of this type of sentence which characterises them as meaningless. In the first place, the set of examples (iii) remain unexplained on this view and special caveats have to be added to prevent the prediction of deviance in these cases. Moreover without such a special caveat an analysis of sentences such as *Rocks get diabetes* and *Stones have babies* as having no meaning will have as a consequence the prediction that sentence pairs such as (17)–(18) and (19)–(20) will be synonymous in each case, because the contribution of the complement sentences to the interpretation of the whole would be the same, namely nothing, their being meaningless. The set of sentences listed under (iv) presents a similar problem, and a further different caveat would have to be added to the account to prevent the prediction of anomaly in these cases.

(17) James said that rocks get diabetes.
(18) James said that stones have babies.
(19) Our five-year-old son told Mavis that stones have babies.
(20) Our five-year-old son told Mavis that his toothbrush tells lies.

Finally, there are examples which suggest that any analysis which assesses anomalous sentences such as (5)–(7) as ungrammatical and not generated by the grammar must be wrong. Consider the pair of sentences (21)–(22).[1]

(21) Priestley's most important discovery supports combustion.
(22) Einstein's most important discovery supports combustion.

Only one of these sentences is anomalous. Einstein's most important discovery was not an object but an abstract proposition. It is thus arguable that it is not merely false to say that his most important discovery supports combustion, but anomalous. Yet the distinction between these two sentences depends solely on our knowing what the respective discoveries of Priestley and Einstein were. If therefore our characterisation of anomaly is to include an explanation of the difference between these two, then it appears that any characterisation of anomaly in terms of a semantically based ungrammaticality will be insufficient, for the distinction between (21) and (22) is not even semantic but depends solely on what we know about Priestley and about Einstein. The problem is not restricted to such rarified topics as scientific discoveries. All sentences containing pronominal noun phrases present a similar problem. If the sentence *It likes cakes* is said by someone indicating that

---

[1] These examples are from Thomason 1972.

it refers to a stone in his back garden, the utterance of his sentence will be anomalous in just the same way and for the same reason as the sentence *The stone in my back garden likes cakes* is anomalous. If therefore a uniform account of anomaly is to be provided, the evidence seems to suggest that such an account cannot be solely in terms of semantic rules of the grammar, but must include non-linguistic considerations. But, according to the view expressed in chapter 5 (cf. 5.5 above in particular), such an account would therefore be outside the bounds of semantics. The semantic characterisation of *Colourless green ideas sleep furiously* would therefore be no different in kind from a sentence such as *John walked in*, the entire phenomenon of anomaly being pushed aside as pragmatic. This conclusion seems unfortunate, for whatever the status of the oddity of a sentence such as *Colourless green ideas sleep furiously*, it is surely at least in part due to the conflict in the semantic interpretation of the lexical items the sentence contains.

We have briefly considered three alternative suggestions about sentences such as (5)–(7): that they are syntactically deviant, that they are semantically deviant, and that their oddity is due to the way the world is structured rather than to the way the language is structured. There is yet one further alternative. Consider again the sentences listed under (iv) (p. 114). I pointed out there that if a verb places a certain constraint on the semantic category of noun phrases it can co-occur with, then when the noun phrase following it is unmarked for the specification in question, as with a pronominal noun phrase, the noun phrase is nevertheless understood to imply the specification in question. So, for example, *Bill killed it* implies that the object referred to by *it* was animate. In line with sentences such as this, suppose then we say that such selectional specifications are simply part of the contribution the verb, or adjective, makes to the truth conditions of the sentences in which it occurs. *Kill* for example would be listed in the lexicon as contributing to the truth conditions of the sentences in which it occurs not only the complex '$[CAUSE]X_{NP,S} ([DIE]X_{NP,VP})$' but also the component '$[ANIMATE]X_{NP,VP}$'. On this view, the specification in question is not a well-formedness condition on sentences, or on semantic representations, but is one aspect of the meaning of a lexical item, no different in kind from other aspects of lexical meaning. Such a view would predict that sentences such as (5)–(7) are necessarily false, there being conflicting truth conditions in each case, that *The stone in my back garden likes cakes* is necessarily false for the same reason, and that *It likes cakes* said of a stone is merely false. What this analysis relinquishes is the distinction between a contradictory sentence and an anomalous sentence. All such sentences are described as necessarily false. Accordingly, (5)–(7), and (15)–(16) (see p. 114 above), would be characterised identically. What this analysis appears not to provide either is any distinction between (21) and (22). The semantic representations of both differ only in that they contain different proper names. However it is possible that this omission is not incorrect. Both (21) and (22) contain the noun *discovery*, and *discovery* is an item like *book* which we have to describe as having a multiple meaning, varying according to context (cf. p. 83 n. 1 above). Recall that *book* could be used either as a concrete noun (referring to such properties as its length and weight), or as an abstract noun (referring to its subject matter). In these two particular examples, (21) and (22), we face a similar problem. Our knowledge of what the respective discoveries of Priestley and Einstein were rules out one way in which *discovery* can be understood, and a different way in each case. But in (22) this causes a conflict, for the predication *supports combustion* demands the opposite interpretation of its subject. This property of *discovery*, that it is open to different interpretations according to context (linguistic or otherwise), thus provides us with grounds within the theory for explaining the difference between (21) and (22), since the context does evoke different interpretations in these two cases. These examples do not therefore force the conclusion that anomaly itself cannot be accounted for within semantics.

We have considered four alternative accounts of anomalous sentences such as *Green ideas sleep furiously*: (i) that they are ungrammatical and that their deviance is due to constraints on noun–verb co-occurrences, (ii) that they are ungrammatical and that their deviance is due to their having no possible semantic interpretation, (iii) that they are grammatical but contradictory, and no different in kind from contradictions such as (15) and (16), (iv) that they are grammatical, and their oddity is due to the oddity of the situation they describe. Of these four, the last three remain as possible alternative solutions, each with its advantages and disadvantages. The final choice between them I must leave open as a decision would involve considerably more detailed discussion than we have time for here.

7.3 Negation
So far we have seen the outlines of a component-based

semantics functioning as part of a general competence model. This form of semantic representation depends on the theoretical model containing (i) a lexicon with lexical entries giving sets of semantic components which represent the contribution of the lexical items to the meaning of the sentences in which they occur; (ii) an infinite set of deep structures characterised by a (finite) set of phrase structure rules; and (iii) a projection rule which for any sentence combines these semantic representations of the lexical items in the sentence with syntactic information given in the sentence's deep structure to form a semantic representation for the sentence, which takes the form of a conjoint set of abstract conditions.

The projection rule we have so far considered is not the one and only semantic projection rule. Separate rules are needed for the so-called opaque contexts (cf. chapter 2 pp. 14–15 above). In particular there is the problem of interpreting negative sentences. How can we reconcile the claim that to give the meaning of a lexical item is to state the conditions which that item contributes to the set of truth conditions of all sentences in which it occurs, with sentences such as (23)–(26), none of which has as a necessary condition for its truth the contribution made by any single lexical item.

(23) John didn't kill Mary.
(24) Sue wasn't strangled.
(25) There aren't any spinsters in the village.
(26) Susie didn't chase the cat.

It is not a necessary condition for the truth of (23) that John caused Mary's death, or indeed that Mary died, nor is it a necessary condition of (24) that Sue was killed by an obstruction of her windpipe, nor of (25) that there be any unmarried women in the village, nor of (26) that Susie either intended to follow the cat, or that she followed it, or indeed that she moved at all. Though there are a number of problems over the exact interpretation of negative sentences which we shall return to in the following chapters, the basis of the solution is relatively uncontroversial.[1] Unlike positive indicative sentences which are used to assert some proposition, negative sentences are used to claim that their corresponding positive proposition is false. Accordingly, for example, just as the

---

[1] I shall consider in chapter 9 the problem of whether negative sentences should be subdivided into two categories, denial negation and descriptive negation.

necessary and sufficient conditions for the truth of *It was a woman* (ignoring tense) are that there be someone who was human, female, and adult, so the necessary and sufficient conditions for the truth of *It wasn't a woman* are that the conditions required for the truth of *It was a woman* are not in fact met in the world. Thus *It wasn't a woman* is true if, for example, either there was someone but it was a girl (not an adult), or if there was someone but it was a man (not female), or if there was someone but it was a boy (not female and not adult), or if there was something but it was a dog (not human), etc. In other words, unlike positive sentences (unless these are ambiguous), there are a number of alternative ways in which negative sentences can be said to be true. There is no one single set of conditions which guarantees the truth of any negative sentence; but there are a number of conditions the satisfaction of any of which will guarantee its truth. In the case of *It wasn't a woman* I listed four such alternatives. Consider also *Maisie didn't murder Mr Smith*. This is true either if she killed him but didn't intend to, or if she didn't actually manage to cause his death though it took him four months to get better, or if Mr Smith was murdered but not by Maisie, or if it wasn't Mr Smith that Maisie murdered but somebody else, among other possibilities. Equivalently what this sentence indicates is that the sentence *Maisie murdered Mr Smith* does not correspond to the state of affairs in question. This failure of correspondence may have one of several causes, as I have just indicated: which of these is the cause of the lack of correspondence is not specified in the sentence, but is left vague. All that the sentence implies is that the correspondence between the sentence *Maisie murdered Mr Smith* and the state of affairs at the time of utterance required for the truth of that sentence fails to hold. Now this property of negative sentences, that they imply, and are true under, a disjunction of conditions can be captured quite straightforwardly if we adopt a well-known rule of logic, an equivalence known as de Morgan's law. This states that for any proposition P and any proposition Q, the logical negation of the conjunction of P and Q is equivalent to the negation of either P or Q:

$$-(P \ \& \ Q) \equiv -P \ v \ -Q^1$$

To see how this applies in the case of negation, look back at the interpretation of *It wasn't a woman* that we have already discussed. This was

---

1 The so-called vel operator 'v', corresponding to *or*, has to be understood inclusively as allowing either one of $-P$ and $-Q$ to be true, or both.

that the sentence was true if either it was not a female person (but a man) or that it was not an adult (but a girl) or that it was not a person (but an animal), etc. But this is precisely what the de Morgan equivalence captures: that a claim that some conjoint set of propositions is false is equivalent to a claim that one or more members of that set is false. Thus the interpretation of a negative sentence is a disjunction (a series in which each item is joined to its fellows by 'v', the logical operator corresponding to *or*) of the negations of each condition which is part of the corresponding positive sentence. Thus if we have a sentence *P* whose semantic representation (the output of the projection rule forming sentence interpretations) is the set of conditions

$$[M_1] \ \& \ [M_2] \ \& \ [M_3] \ \& \ [M_4]$$

the negation of that sentence will have as its semantic representation (the output of the projection rule for negative sentences)

$$-[M_1] \ v \ -[M_2] \ v \ -[M_3] \ v \ -[M_4]$$

In other words the projection rule of negation has as input a conjoint set of conditions and as output a disjunct set of conditions.

Now clearly this formulation does not provide a complete answer to the problem of negation.[1] We have only considered conjoined components, yet we saw previously that components could stand in other relations: predicates could function as arguments to other predicates such as in *rush*: ([[FAST]MOTION]X); and they could also be embedded within a proposition as in *kill*: ([CAUSE]X([DIE]Y)). The rule of negation has to be complicated to allow for these different dependencies. Furthermore, though we are not concerned with which particular component fails to hold on any particular occasion, any more than we are interested in whether on any particular occasion a given sentence is true or not, we are concerned to know whether there is any limit to the disjunction involved in negation. Are there some components in the semantic representation of a sentence which cannot be interpreted as being denied? Equivalently, is there any entailment of the positive sentence which is also an entailment of the corresponding negative sentence? This is the problem we shall be facing in chapter 9. There is yet another problem about negation to be solved. In chapter 3 (p. 40 above) I gave a characterisation of ambiguity within a truth-

---

[1] For more detailed accounts within a Bierwisch-style model, cf. Bierwisch 1969, and Kempson 1975.

conditional semantics, namely that a sentence is ambiguous if it can be true under two different sets of conditions. Thus to recall the original discussion, a sentence such as *Washing machines can be tiresome* is characterised as ambiguous because it is true either under the condition (set of conditions) that the action of cleaning machines with water can be tiresome or under the condition (set of conditions) that machines which do the washing can be tiresome. But we have just seen that negative sentences are true under more than one condition. It seems prima facie that we are committed to predicting that all negative sentences are many ways ambiguous. This last problem, the problem of distinguishing ambiguity and vagueness, lies at the heart of much misunderstanding in semantics, and it is therefore important to clarify the problem as much as possible before embarking on the detailed problems that await us in the final chapters of the book.

RECOMMENDED READING

There are now many introductory books on transformational grammar. On the justification and definition of deep structure, students should still consider Chomsky *Syntactic Structures* and *Aspects of the Theory of Syntax* essential reading. A particularly good introduction to detailed syntactic argument is Akmajian and Heny *An Introduction to the Principles of Transformational Grammar*. A clear though by no means elementary introduction is given in Bach *Syntactic Theory* (see especially chs. 3, 5, 6, 7). Other expositions of the 1965 version of transformational grammar which can be recommended are given in Grinder and Elgin *Guide to Transformational Grammar* and Fromkin and Rodman *An Introduction to Language*. The first specification of semantic generalisations within transformational grammar was given by Katz and Fodor in 'The structure of a semantic theory', shortly to be followed by Katz and Postal *An Integrated Theory of Linguistic Descriptions*. Another formulation related to these is Weinreich's 'Explorations in semantic theory'. The account given here is based on that of Bierwisch: see his 'On certain problems of semantic representation' and 'On classifying semantic features'. A similar account, though using a more idiosyncratic formalism, is given by Katz: see his *Semantic Theory*. The use of referential indices on noun phrases to imply distinctness of the referent indicated by the noun phrase is common practice among linguists, but see in this connection Karttunen 'Definite descriptions with crossing coreference' and Hall-Partee 'Deletion and variable binding' (and references cited there). For references on the relation between syntactic structure and semantic representation, see the recommended reading for chapter 10.

7.2 The problem presented by sentences such as *Colourless green ideas sleep furiously* has been discussed both in the philosophical and the linguistic literature. The philosophical account which is perhaps most helpful to linguists is Thomason 'A semantic theory of sortal incorrectness', but see also Drange *Type Crossings*, Sommers 'Types and ontology', Ziff 'About ungrammaticalness' (reprinted in Ziff *Philosophic Turnings*). This problem has been discussed at some length within transformational grammar. Much of what Chomsky has written on the subject is usefully collected together in Allen and Van Buren (eds.) *Chomsky: Selected Readings* ch. 5. McCawley was the first transformational linguist to point out the inadequacies of Chomsky's syntactic approach with McCawley 'The role of semantics in grammar', 'Where do noun phrases come from?'. For a disagreement between Katz and McCawley on this topic, see Katz 'Generative semantics versus interpretative semantics' and McCawley 'Interpretative semantics meets Frankenstein'. Chomsky's position has been in part defended by Kuroda 'Remarks on selectional restrictions and presuppositions'. That these restrictions depend on pragmatic speaker-dependent factors is argued by G. Lakoff in 'Presupposition and relative well-formedness'.

7.3   The exposition of the projection rule for negation is taken from Bierwisch 'On certain problems of semantic representation'. A detailed discussion of this rule is also given in Kempson *Presupposition and the Delimitation of Semantics* ch. 1. For a related account by Katz see Katz *Semantic Theory* ch. 4. s. 4. Other references relevant to negation are given in the recommended reading for chapters 8 and 9.

8

Ambiguity and vagueness

It may seem as though little need be said about ambiguity in that it is a clear-cut phenomenon: both words and sentences can have more than one meaning, and the semantic rules a linguist sets up must state correctly for each language which words and sentences have more than one meaning – what more is there to it than that? This view of ambiguity is not incorrect, but it is entirely mistaken to think that there is little problem in deciding of a given sentence whether or not it is ambiguous. The problem lies in deciding what counts as ambiguity, as we have already partly seen in chapter 6 (cf. 6.1 above). While there are some clear cases – for example *Flying planes can be dangerous*, *We saw her duck* – there are many cases where it is not at all clear whether the word, phrase, or sentence in question is ambiguous or not. Take the word *good*. Is it ambiguous? One might think not. But consider the sentence *She has good legs*. This can either mean that she has healthy legs (no varicose veins, no broken or badly mended bones, no weak ankles, etc.), or it can mean that she has beautiful legs, or it can mean that she has legs which function well (as an athlete's, say, or a gymnast's, or indeed if the object referred to is a horse her legs may be understood to function well from the point of view of racing). So we have to grant that the word *good* may be used in sentences with different interpretations where the difference lies solely in the basis of the evaluation the word *good* has been used to make. The question remains: do we wish to say that the meaning of the word *good* differs as the basis of the evaluation differs, or do we say that the word *good* corresponds to one single lexical item, whose meaning is common to all these different bases of evaluation? If we think of the word *good* in isolation, there is I think a tendency to consider it as a single lexical item with a single interpretation, however hard that interpretation may be to state; but if we think of sentences containing *good* then there is a conflicting tendency to see the sentences as ambiguous. And indeed those who have discussed the problems presented by this word are divided as to whether or not it is ambiguous. The problem is compounded when we look at other phrases containing *good*. *A good student* describes either someone who behaves well, or someone who works well, or even someone who works haphazardly but shows a high level of ability: a good film is either one which gives enjoyment or one which is thought to be of lasting value. What has to be decided is whether the meaning of *good* is homogeneous and neutral between all these different specifications, or whether *good* has different meanings according to its use in describing different things. In more general terms, this presents an example of the difficulty of distinguishing ambiguity from lack of specification, or vagueness.

8.1 Four types of vagueness

To see the extent of the problem of distinguishing ambiguity from vagueness, let us consider the different types of vagueness which languages present us with. Broadly speaking there are four main types, though they are not unrelated to each other: (i) referential vagueness, where the meaning of the lexical item is in principle clear enough, but it may be hard to decide whether or not the item can be applied to certain objects; (ii) indeterminacy of meaning, where the meaning itself of an item seems indeterminate; (iii) lack of specification in the meaning of an item, where the meaning is clear but is only generally specified; (iv) disjunction in the specification of the meaning of an item, where the meaning involves an either–or statement of different interpretation possibilities.

Firstly, referential vagueness. Take for example the lexical items *city* and *town*. Presumably we can at least roughly agree that a city is a place where a large collection of people live,[1] and it is made up of a large number of houses; whereas a town is simply any place where a collection of people live, made up of a certain number of houses. Towns can be small or large, but cities are big by definition (just as villages are small by definition). Now even if we can agree that the meanings of the items need to have a specification along these lines, we shall certainly find difficulty in individual cases in deciding whether or not some place is a city, or a town. Is Salisbury a city? Most of us would say not. Is Bradford a city? Or Aberdeen? Notice that it will not do to specify as part of the

---

[1] There is an alternative interpretation of *city* as a town with a cathedral but this is gradually being superseded by the interpretation discussed here.

meaning of the item that a city must contain a minimum number of inhabitants, for we can talk of Roman cities or the cities of Minoan Crete where the numbers might scarcely exceed that of a present-day village. There are many examples of this kind of vagueness. When is a mountain not a mountain but merely a hill? When is a forest not a forest but a wood? What crucially distinguishes a house from a cottage? And so on.

The second type of vagueness is indeterminacy of the meaning of an item or phrase, where the interpretation seems itself quite intangible and indeterminate. Perhaps the most extreme example of this in English is the possessive construction – *John's book, John's train, John's sheets*. *John's book* can be used to describe the book John wrote, the book he owns, the book he has been reading, the book he has been told to read, the book he was carrying when he came into the room, etc. *John's train* can be used to describe the train he normally goes to work on, the train he is going to catch, the train he drives, the train he is guardsman of, the train he owns, the train he made, or is making, the train he designed, etc. *John's sheets* may be used to describe not only the sheets John owns, made, or designed, but also the sheets which go on the bed which he is going to sleep in. In the face of this variety, it seems clear that we can say little about the meaning of possessive constructions other than that there must be some relation of association between the 'possessor' and the 'possessed'. The meaning is otherwise quite indeterminate. Into this class too, we might wish to enter *good*, since its meaning seems, while intuitively at least in the main homogeneous, to be so variable.

The third type of vagueness that I isolated was lack of specification in the meaning of an item, where the meaning though in principle quite clear is very general.[1] The simplest example of lack of specification is an item like *neighbour* which is unspecified for sex, or for that matter, race, or age, etc. It can be applied to people as disparate as a tiny, five-foot Welshman studying Philosophy, and a six-foot Ghanaian girl who has seven children and who only did four years of schooling. Perhaps less obvious examples are verbs such as *go* and *do* which both have a clearly specifiable meaning and yet cover a wide variety of actions, since this meaning is so general. The sentence *He went to the station* can be used to

---

[1]   It is arguable that lack of specification itself does not necessarily cause vagueness, but since examples of this type are often confused with ambiguity, I have included it here.

describe actions as dissimilar as walking, running, going on a bicycle, going on a motor-bike, or going in a Rolls-Royce, to mention but a few, for *go* is quite unspecified as to the specification of the action. It simply has a meaning of directional motion.[1] *I've done the sitting-room* can be used by the speaker to imply that he/she has dusted the sitting-room, cleaned it, painted it, laid the floor in it, emptied it, set alight to it, stolen the silver out of it, etc., depending on whether the speaker is a cleaner, a painter, a floor-layer, a furniture remover, a pyromaniac, or a thief. Despite this, the meaning of the item *do* is not itself indeterminate. The expression *to do some object – to do the engine, to do the dishes, to do the cupboard –* means to carry out some action involving that object; but what the action is is quite unspecified.

A rather different kind of lack of specification is involved in the fourth type of vagueness I have isolated: the cases where the meaning of an item involves the disjunction of different interpretations. Now it may seem as though this distinction between a disjunct specification within a single lexical item, and cases of ambiguity characterised by discrete lexical items remains quite unclear, particularly as I argued in chapter 6 (6.1 above) against such disjunct specification in the case of an item such as *run*, which is a central example of a word with multiple interpretations. In that chapter I suggested that disjunction within a single lexical item leads to a prediction that where more than one of these disjunctions can be interpreted, then such interpretations should be possible simultaneously. This I argued was not so for most cases of multiple meaning. However, as I pointed out there, there are a few cases of lexical items which have this property, and this is the fourth type of vagueness that needs to be isolated. To see the validity of this type of characterisation consider what is perhaps the central example: *or*.

(1) The applicants for the job either had a first-class degree or some teaching experience.
(2) All competitors must either be male or wear a one-piece swimming costume.

In each of these cases, the implication that *or* contributes to the sentence as a whole is that one of the two conjuncts is true. In (1), the applicants are implied to have had either a first-class degree but no teaching

---

[1] It also has extended senses as in *The freezer has stopped going, His work is going well*, but I have already argued that these are quite separate (cf. pp. 81–3).

experience, or teaching experience but not a first-class degree, or possibly both. That is to say, there is an interpretation in which both implications can be held simultaneously. In (2), the implication is similar. The utterer of such a sentence would certainly not be excluding the possibility of both of the conjuncts being true, for this would imply that a male competitor had either to wear nothing or a two-piece costume! On the contrary, the sentence allows the following types of competitor: male competitors (whether wearing a one-piece costume or not) and non-male competitors wearing a one-piece costume. This disjunction in the characterisation of *or* can be stated more formally in terms of truth conditions. The logical operator *v*, corresponding to *or*, has been defined in the following way:

> Any sentence of the form P v Q (where P and Q each represent sentences) will be true if and only if either P is true, or Q is true, or P and Q are true.

This definition can be more conveniently displayed in a truth-table definition:[1]

P	Q	P v Q
T	T	T
T	F	T
F	T	T
F	F	F

What this definition captures is that *P or Q*, which corresponds to P v Q (though cf. n. 2 of this page), can be true under different conditions without these different conditions being themselves the basis for an ambiguity in *or*. *Or* is not three-ways ambiguous according as P is true but not Q, Q is true but not P, and both P and Q are true.[2]

[1] The table has to be read from left to right, the particular truth value of P v Q being in each case dependent on the truth values of P and Q (stated on the left of the vertical column).

[2] It is however commonly assumed that *or* is ambiguous between the sense I have characterised here, called inclusive *or*, and exclusive *or* which only allows the possibility of either one of its conjunct sentences being true but not both. Since this second sense of *or* also involves a disjunction, it provides another example which requires a disjunct specification.

Another important example of disjunction in a single semantic representation is provided by negation, which we have already briefly considered. What we can now see is that the disjunction in the statement of meaning of negative sentences is directly dependent on the characterisation of *or*. For, as we saw in chapter 7, negative sentences are logically equivalent to corresponding sentences containing *or* by virtue of the de Morgan equivalence

$$-(P \ \& \ Q) \equiv -P \ v \ -Q$$

and it follows automatically that the semantics of negation like the semantics of *or* involves a disjunction of interpretation possibilities, rather than being ambiguous in as many ways as the negative sentence in question can be true.[1] Now cases such as *or* and negation, which involve such a disjunction of truth conditions as an inherent part of their specification of meaning, are cases which are most commonly confused with ambiguity. And as we shall see in chapters 9 and 10, theoretical arguments of considerable substance are often based on what is alleged to be ambiguity. For this reason, it is of central importance to linguists to distinguish the various types of vagueness from true cases of ambiguity.

8.2 **An ambiguity test**

In order to be certain of separating out cases of vagueness from cases of ambiguity, we need a test which distinguishes clear cases of vagueness and ambiguity, and which will give us some basis for deciding on the less clear cases. Let us look first at the preliminary truth-conditional definition of ambiguity (cf. p. 40 above): does this provide a basis for distinguishing the two phenomena? Unfortunately the answer is clearly 'No'. Our definition of ambiguity, which is a standard truth-conditional definition, is that a sentence is ambiguous if it can be true in quite different circumstances. But this would predict that in all cases where the meaning is unspecified, the sentence in question would be as many ways ambiguous as the contrasting circumstances which that unspecified meaning allowed the sentence to be true in. There is an alternative, equivalent formulation of this definition: that a sentence is ambiguous if it can be simultaneously true and false, relative to the same state of affairs. But this alternative characterisation is no more helpful

---

[1] As with *or*, this over-all disjunction does not exclude the possibility of negative sentences being in part ambiguous, as we shall see in chapter 9.

in unclear cases. For suppose we are uncertain whether a given sentence is ambiguous with respect to some contrast, or merely unspecified as to that contrast. Take for example *John killed Bill*. Is this sentence ambiguous, one interpretation being that John killed Bill intentionally, the other interpretation being that John killed Bill by accident? Or is the sentence merely unspecified as to whether the action is intentional or not, as I suggested in chapter 6? The sentence can certainly be used to describe these two rather different kinds of events. It can in other words be true in these two rather different sets of circumstances. We in fact distinguish lexically between *murder* and *manslaughter* which are specified as to intentionality on the part of the agent. Suppose one linguist claims that the sentence *John killed Bill* has no specification in its meaning as to whether the action implied is intentional or not. He would anticipate that the sentence would be true both in circumstances in which the action was unintentional, and in which the action was intentional. He would argue that the question of intentionality is simply not relevant to the assessment of the truth value of the sentence. But suppose also that some other linguist disagrees, claiming that the sentence is ambiguous between an intentional interpretation and an unintentional interpretation. This linguist will say that in circumstances where the action was unintentional, the sentence is true on the unintentional interpretation and, simultaneously, false on the intentional interpretation. In circumstances where the action was intentional, that same linguist would say, conversely, that the sentence is true on the intentional interpretation and, simultaneously, false on the unintentional interpretation. Since, he would argue, this sentence meets the requirement that a sentence be ambiguous if it is simultaneously true and false relative to the same state of affairs, it must be ambiguous. Now these linguists have reached an impasse. The characterisation of ambiguity as the simultaneous assignment to a sentence of the values true and false has not provided a criterion for deciding unclear cases; it merely accentuates the point of disagreement.

For a more helpful way of distinguishing sentences which are ambiguous from those which are not, we have to turn to anaphoric processes, processes which refer back to an earlier part of the sentence. One example of this is the expression *to do so too*. This is used where the action described has already been specified and is being referred to again. For example the sentence *John hit Bill and Jason did so too* implies that Jason also hit Bill. In more linguistic terms, the use of the expression *do so too* demands identity of meaning of the two verb phrases in question.[1] Now this provides us with a test for ambiguity. If some verb phrase (the traditional expression of *predicate phrase* is equivalent to *verb phrase*) is two-ways ambiguous, then we can predict that when it is conjoined to a *do so* or other verb phrase pro-form expression,[2] the entire sentence will be two ways ambiguous – whichever interpretation is implied, the *do so* expression must be identical to that interpretation. More formally, a sentence which is two-ways ambiguous must be given two semantic representations to characterise its two meanings. Since a *do so* expression or any other verb phrase pro-form demands identity of meaning, a two-ways ambiguous sentence together with such an expression can only be two-ways ambiguous – in both of the two representations of the sentence's meaning, the pro-form expression will always be identical to it. So for example we predict that (3) is only two-ways ambiguous.

(3) Johnny saw her duck and Will did so too.

Either it means that Johnny saw the duck which belonged to her and Will also saw the duck which belonged to her; or it means that Johnny saw her quickly lower her head and Will also saw her quickly lower her head. What we predict that it cannot mean is that Johnny saw the duck which belonged to her and Will saw her quickly lower her head, because in such a case, the meaning of the two verb phrases would not be identical. And so it is. Except as a pun (see p. 82 above), there is no possibility of such crossed interpretations when the verb phrase to which *do so* is added is ambiguous. In the case of an unspecified or vague verb phrase, we have a contrary prediction. *Do so* expressions require identity of meaning, and where the meaning in question is unspecified with respect to some contrast, there is no reason to expect that non-identical interpretations are excluded. For example, the sentence *John is my neighbour and Sue is too* does not imply that because Sue is also my neighbour she must have all the properties that John has – being, say, a six-foot male West Indian. Or, to take our previous example of *do the room*, *The painter has done the sitting-room and the carpet-man has too* does not imply that the carpet-man must also have painted the sitting-room. On the contrary, the natural interpretation

---

[1] There are problems in stating the precise requirement of identity: cf. Dahl 1973, Bach, Bresnan and Wasow 1975, and Hall-Partee 1975.
[2] Other verb phrase pro-forms are *so did X, X did/has/will/is too*.

is that different actions have been carried out. If the expression *to do the sitting-room* were said to be ambiguous according as the actions it described differed, we would predict that such different interpretations of the expression could not be conveyed in the above example. But they can; and they can because the expression *to do the sitting-room* is not ambiguous but merely unspecified.[1]

We are now in a position to see how this test works in slightly less obvious cases. Let us return to *kill* and the problem of the specification of unintentionality. Given that *kill* can be used to describe actions which are intentional on the part of the instigator and actions which are quite accidental, the point of disagreement is whether the word *kill* is correspondingly ambiguous, or whether it is merely unspecified as to intentionality. If it is ambiguous, one should not be able to interpret sentence (4) as having conflicting interpretations of intentionality on the part of Johnny and Susie. If *kill* is merely unspecified as to whether or not the action of killing is intentional, then such conflicting interpretations will be possible.

(4) Johnny killed a bird today, and so did Susie.

Can this sentence be used to describe an occasion on which Susie came in heart-broken because she had ridden her bicycle over a lark's nest quite by mistake and killed a young lark; but Johnny, the little horror, was thrilled when he finally managed to shoot down a pigeon with his air-gun? It surely can. Similarly there is nothing odd in (5) despite the fact that, of the two actions described, only one was intentional.

(5) Gesualdo killed his wife, and so did Orpheus.[2]

To take another somewhat unclear case, which has been used as the

---

1   It might be argued that *do* must after all be ambiguous on the basis of the oddity of sentences such as *The painter has done the sitting-room and so has the burglar*, where the action referred to by the verb phrase pro-form is not the same as that of the first verb phrase. In this case, however, I think the oddity is not semantic but pragmatic, stemming from the unlikelihood of referring at the same time and in the same manner to the action of a painter and of a burglar. This sentence certainly seems very much less odd if envisaged as describing a state of affairs in which the owner planned both actions – first having the house painted so that it appeared to be of considerable value, secondly arranging for it to be burgled in order to get money out of the insurance company.

2   For those not familiar with Italian madrigals, Gesualdo was a late Renaissance Italian composer who was not only a prince but an extremely corrupt one.

basis for an argument in the recent syntax–semantics controversy (cf. pp. 167–8 below), consider the word *almost*. The sentence *John almost killed the hostages* can be used to describe an occasion on which John was on the point of carrying out some action which would have caused the hostages to die, or it can be used to describe an occasion on which John *did* carry out some action which brought the hostages to the point of death. What we have to decide is whether the sentence is ambiguous, and has two quite separately specifiable meanings, or whether it has a meaning which does not specify exactly how *almost* interacts with the remainder of the sentence. For example, what does sentence (6) mean?

(6) John almost killed the hostages and so did Manuel.

As a first approximation let us agree that the hostages were almost brought to the point of death by both John and Manuel. But can it be used to describe an occasion on which John severely wounded the hostages and Manuel was on the point of finally killing them when the police burst in and tore the gun away from him? It seems clear that it can: there is nothing contradictory about the sequence of sentences in (7).

(7) John almost killed the hostages and so did Manuel. John first severely wounded them and then Manuel was on the point of finally killing them when the police burst in and tore the gun from him.

Yet if the sentence *John almost killed the hostages* was ambiguous such a sequence would be contradictory since the *do so* expression would be being used where there was no identity of meaning. The test therefore seems to show that *John almost killed the hostages* is not ambiguous, but merely unspecified. Whether this non-ambiguity involves complete lack of specification or a representation of disjunct possibilities (analogous to *or*) remains an open question. But what the tests indicate quite clearly is that though *almost* can be used in a sentence to convey rather different interpretations, such a sentence is not ambiguous.

8.3 Ambiguity and negation

What of negation? In the previous chapter I argued that the semantic representation of negation had to represent the claim that the conditions for the truth of the corresponding positive sentence were not met, and that this representation had to be in the form of a disjunction of the negation of each of the conditions for the truth of the corresponding positive sentence. So for example I suggested that the interpretation of the sentence *It wasn't a woman* had to characterise the implication that either the item described was not female or not adult or not human, this being a disjunction of the truth conditions of its positive congener.[1] I pointed out at the end of that chapter that such a characterisation of negation conflicted with the truth-conditional definition of ambiguity that a sentence is ambiguous if it is true under different sets of conditions. But we have just seen in this chapter that that characterisation is in any case insufficient in that it predicts that all cases of only generally specified interpretations are ambiguous. What prediction does the verb phrase pro-form test make about negation? We have seen that negative sentences, at least in general, have a single representation of meaning, given by a disjunction. This being so, we should predict that negative sentences are unambiguous; and this the pro-form test confirms.

(8) On Monday it wasn't a woman that came to the door, and on Tuesday it wasn't either: on Monday it was a man and on Tuesday it was a young girl.

In (8), the sentence *It wasn't a woman that came to the door* is used for two purposes – firstly to assert that the reason why on Monday it was false that a woman came to the door was that the person who came was not a female adult but a male; secondly to assert that the reason why on Tuesday it was false that a woman came to the door was that the person who came was not a female adult, but a non-adult female. Thus there are claimed to be different bases for the truth of *It wasn't a woman that came to the door*, in the first place that the condition of femininity required for the truth of the positive sentence was not met, in the second place that the condition of adult-hood also required for the truth of the positive sentence was not met. Yet this difference does not demonstrate a difference in the meaning of the negative sentence in question. The phenomenon we are dealing with here is called the scope of negation, the scope of negation being those elements to which the negative element is applying. In the case of *It wasn't a woman that came to the door – it was a man* the scope of negation is restricted to the condition of femininity – no other part of the sentence is denied: in the case of *It wasn't a woman that came to the door – it was a young girl*, the scope of negation is restricted to the condition of adult-hood. The

1 This is only an approximate characterisation: cf. also pp. 118–20 above.

pro-form test for ambiguity shows clearly that differing scope of negation, at least for sentences of this type, does not result in ambiguity.
Now this is an important result for it is a common mistake among
linguists to argue for a conclusion on the basis of scope of negation
ambiguity. But these are non-arguments, for, at least in general, negative
sentences are not ambiguous with respect to variations in the scope of
negation. (9)–(11) provide us with further demonstration of this.

> (9) Edwin didn't kill the mice and Bill didn't do so either.
>   Edwin is always kind to animals and wouldn't have anything
>   to do with the experiment and though Bill used to make them
>   very ill, they never actually died.
> (10) The professor didn't accuse her of taking drugs and her tutor
>   didn't do so either. The professor didn't say anything at all
>   because he didn't think she was taking them and her tutor,
>   who also takes them, merely suggested that she should be
>   more careful about it in future.
> (11) The chairman didn't sell any shares to the new firm and the
>   secretary didn't do so either. I know the chairman didn't
>   because he specifically told me that he had given them some as
>   a free gift, and the secretary didn't because he didn't have
>   any to sell.

In (9) we have a case of a negative sentence containing *kill* in which the
scope of negation differs in the two sentences, in the first applying to
the whole complex representation of meaning of *kill*, in the second
applying to merely a sub-part of it: the fact that Bill carried out some
action on the mice which caused some reaction in them is not negated;
what is negated is the causation specifically of death. This difference is
not however sufficient to exclude the identity-requiring *do so* verb
phrase. In (10) we have a difference of scope in a sentence containing
accuse. Now it is arguable that a characterisation of the meaning of
accuse must include the implications that the referent of the subject of
the verb assume that the action involved was bad and that the referent
of the subject of the verb state that the person accused was responsible
for the action in question. And in (10) the scope of negation varies across
these two implications: the first conjunct is taken to imply that the
second of these implications falls within the scope of negation; the second
conjunct implies that the first of these implications falls within the scope
of negation. Again this difference in scope provides no evidence of

consequent ambiguity of the negative sentence. (11) is parallel. The selling of shares by both the chairman and the secretary is denied but for different reasons – firstly the scope of negation is restricted to the transaction of money involved in selling (this was a gift); secondly the scope of negation encompasses the whole action depicted by the item *sell* (there was no exchange of any sort – either of goods or money). In each of these cases, though the scope of negation varies, the sentences, according to the test, are unambiguous. Thus our representation of negative sentences as involving a single semantic representation which is itself a disjunction of conditions receives confirmation from this test. The significance of this result will become clear in the following chapters, particularly chapter 9.

8.4 Quantifiers and problems in testing ambiguity

What has this one verb-phrase pro-form test shown us? First, it provided a test for ambiguity because ambiguity of a sentence is by definition due to the existence of two non-identical interpretations of a single sentence (where these interpretations correspond to non-identical sets of truth conditions): since the occurrence of *do so* or any other verb phrase pro-form demands identity of interpretation between two verb phrases, it follows that an ambiguous sentence should allow only two interpretations of any verb phrase pro-form expression conjoined to it. This is in contrast to a sentence whose interpretation is unspecified for certain contrasts since the identity requirement of the pro-form expression is between the two general, under-specified, semantic interpretations. If some specification, linguistic or contextual, is added to clarify what precise use is being made of some unspecified expression, there is no reason therefore to anticipate that a verb phrase pro-form must be interpreted identically at this level of detail. This test distinguishes successfully between clear cases of vagueness,[1] and clear cases of ambiguity. In rather more controversial cases, the results suggest that neither *kill* nor *almost* create ambiguity in a sentence; nor does negation.

Heavy reliance has without doubt been placed on the test itself, and there is some reason to think that it is not quite so reliable a test as I have so far assumed it to be.[2] However the problems which other

---

[1] The reader can check for himself other cases of vagueness which have been mentioned but not put through the test.

[2] Cf. Zwicky and Sadock 1975 for a detailed evaluation of this and other tests.

linguists have raised concerning the test do not I think affect the examples we have so far considered in this chapter. There is though one more case to consider, which has special significance in connection with the issues to be raised in the following chapters, and which provides a case where the verb phrase pro-form test fails entirely to distinguish between ambiguity and vagueness. As a preliminary to this case, consider the word *dog*. This is a word which according to the view expressed in chapter 6 (cf. 6.1 above) would be said to be ambiguous as between the item *dog* which is unspecified for sex, and the item *dog* which implies a male dog. In other words, one item *dog*, with the sense marked for masculinity, is a hyponym and is included in the second, more general, use of *dog*. Suppose we seek to test this ambiguity by the verb phrase pro-form test. Consider (12).

> (12) Mary has bought a dog and so has Will: Mary's got a bitch because she wants to look after puppies, but Bill was careful to get a male.

At first sight, this example appears to provide a case of crossed interpretations, the first conjunct implying the more general sense of *dog*, the second conjunct implying the more specific sense of *dog*. Can we therefore conclude that the word *dog* is not ambiguous, despite the arguments of chapter 6 (6.1 above)? The answer is 'No', and for good reason. If a sentence is ambiguous between two interpretations, one of which is more general than and includes the other, a verb phrase pro-form test frame will always provide results which appear to demonstrate a crossed interpretation and hence lack of ambiguity, because the sentence can always be understood on the basis of the more general interpretation which *allows* crossed interpretations. This means that where a sentence is ambiguous between two such interpretations it will always fail the ambiguity test, by default as it were.

The problem which we now turn to involves precisely such a case. Consider (13).

> (13) A hundred students shot twenty professors.

This sentence is sometimes said to be ambiguous between two interpretations. On the one hand it can mean that there were twenty professors each of whom was shot by a hundred students; or it can mean that each member of a group of one hundred students shot twenty professors (in which case the total number of professors shot might be considerably larger than twenty). If we consider this second interpretation rather more closely we find that what is implied is the existence of a group of one hundred students each of whom shot twenty professors, with no specification as to how many professors were shot only once, how many professors were shot twice, etc. In other words, the second interpretation allows not only the possibility that twenty times one hundred professors were shot, each one only once, but all the different possibilities ranging between a total of two thousand professors shot and a total of twenty professors shot. But if this interpretation includes the possibility of one hundred students shooting a total of twenty professors, which it does, then it includes the other reading of the sentence, namely that there were twenty professors each of whom was shot by one hundred students. This being so, it seems that sentences such as (13) which involve the interaction of two quantified noun phrases, because their putative ambiguity involves the inclusion of one interpretation within the second more general interpretation, are not amenable to any known ambiguity test.

The two most important phenomena that we have considered in this chapter are, from a theoretical point of view, negation and quantifiers. In the first case, we saw how the disjunctive nature of the semantic representation of negation was not in general sufficient to cause ambiguity. And in the case of quantifiers, we found that they provide a test case for the ambiguity test itself, a test which it signally fails to pass. As we shall see in the following chapters, these results bear directly on arguments concerning two major issues in semantics: the nature of the logic of natural language; and the nature of the relation between semantics and other components of a linguistic theory, in particular the syntactic component.

RECOMMENDED READING

A detailed discussion of ambiguity and the problems in deciding on particular cases is presented in Kooij *Ambiguity in Natural Language* (see especially chs 3–5). Zwicky and Sadock 'Ambiguity tests and how to fail them' give an excellent evaluation of the criteria on which ambiguities have been decided, and they include a consideration of the *do so* test discussed here.

8.1 For an introductory discussion of types of vagueness, see Alston *Philosophy of Language* ch. 5. The general problem of distinguishing ambiguity from vagueness, or indifference as Reeves calls it, is discussed in Reeves in 'Ambiguity and indifference', which was written in answer to Hall-Partee's invocation of ambiguity in 'Opacity, coreference and pronouns'. Hintikka in 'Grammar and logic: some borderline problems' also takes up Hall-Partee's claim of ambiguity. The problem of ambiguity in connection with *good* is discussed in Wiggins 'On sentence-sense, word-sense and difference of word-sense', and Ziff *Semantic Analysis* ch. 6. For an argument that *or* is not ambiguous between the inclusive sense of *or* and the exclusive sense see Barrett and Stenner 'On the myth of the exclusive "or"'.

8.2   The *do so* test for ambiguity was first discussed in print by G. Lakoff 'A note on ambiguity and vagueness' in which he used examples similar in all important respects to *John killed Bill*. Replies to this have been made by Catlin and Catlin 'Intentionality: a source of ambiguity in English', Mistler-Lachman 'Comments on vagueness', and Kuno 'Lexical and contextual meaning'. On the problem of the identity requirement of such processes as pronominalisation, see Dahl 'On so-called "sloppy identity"', Hall-Partee 'Opacity, coreference and pronouns' and 'Deletion and variable binding', Bach, Bresnan and Wasow '"Sloppy identity": an unnecessary and insufficient criterion for deletion rules', and Karttunen 'Pronouns and variables'. The articles that use sentences containing *almost* as ambiguity data are listed in the recommended reading for chapter 10.

8.3   A number of linguistic arguments have assumed that negative sentences are ambiguous. These include G. Lakoff *Irregularity in Syntax*, and Jackendoff *Semantic Interpretation in a Generative Grammar*. Jackendoff's discussion of negation is an attempt to demonstrate the relevance of surface structure to semantic interpretation. For another argument along these lines, using negation as evidence, see Chomsky 'Deep structure, surface structure and semantic interpretation'. I have argued in more detail in Kempson *Presupposition and the Delimitation of Semantics* that, contrary to these views, negative sentences are unambiguous. For a detailed discussion of verbs such as *accuse*, see Fillmore 'Verbs of judging: an exercise in semantic description'.

8.4   On the ambiguity caused by quantifiers, G. Lakoff 'Linguistics and natural logic' and Carden *English Quantifiers: Logical Structure and Linguistic Variation* are perhaps the most detailed discussions, but see also Hall-Partee 'Negation, conjunction and quantifiers' and 'Linguistic metatheory'. This last reference is incidentally an excellent introduction to the syntax–semantics controversy within the framework of transformational grammar. On some fundamental problems in connection with quantifiers, see Hintikka 'Quantifiers *v.* quantification theory'.

9

The logic of natural language

In chapter 3 I argued that the semantic representation of a sentence was a specification of its logical form. In the ensuing chapters I have assumed without discussion that the system of logic on which these logical forms are based is two-valued. That is to say, in talking of truth conditions on sentences, I have assumed that a sentence has two possible truth values relative to a given situation – either it is true or it is not, in which case it is false (cf. for example the discussion of *or*, pp. 126–8). Recently however, it has been suggested that the logic on which the semantic representations (logical forms) of natural language depend is not two-valued but allows for a third possibility: neither true nor false. So we are faced with a choice between two alternatives – that the basis of natural language semantics is a two-valued logic; or that its basis is such a three-valued logic, called a presuppositional logic.[1]

To see what is involved in the two contrasting systems of logic, consider the sentence which formed the centre of the disagreement between Russell and Strawson, *The King of France is bald*. The two analyses do not differ in their evaluation of the sentence when it happens to be true. But suppose the required correspondence, specifically that there be a single individual who is King of France and who is bald, does not hold. If for example there is a king of France but he has lots of hair, then there is still no disagreement – the sentence is agreed under such circumstances to be false: anyone who uttered the sentence *The King of France is bald* under these circumstances would have spoken falsely. However, suppose the sentence *The King of France is bald* is uttered at a time when there is no king of France: it is here that the two analyses

---

[1] The term *three-valued* is perhaps a little misleading, since though there are three possible relations which may hold between a sentence and some state of affairs – true, false, and neither true nor false – only two of these – true and false – are truth values.

diverge. On one view, held by Russell, the sentence is again false: the relation between the sentence and the state of affairs required for the value true to be assigned is not met, rather strikingly so. On the other view, held by Frege and Strawson,[1] the sentence cannot be assessed either for truth or falsity – it is neither true nor false. As Strawson suggested (1950: 330), 'suppose someone were in fact to say to you . . . "The King of France is bald"[2] . . . and went on to *ask* you whether you thought that what he had just said was true, or was false . . . I think you would be inclined to say . . . that the question of whether his statement was true or false simply *did not arise*, because there was no such person as the King of France'. The difference between the two views, that founded on a traditional logic and that founded on a three-valued logic is that the former, in allowing only two assignments to a sentence, must give a broader characterisation to what it means for a sentence to be false than the presuppositional logic, which, with a third assignment possibility of 'neither true nor false', can maintain a rather narrower delimitation of what it means for a sentence to be false.[3]

Before we enter into the detailed arguments for a presuppositional analysis of natural language, it is important to make clear the theoretical consequences for linguistics of adopting such a position. The first of these is the need to recognise an additional relation between sentences – presupposition. In chapters 1 and 3, I pointed out that a semantic theory must be able to predict the relation of entailment between sentences, the entailments of a sentence being all the sentences whose truth follows from the truth of that sentence. A three-valued logic recognises a second relation between sentences, the relation of presupposition, the presuppositions of a sentence being all the sentences that follow both from the truth of that sentence and also from its falsity. To take the original

[1] As early as 1892 in Germany, Frege had given a presuppositional account of definite noun phrases, but Strawson's account is more detailed and better documented, at least in the English literature.

[2] Strawson in fact changed Russell's example of *The King of France is bald* to *The King of France is wise.*

[3] This third possibility of a statement or sentence being neither true nor false is used by Strawson only for cases of statements being further from the truth than being simply false. It should not be confused with the difficulty of truth-value assignment in a situation where it is uncertain whether a given statement is true or false. To say of a statement in such a situation that "it's neither true nor false but somewhere in between" is not the sense of *neither true nor false* that is characterised by a presuppositional logic.

example again, if we agree that *The King of France is bald*, then on Strawson's view it must still be the case that there is a king of France. Thus to a presupposition-supporter the sentence *The King of France is bald* does not entail the truth of the sentence *There is a king of France* even though this latter sentence follows from its truth, but it presupposes it, because on this more restricted view of what it means for a sentence to be false, it being true that there is a king of France is a necessary condition both of the truth *and* of the falsity of the sentence *The King of France is bald*. This additional relation of presupposition must be captured in the theory by a mechanism which distinguishes between the presuppositions of a sentence and its entailments, and we can expect that this will necessitate setting up rather different projection rules (cf. chapter 7 above) to characterise the meaning of a sentence as having two distinct parts, that which corresponds to its entailments and that which corresponds to its presuppositions. So if we agree with a presuppositional analysis of sentences, the interpretive rules for stating the relation between the meaning of a lexical item and the meaning of sentences which were provisionally set up in chapter 7 will have to be radically revised. Not only this, the interpretation of negative sentences has to be reconsidered and reformulated, for the de Morgan equivalence which was the basis of the projection rule for negative sentences was formulated within a two-valued logic and no longer holds in the form given earlier (p. 119) in a three-valued logic. Finally, all those items which have been said to correspond to logical connectives, such as *and*, *or*, *if-then*, *unless*, as well as negation, which have in the past been given truth-conditional definitions within a classical two-valued logic, will have to be redefined in terms of the three values available in a presuppositional logic. In short, the entire mechanism of stating semantic interpretations of lexical items and of sentences depends on the logic which underlies the semantic system, and any change in the logic on which the semantic rules are based requires corresponding changes in the rules themselves.

9.1 Presupposition and entailment defined

The basis of the disagreement lies in whether the truth-conditional implications on sentences should be divided into those which are entailments and those which are presuppositions, or whether such implications form a homogeneous set of entailments. In order to test these two alternatives, it is essential to have clear-cut definitions of the two relations. Entailment I defined earlier as a relation between sentences such that the truth of the second sentence necessarily follows from the truth of the first.[1] Thus any sentence S_1 will entail a sentence S_2 if when S_1 is true, S_2 must also be true. Furthermore if S_2 is false, its entailing sentence S_1 will also be false. For example the sentence *That person is a bachelor* (S_1) entails the sentence *That person is a man* (S_2) since if S_1 is true of some individual then S_2 must also be true; and if S_2 is false of some individual, then S_1 must also be false. However if S_1 is false, nothing follows about S_2 – it can be either true or false. So, to return to our example, it may be false to say of someone *That person is a bachelor* without its necessarily being false to say of that person *That person is a man*. It might for example be false to say of John *That person is a bachelor* even though it be true to say of him *That person is a man*. But equally it would be false to say of my teenage daughter Susie *That person is a bachelor* (with the same interpretation of *bachelor*) while also being false to say of her *That person is a man*. When an entailment relation holds between two sentences S_1 and S_2, the truth value of S_2 is independent of that of S_1 *if* S_1 is false. To put it in more linguistic terms, when S_1 entails S_2, S_2 is a necessary implication of S_1; but the negation of S_1 (which implies the falsity of its positive congener)[2] does not imply S_2. Thus though *That person is a bachelor* implies *That person is a man*, *That person isn't a bachelor* does not – it can be used to describe both people who are men and people who are not (recall its disjunct specification discussed in 7.3 and 8.3 above).

Presupposition differs from entailment in only two ways: the consequence of S_1 being false, and the consequence of S_2 being false. For S_1 to presuppose S_2, the truth of S_2 must follow from the truth of S_1, but if S_2 is false then S_1 will have no truth value, i.e. will be neither true nor false. It follows from this that if S_1 is false, S_2 must be true. The original example *The King of France is bald* is thus said to presuppose the sentence *There is a king of France* since, as Strawson argues, one judges the truth or falsity of this statement by assuming the existence of the King of France and by assessing on the basis of this assumption whether or not he actually is bald. If there is no king of France, then the statement *The King of France is bald* is neither true nor false. It follows from this

---

[1] As with all relations defined within logic, the logical definition concerns statements, not sentences (cf. 3.4.1 above).

[2] This characterisation of negation is not uncontroversial, as we shall see (cf. 9.3 below). However it does correspond to the central use of negation.

that the sentence *The King of France is not bald* (which implies the falsity of the sentence *The King of France is bald*) is also said to be either true or false only if there is a king of France. If there is no king of France it is said to be just as odd to say *The King of France is not bald* as it is to say *The King of France is bald*. As Strawson expressed it, the question of whether these sentences are true or false simply does not arise if there is no such person as the King of France. This characteristic is translated into a linguistic criterion for presupposition that a purported presupposition must be a necessary implication of the positive and the corresponding negative sentence. The difference between entailment and presupposition is summarised in table 1:

Table 1

Entailment	Presupposition
S_1 S_2	S_1 S_2
$T \rightarrow T$	$T \rightarrow T$
$F \leftarrow F$	$-(T \lor F)^1 \leftarrow F$
$F \rightarrow T \lor F^2$	$F \rightarrow T$

It now becomes evident that the problem of interpreting negative sentences forms a central issue in the controversy of semantics with presuppositions v. semantics with no presuppositions. But before turning once again to negative sentences, let us look at a second point of difference between the two systems of logic underlying the controversy, which will provide us with a further criterion against which to judge the two analyses. Consider the word *and*. The standard truth-conditional account of *and*, given in a two-valued logic, is that any sentence formed by joining two sentences together with *and* (i.e. of the form *P and Q*, where *P* and *Q* represent sentences) will be true if, and only if, both of those two sentences are true. If either one is false, the whole conjoined sentence will be false. In logic, this is given in what is called a truth-table format, as follows:

Table II

P	Q	P and Q^3
T	T	T
T	F	F
F	T	F
F	F	F

[1]   This is the symbol standardly used for the value *neither true nor false*.
[2]   In this case, in other words, there is no consequence for the truth value of S_2 if S_1 is false.
[3]   In the two left columns, reading across, are truth-value assignments for

In a three-valued logic, the statement of truth conditions of any sentence must take into account the three possibilities. So for *and* we shall have to decide what the truth value of *P and Q* is if one of its conjuncts, either *P* or *Q*, should have this third value, neither true nor false. The decision presumably lies between whether the whole conjoined sentence is neither true nor false if one conjunct is neither true nor false, or whether such a sentence is merely false under these conditions. In a truth-table format, the problem becomes a choice between table III and

Table III

P	Q	P and Q
T	T	T
T	F	F
F	T	F
F	F	F
$-$(T v F)	T	$-$(T v F)
T	$-$(T v F)	$-$(T v F)
$-$(T v F)	F	$-$(T v F)
F	$-$(T v F)	$-$(T v F)
$-$(T v F)	$-$(T v F)	$-$(T v F)

Table IV

P	Q	P and Q
T	T	T
T	F	F
F	T	F
F	F	F
$-$(T v F)	T	F
T	$-$(T v F)	F
$-$(T v F)	F	F
F	$-$(T v F)	F
$-$(T v F)	$-$(T v F)	$-$(T v F)

table IV. The details of how this decision should be made we shall go into shortly. For the moment all that matters is that the characterisation of *and*, and indeed the other connectives such as *or* and *if-then*, is not the same under the two analyses: it therefore provides a potential test case for the two alternatives.

P and Q, in the right column is the truth value of *P and Q* which follows from those truth-value assignments.

9.2 Presupposition and the negation test

The original Strawsonian account of presupposition was, as we saw, restricted to definite noun phrases. However linguists have recently given presuppositional accounts to a rather wider range of sentences. In particular, it has been suggested that sentences containing verbs such as *regret* and *realise* presuppose the truth of the complement sentence following the verb. So it is argued that the sentence *John regrets that the captain was in prison* presupposes the sentence *The captain was in prison*. The basis of all such linguistic accounts of presupposition is the interpretation of negative sentences. It is argued that some necessary implications of positive sentences are also necessary implications of their negative congener, and as we saw in section 1 of this chapter, such implications are central cases of presupposition. Consider sentences (1)–(6).

(1) Edward regretted that Margaret had failed.
(2) Edward didn't regret that Margaret had failed.
(3) Sue realised that Bill had been unfaithful to his wife.
(4) Sue did not realise that Bill had been unfaithful to his wife.
(5) Malcolm regretted that his sister caused a lot of trouble.
(6) Malcolm didn't regret that his sister caused a lot of trouble.

In each of these cases, it has been argued, the positive sentence has some implications which are shared by the negative sentence. Thus both (1) and (2) are said to imply that Margaret had failed, (3) and (4) that Bill had been unfaithful to his wife, (5) and (6) that Malcolm's sister caused a lot of trouble. In other words, it is predicted that both the positive and the negative sentence display a symmetrical behaviour: both are said to contain the same implication and accordingly it should be impossible and contradictory in each case both to assert the sentence (whether positive or negative) and simultaneously to deny the implication in question (cf. 6.2.4 above for a discussion of this criterion to test truth-conditional analyses). This is certainly true of (1). (7), which is an assertion of (1) but simultaneously an assertion of the falsity of the complement sentence *that Margaret had failed*, is a contradiction. But what of (8)?

(7) † Edward regretted that Margaret had failed but she hadn't.
(8)   Edward didn't regret that Margaret had failed because, as he knew full well, she hadn't.

Though *Edward didn't regret that Margaret had failed* would not normally be used in circumstances where Margaret had not failed, (8) is not, like (7), a contradiction. Thus the predicted symmetry of (1) and (2) appears not to hold. This predicted symmetry also fails for (3)–(6). Consider (9)–(12).

(9) † Sue realised that Bill had been unfaithful to his wife, though he had in fact never been unfaithful.

(10) Sue did not realise that Bill had been unfaithful to his wife – how can she have done when he never has?

(11) † Malcolm regretted that his sister caused a lot of trouble though he knew she hadn't.

(12) Malcolm didn't regret that his sister caused a lot of trouble because he knew she hadn't.

The question that now arises is the significance of (8), (10) and (12). These certainly do not represent the normal interpretations of the negative sentences they contain: are they indeed quite a separate sense of negation from the normal interpretation of these sentences? This is what presuppositionalists argue – that sentences such as (1)–(6) *do* presuppose the truth of the complement in each case, and that examples such as (8), (10) and (12), where the presuppositions are not carried in the negative sentences, constitute a separate sense of negation. Thus they are relying on the ambiguity of these negative sentences, between an interpretation in which the implication of the positive sentence is maintained and is indeed presupposed, and an interpretation in which the presupposition is not maintained. An alternative account of this same data in terms of entailment makes different predictions and does not have recourse to claims of ambiguity in negative sentences. To recapitulate, entailments of a (positive) sentence are those sentences which follow from the truth of the entailing sentence. If that entailing sentence is implied to be false, as it is standardly said to be in negative sentences,[1] nothing follows about the truth value of the entailed sentence. To put it more informally, if what one claims turns out to be false, it does not follow that all the consequences of that claim will also be false – they may be false, but they may not. In other words, an entailment analysis of those implications which have been said to be presuppositional predicts an asymmetry in the behaviour of positive and negative congeners of the same sentence: it predicts that a sentence

[1] Cf. p. 142 n. 2.

entailed by the positive sentence cannot be denied without contradiction if the positive sentence is implied to be true, but that it can be denied without contradiction if the negation of that sentence is implied to be true. And this is what we have found in these cases. It thus seems likely that, at least in these cases, the entailment account is to be preferred, unless the negative sentences in question can, despite a general lack of specification in negative sentences, be shown to be ambiguous.

Before looking at this problem in more detail, let us reconsider the original source of the presuppositional account, definite noun phrases. If the presuppositional account is correct, there should be no asymmetry in the behaviour of the presupposed implication of existence in positive sentences and in negative sentences. If an entailment account of these implications is correct, then there should be just such an asymmetry. In the light of these contrasting predictions, consider (13)–(18).

(13) † The Mayor of Liverpool visited the exhibition this year, but there was no exhibition.

(14) † The Mayor of Liverpool visited the exhibition this year, though there is no mayor of Liverpool.

(15) The Mayor of Liverpool did not visit the exhibition this year, as there was no exhibition this year.

(16) The Mayor of Liverpool did not visit the exhibition this year, as there is no mayor of Liverpool any longer.

(17) † John has spent the morning at the local swimming pool though there is no swimming pool here.

(18) John has not spent the morning at the local swimming pool – there isn't a swimming pool in this town.

Unlike the prediction of the presuppositional analysis, and in accordance with an entailment analysis of the same implication, the positive and negative congeners of the same sentence do not behave symmetrically. Yet it remains a fact that the normal interpretation of *John has not spent the morning at the local swimming pool* does imply that there is a local swimming pool, and similarly with the use of all definite noun phrases in negative sentences. If then it could be argued that a negative sentence, such as *John has not spent the morning at the local swimming pool*, is ambiguous between an interpretation (the natural one) which retains the implication that there is a local swimming pool and a special use of negation in which this interpretation does not hold, then the presuppositional account would be vindicated.

9.3   Internal negation v. external negation

9.3.1   *Negation and the ambiguity test revisited*

Suppose that we postulate that negative sentences are ambiguous if they contain a verb such as *regret*, or if they contain a definite noun phrase. The one interpretation, often called 'internal negation', would retain the implication of the truth of the *regret* complement or of the existence of the referent implied by the definite noun phrase: the other, called 'external negation', would have no such implication. Is such a postulated ambiguity testable by our verb-phrase pro-form test discussed in chapter 8? Unfortunately, the answer is 'No', despite the fact that this test was used in chapter 8 as evidence that negative sentences are not in general ambiguous according as the scope of negation varies (cf. 8.3 above). Consider the sentence *The Mayor of Liverpool visited the exhibition*. This entails such sentences as *The Mayor of Liverpool went to the exhibition* (e_1), *The Mayor of Liverpool went to an exhibition* (e_2), e_3, e_4 . . . However under the presuppositional analysis it would presuppose such sentences as *There is a mayor of Liverpool*, *There was an exhibition*.[1] On this basis, the negative sentence *The Mayor of Liverpool did not visit the exhibition* would have two interpretations with implications whose significance can perhaps be most easily grasped if displayed as follows:

Internal Negation:

(A) Either the Mayor of Liverpool did not go to the exhibition (not e_1) or the Mayor of Liverpool did not go to an exhibition (not e_2)[2] or not-e_3 or not-e_4 or . . .

(B) There is a mayor of Liverpool

(C) There was an exhibition[3]

External Negation:

(A) Either the Mayor of Liverpool did not go to the exhibition or the Mayor of Liverpool did not go to an exhibition

---

[1]   The fluctuation in tense in these two sentences is an awkwardness which arises only in a presuppositional account.

[2]   If this second condition, e_2, falls within the scope of negation then the first condition, e_1, will of course do so too.

[3]   According to Strawson 1964b, this implication of existence is not a presupposition since the definite noun phrase is not in subject position, and is not therefore an implication of this negative sentence. But this is an additional complication for presuppositional analyses which I shall ignore here.

or not-e₃ or not-e₄ or . . .
or there is no mayor of Liverpool
or there was no exhibition.

The problem is that external negation, said to correspond to a special denial use of negation, has an interpretation which follows the pattern of the negative sentences we considered in chapters 7 and 8 (cf. 7.3 and 8.3 above): the interpretation is a straightforward disjunction of the negation of each of the implications of the positive sentence. Moreover this disjunction is more general than, and includes, the interpretation corresponding to internal negation. That is to say, since the interpretation specific to so-called external negation states that the negative sentence in question will be true if any one (or more) of its disjuncts is true, without its being necessary for all of these disjuncts to be true, this allows the possibility that on the *external* reading of the sentence, it will be true if the Mayor of Liverpool did not go to the exhibition, indeed if the Mayor of Liverpool did not go to an exhibition at all, but there is a mayor of Liverpool and there was an exhibition (i.e. two of the disjunct conditions happen to be fulfilled, two of them happen not to be). But if this is so, the external interpretation of such a negative sentence includes the internal interpretation; and our verb-phrase pro-form ambiguity test is of no help at all. For it is precisely in cases of this sort that the test fails to distinguish between ambiguity and vagueness.[1]

9.3.2 *The three-valued definition of* and

What other evidence can we turn to? At the beginning of this chapter, I pointed out that commitment to a presuppositional analysis of negative sentences involved a commitment to a presuppositional logic distinct from classical two-valued logic in that it allowed a third possibility, neither true nor false, and that such a commitment involved a re-definition of such connectives as *and*, *or*, and *if-then*, within this new kind of logic. As I pointed out earlier, one problem is to decide the details of the truth table for these connectives. Let us take the problem of *and*. Presumably, as in two-valued logic, any sentence of the form *P and Q* (where *P* and *Q* represent sentences) will be true if and only if

---

[1] Notice that this negative conclusion as to whether negative sentences are ambiguous as between an external and internal scope of negation does not apply to differences of scope in general. For the scope of negation can vary along mutually exclusive parameters, a distinction which the ambiguity test is sensitive to.

both *P* and *Q* are true. But what if either *P* or *Q* is neither true nor false? Recall the intuitions which a presuppositional logic is said to capture in simple sentences, sentences merely of the form *P*. *The Mayor of Liverpool visited the exhibition* was said by Strawson to be judged as to whether it was true or not on the assumption of there being a mayor of Liverpool. If there is no such man, then such a claim could no longer be assessed at all. Corresponding to this, the claim that such a sentence is false – i.e. that *The Mayor of Liverpool did not visit the exhibition* is true on the internal reading of negation – must also imply that there is a mayor of Liverpool. If such a claim is made in the event of there being no such man, it is just as odd a claim as the claim that the Mayor of Liverpool visited the exhibition. In the event of the sentence *The Mayor of Liverpool did not visit the exhibition* being deliberately used in the knowledge that there is no mayor of Liverpool, quite a different use of negation is involved, the denial use of negation. In other words, in simple sentences of this type, a presuppositional analysis purports to explain four facts: (i) that in asserting (being committed to the truth of) a positive sentence such as *The Mayor of Liverpool visited the exhibition* a speaker will be assuming that there is a mayor of Liverpool, (ii) that in asserting the falsity of such a sentence, i.e. being committed to the truth of *The Mayor of Liverpool did not visit the exhibition*, a speaker will also under all normal descriptive uses of the sentence be taking for granted that there is a mayor of Liverpool, (iii) that there is something odd about using either of the sentences, positive or negative, if there is no such person as the Mayor of Liverpool, and (iv) that if such a negative sentence *is* used when there is no implication of there being a mayor of Liverpool, this is always in denial of some immediately previous assertion.

As these intuitions (particularly (i)–(iii)) provide the semantic data which a presuppositional analysis was set up to explain, one might anticipate that they carry over to more complex sentences. To what extent do they? Consider (19)–(24).

(19) John beats his wife and he is a boxer.
(20) Susie was sick and James regretted going to the circus.
(21) The Mayor of Liverpool is coming to the exhibition and Mary has got a head-ache.
(22) John is married and he beats his wife.
(23) James went to the circus and he regretted going to the circus.

(24) There is a mayor of Liverpool and he is coming to the exhibition.

If we are to maintain the view that the concept of presupposition corresponds to and explains assumptions made in asserting a sentence, then it would seem that just as anyone asserting *John beats his wife* would be assuming that he has a wife, i.e. that he is married, so too would anyone asserting (19). It is just as odd, presumably, to assert (19) if John isn't married as it would be to assert the more simple sentence *John beats his wife*. Similarly with sentences (20) and (21). In accordance with these intuitions, it appears that a three-valued truth-conditional definition of *and* should incorporate the claim that if one of the conjuncts P and Q of a sentence P *and* Q is neither true nor false through presupposition failure, then P *and* Q is itself neither true nor false, since it shares the same presupposition. However, examples (22)–(24) do not correspond to this analysis as neatly. Anyone asserting (22) is not assuming that John is married: on the contrary, this is what he is asserting. In this case then, it seems that despite the fact that one of the conjuncts (the second one) presupposes that John is married, the whole conjunction of two sentences does not carry this presupposition. (23)–(24) present similar problems. In all three cases, the first conjunct is a sentence which is a presupposition of the second conjunct, and in these cases the conjunction of the two sentences does not presuppose what one of its conjuncts presupposes, for it asserts it. But both two-valued logics and three-valued logics are in agreement over the truth-value assignment of a statement if what it asserts does not correspond to the state of affairs in question: in both logics the statement is false. So if we wish to assign truth values to these conjunctions in accordance with speakers' intuitions about what is assumed in uttering sentences, then in these cases it appears that even though one of the conjuncts is neither true nor false because its presupposition is false, then because the whole conjunction of P *and* Q asserts the truth of this presupposition rather than assuming it, the conjunction is merely false. Unfortunately, this conclusion presents a paradox, for we have assigned to *and* two conflicting truth tables, one in which a conjunction P *and* Q is neither true nor false if one conjunct is neither true nor false, one in which a conjunction P *and* Q is false if one conjunct is neither true nor false. In other words, if we seek to capture certain intuitions of speakers about what is assumed in asserting sentences in terms of truth-value assignments, then we are committing ourselves to the prediction that *and* is ambiguous, for we have assigned to it two different sets of truth conditions. Yet there is no independent motivation for claiming that *and* is ambiguous in this way. The need to provide two conflicting truth-conditional definitions of *and* arose solely through having made the distinction between the presuppositions of a sentence and the entailments of that sentence in order to provide a semantic analysis which explained assumptions speakers standardly make in saying sentences.

More problems arise when we consider negative sentences as conjuncts of a sentence of the form *P and Q*. Consider (25).

> (25) In 1990 the Pope will not give the annual address and it will be the Prefect of the Sacred College of Rites who gives it.

According to a presuppositional analysis, the first conjunct is ambiguous between internal negation which corresponds to a negative description, and external negation which corresponds to a denial of some previously made assertion. Now suppose I make a bet by uttering example (25) and what in fact happens is that the Pope dies in 1989 and they do not replace him. So in 1990 the Prefect of the Sacred College of Rites gives the annual address. Do I win my bet? It seems clear that I do. What is problematic for a presuppositional approach is that this intuition can only be captured by invoking the denial sense of negation, external negation. For on the interpretation of internal negation, the first conjunct of (25) is neither true nor false under the given circumstances (because its presupposition is false), so on this interpretation the bet cannot have been won. It can only have been won if we assume that negative sentences such as *The Pope will not give the annual address* can be true when there is no pope. Only external negation allows this. But we can hardly say that such a use of this negative sentence in making the bet turns out years later to have been a denial. And this is by no means an isolated case. There are many examples of simple negative sentences too which are clearly not denials but whose truth does not depend on an implication of existence of some definite noun phrase in that sentence. Ironically, the article in which Strawson first discussed presupposition ends with just such an example (Strawson 1950: 344):

> (26) Neither Aristotelian nor Russellian rules give the exact logic of any expression of ordinary language; for ordinary language has no exact logic.

This sentence is an assertion of a negative proposition precisely on the basis of the non-existence of the definite noun phrase of that sentence. Yet such a sentence is not a denial of a previously made assertion: it is a descriptive negative statement finalising the previous argument. The only recourse that a presuppositionalist has at this point is to argue that the concept of denial is not restricted to a contradicting response of some immediately previous statement, and should be generalised to cover such problem cases as these. But if this move is made, the distinction between denial uses of negation and descriptive uses of negation is blurred to such an extent that it forfeits the original advantage of the presupposition-based analysis that it explain the distinction in use between sentences such as *The King of France didn't visit the exhibition, because there's no such man* and *The King of France didn't visit the exhibition because the flight from Paris to Edinburgh was delayed.* Indeed the characterisations of denial and descriptive negation have become effectively non-distinct.

Thus it appears that the independent motivation for invoking ambiguity of negation that uses of negative sentences divide into denial uses and descriptive uses has to be jettisoned. But the only remaining motivation for invoking ambiguity of negation is that it provides a solution to counter-examples to a presupposition-based analysis. This was also the sole motivation for invoking ambiguity of *and*. Thus, despite its apparent ability to explain certain intuitions about simple sentences, it seems that a presuppositional analysis meets considerable problems in accounting for compound sentences. Contrary to this, however, an entailment analysis of the very implications which have been claimed to be presuppositions does not meet with these anomalies. If an entailed sentence is false, the sentence entailing it will also be false. So in all the cases (19)–(24) if one of the conjuncts is false, then the whole conjunction will also be false, irrespective of whatever relation there may be between the conjuncts themselves. In the case of both (19) and (22) for example, if *John is married* is false, *John beats his wife*, which entails it, will also be false, so any conjunction containing the sentence *John beats his wife* will also be false. There is no need to invoke ambiguity of *and*, for the truth-value assignment is consistent despite the difference in the relations between the conjuncts. With negative sentences, there are also no problems. In a homogeneous entailment analysis of the implications of a sentence, negative sentences unlike positive sentences have no specific entailments other than a disjunction.

So *The Pope will not give the annual address in 1990* will be compatible with there being no pope and will indeed be true if there is no pope. For this reason, no problem arises in the analysis of (25). On the contrary, it is predicted that anyone betting on the truth of (25) will win his bet if jointly there is no pope and the prefect of the Sacred College of Rites gives the address, for there being no pope guarantees the truth of the first conjunct, so under these circumstances the success of the bet depends solely on who the annual address is given by. If it turns out that it was given by the Prefect of the Sacred College of Rites, then it is predicted that the bet is won.

9.4 **Summary**

So far, the evidence we have considered tends to provide support for a presuppositional analysis in simple sentences, but contrarily tends to provide support for an entailment analysis in compound sentences such as those which consist of conjunctions by *and*. At this point, we should perhaps review the sequence of arguments. The disagreement lies in whether the implications of natural-language sentences can best be characterised in terms of a two-valued logic, or a three-valued logic. The strongest evidence in favour of an analysis based on a three-valued logic is provided by simple sentences, for such an analysis provides an explanation of why it is that in saying sentences such as *John didn't regret that Mabel went to the party* a speaker would normally be committed to the truth of the complement sentence *Mabel went to the party*, and similarly of why in saying sentences such as *The Queen of Togoto does not have six husbands* a speaker would generally be committed to the truth of the sentence *There is a queen of Togoto*. It is for these cases that an analysis in terms of a two-valued logic gives a weaker characterisation. For this latter analysis would merely claim that *John didn't regret that Mabel went to the party* was compatible both with Mabel having been to the party and with her not having been to the party, and that *The Queen of Togoto does not have six husbands* was compatible both with there being a queen of Togoto and with there not being such a person, or even such a place. In particular, an entailment analysis would give no account of why one possibility in each case is so much the preferred interpretation. However in the first place, a presuppositional account of natural language has to embrace an analysis of negative sentences as ambiguous, an analysis which depends on a dubious distinction between denial and descriptive negation. In the second place, a presupposition-based analysis appears to necessitate the acceptance of an equally unmotivated ambiguity in the conjunction *and*. Furthermore, this problem of unmotivated ambiguity arises in the case of all the logical conjunctions, *or*, *if-then*, *unless*, as well as *and*, by exactly parallel arguments.[1] It is these cases of compound sentences which provide strongest evidence for the homogeneous entailment account of sentence implications. For in every case, the anomalies which arise for a presupposition-based account stem either from the distinction made between the value neither true nor false and the value false, or from the prediction of symmetry between corresponding positive and negative sentences. Since these are properties only of the presupposition-based analysis, they present problems for this account alone.

There is one additional consequence of a presuppositional analysis, which suggests that the presuppositional analysis even of simple sentences is not as plausible as it might at first appear. If one argues that a sentence such as *The Mayor of Liverpool did not visit the exhibition* is ambiguous between an interpretation in which the existence of the exhibition is implied, and an interpretation in which it is not, and also ambiguous between an interpretation in which the existence of the Mayor of Liverpool is implied, and one in which it is not, then it follows that the positive sentence *The Mayor of Liverpool visited the exhibition* must also be said to be correspondingly ambiguous. For on the reading of the negative sentence that maintains the existence implication(s) the positive sentence will presuppose that there is a mayor of Liverpool or that there is an exhibition, but on the reading of the negative sentence that does not maintain the existence implication(s), the positive sentence will entail that there is a mayor of Liverpool or that there is an exhibition. In other words, the positive sentence will be predicted to be at least four-ways ambiguous.[2] This is hardly a plausible claim.

Thus we are faced with two alternatives. An entailment analysis appears to make the correct predictions with respect to the semantics of compound sentences, but it gives only a weak characterisation of negative sentences, with no explanation whatever of their preferred interpretations. A presupposition analysis explains the distinction

---

1 The details of these arguments are given in Kempson 1975 chs. 4–5. For independent arguments against a presuppositional account of these compound sentences, cf. Wilson 1975.

2 It is not possible for a sentence to simultaneously presuppose and entail some other sentence. For a proof of this, cf. Wilson 1975 p. 24.

between these preferred and non-preferred interpretations of negative sentences by making the basis of this distinction a central part of its logic; but in making a category distinction between two kinds of negation, this analysis faces serious anomalies elsewhere in its semantic account. One of the difficulties in assessing these alternatives is the nature of the data upon which the decision rests. Throughout this chapter, I have had to have recourse to intuitions which are by no means clear-cut. In particular, in discussing the presupposition-based analysis, I have referred to some interpretations as preferred, or normal. One of the advantages of the entailment-based analysis over the presupposition-based alternative is that it does not force judgments between normal and highly marked interpretations. The advantage of the presupposition-based analysis on the other hand is that it incorporates within the semantic account of natural language an explanation of a wider range of data, but since this data is by no means as clear-cut as it at first appears, this is only a spurious advantage. For this analysis there also remains the burden of explaining away the anomalies of multiple, unmotivated ambiguity. Since the anomalies seem in my view less serious for an entailment-based account, in the remaining chapters of this book I shall assume the more conservative solution presented by the account which does not recognise a distinct relation of presupposition, requiring of the semantics of natural language that it provide a representation of the truth conditions for the sentences of a language in terms of the two values, true and false.

RECOMMENDED READING

The original Fregean account of presupposition is given in Frege 'Über Sinn und Bedeutung'. Russell's reply to this in 'On denoting' was later answered by Strawson in 'On referring' (reprinted in Parkinson (ed.) *The Theory of Meaning*, Rosenberg and Travis (eds.) *Readings in the Philosophy of Language*, and Olshewsky (ed.) *Problems in the Philosophy of Language*). Strawson compared his view with the Russellian view in rather more detail in 'Identifying reference and truth values' (reprinted in Strawson *Logico-Linguistic Papers* and in Steinberg and Jakobovits (eds.) *Semantics*). Since then a large amount of philosophical, logical, and linguistic literature has emerged. In direct response to Strawson's 'On referring' was Sellars 'Presupposing', answered in its turn by Strawson 'A reply to Mr Sellars'. Other philosophical articles on the subject since then include Geach 'Russell on meaning and denoting', Baker 'Presupposition and types of clause', Cassin 'Russell's

discussion of meaning and denotation', and 'Russell's distinction between the primary and secondary occurrence of definite descriptions', Caton 'Strawson on referring', Jacobson 'Russell and Strawson on referring', Nerlich 'Presupposition and entailment', Roberts 'A problem about presupposition', Schnitzer 'Presupposition, entailment, and Russell's theory of descriptions'. More formalised logical accounts are given by Van Fraassen in 'Presupposition, implication and self-reference', 'Presuppositions, super-valuations, and free logic', 'Truth and paradoxical consequences'. The first main linguistic accounts of presupposition were Kiparsky and Kiparsky 'Fact' and Fillmore 'Types of lexical information', and Morgan 'On the treatment of presuppositions in transformational grammar'; and *presupposition* then became a fashionable term in linguistic analysis. Fillmore and Langendoen (eds.) *Studies in Linguistic Semantics* is almost entirely devoted to presuppositional analyses in terms of *presupposition*, where it is used in a large number of different ways. Linguists have often failed to distinguish *speaker-presupposition* and the logical term *presupposition*. Among articles where the difference is either not made or ignored are G. Lakoff 'Linguistics and natural logic', R. Lakoff 'If's, and's, and but's about conjunction', Fraser 'An analysis of "even" in English', Karttunen 'Presuppositions of compound sentences', 'Some observations on factivity', and 'Presupposition and linguistic context', Chomsky 'Deep structure, surface structure and semantic interpretation' (reprinted in *Studies on Semantics in Generative Grammar*). More rigorous attempts to give a characterisation to the term *presupposition* are Garner '"Presupposition" in philosophy and linguistics', Keenan 'Two kinds of presupposition in natural language', Katz 'On defining presupposition'. Presuppositional analyses of questions have also been given. See Katz *Semantic Theory* ch. 5, Keenan and Hull 'The logical presuppositions of questions and answers', Hull 'A semantics for superficial and embedded questions'. Attacks on the concept of presupposition have been given both by logicians and linguists. See Nerlich 'Presupposition and entailment', Schnitzer 'Presupposition, entailment, and Russell's theory of descriptions', Mates 'Descriptions and reference', Wilson *Presuppositions and Non-Truth-Conditional Semantics*, Kempson *Presupposition and the Delimitation of Semantics*, O. Cohen 'On the mis-representation of presuppositions'. For a rather different form of attack, see Katz and Langendoen 'Pragmatics and presupposition'.

9.1   On definitions of '&' within a three-valued logic, see Herzberger 'Truth and modality in semantically closed languages'.

9.2   The negation test for presuppositions is discussed in detail in Kiparsky and Kiparsky 'Fact', and in Kempson *Presupposition and the Delimitation of Semantics* chs. 4–5, from whence this chapter derives.

9.3   Discussions of internal and external negation include Russell 'On denoting', Herzberger 'Truth and modality in semantically closed languages', Sommers 'Predicability', Martin 'Sommers on denial and negation', Kempson *Presupposition and the Delimitation of Semantics* ch. 5 s. 5.2.

9.4 Karttunen 'Presuppositions of compound sentences' discusses the alternative three-valued definitions of *and* available.

For pragmatic accounts of phenomena sometimes argued to be semantic, see Wilson *Presuppositions and Non-Truth-Conditional Semantics*, Kempson *Presupposition and the Delimitation of Semantics* ch. 8, Ducrot *Dire et Ne Pas Dire*, R. Lakoff 'The pragmatics of modality'.

IO

Syntax and semantics

10.1 'Standard' deep structure and semantic representation

It may seem odd in a book on semantics to see the discussion of the relationship between semantics and the rest of the grammar left until the end of the book. Indeed it will surely disappoint many people that I have so far said relatively little about the detailed formulation of semantic representations: we have not considered a complete semantic specification of so much as a single sentence. Yet such relegations are by no means casual. As I hope the previous two chapters will have shown, there remains a pervasive ignorance about so many aspects of the semantic properties of sentences, that to give a complete semantic account of any sentence is not unfortunately a realistic task at the present time. There is however one problem which must be solved before any semantic properties of sentences can be characterised formally: the problem of the relation between the syntactic generalisations about a language and the semantic generalisations about that language. The over-all problem is this: given that we need to state semantic generalisations about a language, and given that we need to state syntactic generalisations about a language, what is the relation between these two types of linguistic rule? We have so far considered (chapters 6 and 7) one form of semantic generalisation in terms of semantic components combining in different ways to reflect the meanings of lexical items and sentences. And I have up to now assumed the correctness of the so-called standard theory of transformational grammar, in which syntactic generalisations are stated in terms of two syntactically defined levels, deep structure and surface structure, and the relationship between those two levels. We now have to consider in more detail the problem of the relationship between these constructs of deep and surface structure and semantic representations. In chapter 7 I assumed an answer to this question in order to display in a preliminary way the nature of the hierarchical structure of lexical and sentence meaning and the relation between the characterisation of positive sentences and negative sentences. Consideration of this question in more detail demands that we have a clear definition of deep structure, and this is of particular importance in view of the fact that each of the defining conditions of the 1965 concept of deep structure has been challenged.

In 1965, deep structure was defined to be (i) the output of the phrase structure rules (i.e. it was the level at which phrase structure rules could be used to state generalisations about the syntactic structures of a language), (ii) the input to the set of transformational rules (which state the relationship between this level and the surface string of elements making up the sentence), (iii) the level at which relations such as subject and object were defined (recall that it was claimed that deep structure was the level at which *John persuaded Bill to leave* and *John promised Bill to leave* could be structurally distinguished), (iv) the level at which lexical items were inserted (i.e. syntactic generalisations in the form of phrase-structure rules and transformational rules concern either lexical items as groups or lexical items (and sometimes morphemes) as units, but not such minimal units as semantic components), (v) the level at which so-called selectional restrictions were stated (i.e. the deviance of *The speck of dust skipped to the station* would be explained by setting up restrictions on the insertion of lexical items such as *skip* into a phrase marker so that strings containing *the speck of dust* as subject of *skip* were not generated as a well-formed sentence at all), and (vi) the level at which ambiguity in sentences was captured, by assigning a different deep structure corresponding to each interpretation a sentence has (for example the now famous sentence *Visiting relatives can be a nuisance* was said to have two deep structures, one corresponding to the interpretation in which the relatives are the visitors, one corresponding to the interpretation in which they are visited).[1] There was one further defining condition which provides the first answer to the question of the interdependence between syntactic statement and semantic statement which we shall consider: (vii) the level of deep structure was said to be the input to the semantic component.[2]

What, one might ask, is the significance of this claim? In the period

---

[1] For a rather more detailed account of deep structure, cf. 7.1.1 above.
[2] This seventh condition was not explicitly stated to be a defining condition of deep structure in Chomsky 1965, but it was widely accepted as one at about that time. For a discussion of this, cf. pp. 180–1 below.

immediately following 1957, when Chomsky first discussed the need for transformational rules as part of the grammar, many arguments were used to motivate particular deep structure configurations for different sentence types. These arguments followed a consistent pattern. In almost all cases, the suggested deep structure seemed to correspond much more closely to what was required in a semantic representation of the sentence than the actual sequence of elements of the sentence itself. Thus for example it was argued on syntactic grounds that the deep structure of imperative forms such as *Shut the door* should contain a second person subject, information which is certainly required for the semantic interpretation of such forms; it was argued that *John persuaded Bill to leave* and *John promised Bill to leave* be distinguished at deep structure in a way necessary for the semantic interpretation of the sentence; it was argued that *Visiting relatives can be a nuisance* be distinguished at deep structure in a way corresponding to its contrasting semantic interpretations; etc.; etc. In the light of this general consistency, Katz and Postal made a claim in 1964 which is taken to be an essential claim of the 'standard' 1965 model of transformational grammar – that all elements and configurations necessary for the semantic interpretation of a sentence are stated at the level of deep structure. That is to say, the syntactically defined level of deep structure, which was for each sentence a structured hierarchy (a phrase marker) expressing the syntactic relations between the lexical items of that hierarchy, was also the structure on which semantic rules operate to provide an interpretation of the sentence in question. In other words, to recall our final defining condition of deep structure, the level of deep structure was said to be the input to the semantic component. It was on this basis that the projection rules operated which I outlined in chapter 7 for providing a semantic representation of positive sentences and of negative sentences. In all then, we have seven defining conditions of deep structure. Now the combination of these conditions leads to certain paradoxical consequences, and it is the solution of these paradoxes over which linguists are currently divided.

10.2 Surface structure and semantic representation

Let us take first the combination of the defining conditions of deep structure listed above as (ii), deep structure being the input to the transformational rules, and (vii), deep structure being the input to the semantic component. If deep structure provides all the information required for semantic rules to operate to provide a semantic representation corresponding to the interpretation of a sentence, then it follows that any syntactic operation which takes place after deep structure is defined (with a deep structure or some structural modification of a deep structure as input) will not itself modify the semantic interpretation of the sentence. Whatever sequence of transformations is carried out on a particular deep structure, they will not have any effect on the semantic properties of the sentence to which that deep structure corresponds. That is to say, accepting the defining conditions (ii) and (vii) leads to a consequent claim that transformations, and indeed properties of surface structure (in so far as they are not also properties of deep structure), do not play any part in the prediction of meaning for a sentence. This claim is the basis of much dispute. Consider sentences (1)–(6).

(1) John is an informal kind of guy and John is easy to get on with.
(2) John is an informal kind of guy and easy to get on with.
(3) The men who planted the bomb were known to the police and the men who planted the bomb were careful to conceal their identity.
(4) The men who planted the bomb were known to the police and were careful to conceal their identity.
(5) The group went to the shop and the group bought themselves some new gear.
(6) The group went to the shop and bought themselves some new gear.

In each pair of sentences, the second sentence is said to be derived from a structure corresponding to the first sentence by a rule of conjunction reduction, which operates on conjoined sentence structures such as (1), (3) and (5), to form such derived structures as (2), (4) and (6), with a single subject and conjoined verb phrases. The syntactic motivation for this rule of conjunction reduction is extremely strong, but this need not concern us here. What is more important for our purposes is that the sentences in each pair, (1)–(2), (3)–(4), and (5)–(6), are synonymous. That is to say, in line with condition (vii) on deep structures, the rule of conjunction reduction appears to be meaning preserving. And indeed it is, for the majority of cases. But consider sentences (7)–(12).

(7) Many people are married and many people are happy.
(8) Many people are married and happy.

(9) No number is even and no number is odd.

(10) No number is even and odd.

(11) Some cakes are fruity and some cakes are not fruity.

(12) Some cakes are fruity and not fruity.

The syntactic relationship between the sentence pairs (7)–(8), (9)–(10), and (11)–(12), appears to be identical to that in the sentence pairs comprising (1)–(6), but in these cases, there is a meaning change, in two of the pairs a radical change. The source of the problem lies in the fact that these sentences contain noun phrases with quantifiers such as *some, many, no*. Where there seems to be a transformational relation between two sentences containing quantified noun phrases (a relation which is in all other cases meaning preserving), this relation will often not be meaning preserving.[1] This evidence suggests therefore that if the syntactic motivation for relating these sentence pairs remains strong, then their syntactic analysis should be like all other such sentence pairs, and the difference in meaning between the sentences of each pair should be captured at some level after the syntactic rule in question has taken place – i.e. at surface structure. That is to say, the syntactic account should be unitary, even though the semantic account is not, some part of the semantic interpretation being stated upon deep structure configurations, some of it upon surface structure configurations. There is further evidence which supports this conclusion that some information about surface structure is relevant to the interpretation of sentences. Consider sentences (13) and (14) (small capital letters are used to signify heavy stress):

(13) Like most BACHELORS, my husband likes chatty girls.

(14) Like MOST bachelors, my husband likes chatty girls.

(13) implies that my husband is like the majority of people who are bachelors in so far as he likes chatty girls: it does not imply that he is a bachelor himself. (14), however, with contrastive stress on *most*, implies that my husband is like the majority of bachelors in liking chatty girls, and in addition it implies, contradictorily, that he is a bachelor himself. The only distinction between (13) and (14) is in stress placement.

---

[1] For another example, consider the following sentences, related by a rule of Equal Noun Phrase Deletion ('Equi-NP Deletion'), which are also not synonymous:
   Every child wants every child to have a biscuit.
   Every child wants to have a biscuit.

Whatever syntactic operation is required to describe syntactic properties of (13) will therefore also be required to describe (14). The only natural conclusion to draw from this pair of sentences is not that (13) and (14) differ at the level of deep structure, thus preserving condition (vii) and making a distinction in the syntactic account of (13) and (14), but rather that factors such as stress assignment can sometimes alter the meaning of a sentence.[1] In other words, it appears that condition (vii) has to be relinquished as a defining property of deep structure since some aspects of surface structure may be required in predicting the semantic interpretation of sentences.

This conclusion has not yet led us to a paradoxical position. The data have merely suggested that syntactic generalisation in the form of transformational rules does not always correspond to semantic generalisation, which appears to depend on more than one kind of syntactic information. However evidence has been brought forward which appears to confirm the conflicting conclusion that deep structure, the level set up to capture syntactic generalisations about sentences, is not an independently definable syntactic level, but is identical to the level of semantic representation, the level set up to capture semantic generalisations about sentences. But if this is so, one cannot maintain that semantic representation is also dependent on the separate level of surface structure.

10.3 **Deep structure and semantic representation identified: an ambiguity argument**

How could deep structure be demonstrated to be identical to semantic representation? The evidence again involves quantifiers, but this time the problem concerns quantifiers and ambiguity. In chapter 8 (cf. 8.4 above), I discussed cases for which there is no known test for ambiguity; and these were cases where one interpretation of the sentence is more general than and includes the second interpretation. One such was the sentence *A hundred students shot twenty professors*. The ambiguity claimed is between an interpretation in which it is implied that there were one hundred students each of whom shot twenty pro-

---

[1] This argument depends on the assumption that the interdependence of stress and the interpretation of a sentence should be accounted for as part of semantics. If however stress variation is seen as an utterance phenomenon, then this argument can no longer be used. In any case, it might be argued, (14) does not necessarily imply that the referent of *my husband* is a bachelor. If this is so, then this pair of sentences no longer provides a point of controversy.

fessors, and an interpretation implying that there were twenty professors, who were shot by a hundred students. For the moment, let us assume that this sentence is indeed ambiguous. The question becomes: how should the grammar account for this ambiguity? According to the sixth defining condition on deep structure listed above, deep structure is the level at which such ambiguity should be characterised, particularly so since the ambiguity is structural and not due to a lexical item of the sentence being ambiguous. Yet the only way to specify the two interpretations of this sentence is by giving the logical form corresponding to these two interpretations. But I have already argued (3.4) that logical form, as the level from which entailments of a sentence can be deduced by general rules of logic, is indeed the level of semantic representation. It follows that, at least in some cases of ambiguity, the level of deep structure which is required to characterise ambiguity is itself the level of semantic representation (this is the view known as generative semantics). This conclusion is in direct conflict with our earlier conclusion that some aspects of surface structure were required for giving a complete semantic representation of a sentence: if deep structure is itself the semantic representation of the sentence, it cannot follow that some aspects of surface structure that are distinct from deep structure can be relevant to the stating of that deep structure.

10.4 Phrase structure rules, transformations and semantic representation

So far we have seen evidence which casts doubt on deep structure as defined by the conditions (ii), (vii) and (vi), but in two contradictory ways. The conflict does not end here. The other defining conditions of deep structure have been attacked too. Condition (v), that deep structure is the level at which generalisations about co-occurrence restrictions can be captured, has now been very widely jettisoned. As we saw in chapter 7 (cf. 7.2 above), there is strong evidence to suggest that the phenomenon is not one that can be captured at a syntactic level but is entirely semantic. There remain conditions (i) (ii) and (iv) – that deep structure is the output of the phrase structure rules, the input to the transformational rules, and the level at which lexical items are inserted. These conditions together have a consequence which apparently must be rejected, or so it has been argued by those seeking to maintain that deep structure is identical to the level of semantic representation. Consider the derivation of the pair of sentences *The man killed the woman, The woman was killed by the man.* Their deep structure within the standard model would be approximately as in figure I.[1] The phrase structure rules generate the hierarchical structure represented by the phrase marker in figure I,[2] and the lexical insertion

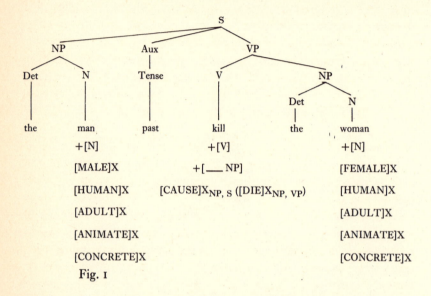

Fig. I

rules place the complex of syntactic, semantic and phonological features which characterise the lexical items from the lexicon into the phrase marker. This complete phrase marker is then subject to transformational rules, in particular the optional rule of passive formation, which operates on the constituent items of the phrase marker to generate the two surface structures corresponding to the sentences *The man killed the woman, The woman was killed by the man.* What is significant about this derivation is that neither the phrase structure rules nor the transformational rules make any reference to the lexical items themselves, let alone to their semantic specification. That is to say, implicit in the definition of deep

[1] Details such as tense, the semantic specification of the articles, and of reference implications in general, are ignored. I am also omitting all specification of the so-called selectional restrictions. Cf. 7.2 above for a discussion of the alternative formulations. I assume here and elsewhere in this section that [DIE] is semantically primitive merely for convenience of presentation.

[2] Cf. p. 111 above for one suggestion as to how the projection rules operate giving a semantic representation of the sentence.

structure as, jointly, the output of the phrase structure rules, the level at which lexical items are inserted, and the input to the transformational rules, is the claim that the mechanisms of phrase structure rules and transformational rules set up to account for the syntactic structure of the sentences of a language are not required to account for the semantic structure of those sentences and the lexical items they contain. This structure is accounted for by an entirely different means of characterisation. In other words, the semantic structure of lexical items and sentences is claimed to be subject to different rules, and different constraints, from the rules and constraints operating on syntactic structures. It is this claim, the consequence of defining deep structure by the joint conditions (i), (ii) and (iv), that has also been attacked.

Evidence has been brought forward purporting to suggest that statements about the internal semantic specification of lexical items such as *kill* require precisely the same mechanisms of description as the syntactic structure of sentences, viz. phrase structure rules and transformational rules, and more specifically that independently motivated rules such as reflexivisation are required in the semantic characterisation of certain lexical items. It has been pointed out, for example, that the specification of meaning for a sentence such as *John killed Bill* is extremely similar to the specification of the syntactic structure of a sentence such as *John caused Bill to die*. This similarity can be accentuated by giving both specifications in the form of a tree structure (figs.

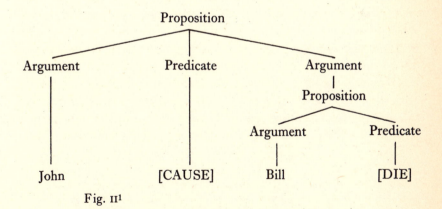

Fig. 11[1]

---

[1] This formulation entirely ignores the problem of the semantic characterisation of proper names, but this additional problem does not affect the argument under consideration.

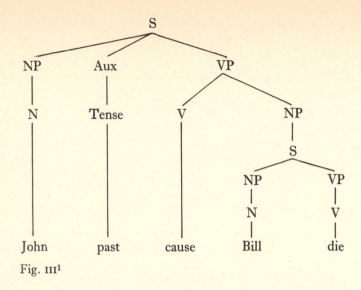

Fig. III[1]

II and III). Though these structures are by no means identical, either in configuration or in labelling, what they share is a parallel hierarchic structure. But hierarchic structure in syntax is captured by phrase structure rules. Because this hierarchic structure is also displayed in semantic representations, it is argued, the phenomenon also requires the application of phrase structure rules to characterise semantic representations. Evidence said to confirm this is provided by the alleged ambiguity of sentences containing *almost*. It is argued that since the sentence *The robber almost killed the woman* is ambiguous between an interpretation in which the robber almost did something which would have killed the woman and an interpretation in which the robber did something which caused the woman almost to die,[2] and since deep structure is the level at which such structural ambiguity is characterised, the deep structure of this sentence in which *almost* has been inserted cannot be simply as shown in fig IV but must correspond to the more complex structure[3] shown in fig. V since it is only at this level of abstraction that the deep structure representation conveys enough structural information to

[1] A generative semantics supporter would in fact claim that the underlying representation of this sentence is more abstract than the representation I have given here, but these details (concerning the order of elements and the characterisation of tense) are ignored here.

[2] It has sometimes been argued that sentences such as these are not two-ways ambiguous, but three-ways ambiguous. Cf. McCawley 1968a, 1972.

[3] Cf. n. 1 above.

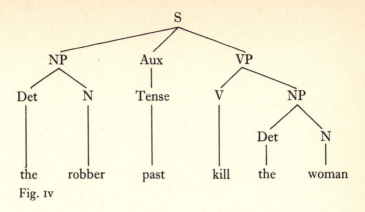

Fig. iv

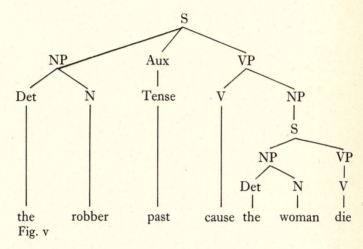

Fig. v

characterise the ambiguity which the addition of *almost* creates.[1] If the deep structure of the sentence *The robber killed the woman* did indeed correspond to this more complex structure, it would follow (*a*) that phrase structure rules would characterise the semantic properties of lexical items, (*b*) that deep structure could no longer be the level at which the lexical item *kill* was inserted, (*c*) that deep structure was in all significant respects identical to the semantic representation of that sentence.[2]

However this particular argument is both flimsy in itself and based on

---

[1] I have assumed here and elsewhere in this book that *kill* means the same as *cause to die*. Wierzbicka 1975 has argued that this is not so.

[2] Though this argument ignores the additional independent problem of the semantic characterisation of the lexical items *robber* and *woman*.

insecure assumptions. In the first place, we have already seen evidence (cf. 8.2 above) which clearly suggests that sentences containing *almost* are not ambiguous in the way suggested, but involve a single semantic representation. So the ambiguity datum on which the arguments depend is unsound. Moreover the argument that evidence of hierarchical structure in both syntax and semantics is evidence of the need to set up the same phrase structure rule mechanism to capture semantic general-isations is extremely weak. For if we look back at figures II and III (pp. 167–8), two points of comparison can be made. On the one hand, the hierarchical configuration is extremely similar. But on the other hand, the labelling of the relations is not. Figure II uses the terms *proposition, argument*, and *predicate*, whereas figure III uses S, *NP, Aux, Tense, VP, V, N*. And this distinction is not merely terminological. All that is conveyed by the terms in figure II is:

> Argument: non-relational term
> Predicate: relational term
> Proposition: combination of argument and predicate

There is no more specification of the properties and relations than this. And apart from the addition of quantifiers and the logical operators, this list constitutes the entire meta-vocabulary required for semantic representations. Now while this is arguably a form of syntax in so far as it relates items syntagmatically,[1] it is a syntax which is so general that it is not even specific to language. What is common to both syntactic structure and the structure of semantic representations is that they use linking and hierarchical relations: there are concatenation relations between argument and predicate and between subject and verb, and there are hierarchical relations between propositions and also between sentences. The difference between them lies in the very much greater abstractness of the relations in the semantic structure and, conversely, in the specification of the relations in syntax – the labelling. Since the information given in the semantic structure is so general, the fact that it can be represented in the form of a phrase marker merely states, trivially, that semantics, like syntax, involves hierarchical relations. Such a conclusion is hardly justification in itself for setting up deep structure as non-distinct from semantic representation, and so renouncing the distinction between syntax and semantics.

---

[1] We shall see in 11.1 below that the description of the structure of logical forms is indeed logicians' conception of syntax.

However there is further, rather more substantial, evidence which suggests the validity of this identification of deep structure with semantic representation. It has also been argued that specific independently motivated transformational rules are required in the semantic characterisation of lexical items, and for this reason deep structure, if it is to remain the input to the transformational rules, cannot also be the point at which lexical items are inserted as minimal syntactic units, but must be a more abstract structural representation, closer to semantic representation. Consider sentences (15)–(22).

(15) This is a door which locks itself.
(16) This is a door which is self-locking.
(17) That is a lock which adjusts itself.
(18) That is a lock which is self-adjusting.
(19) That is a man who employs himself.
(20) That is a man who is self-employed.
(21) That is a man who taught himself philosophy.
(22) That is a man who is a self-taught philosopher.

In these sentences we have examples containing reflexive pronouns, and a range of cases containing morphologically complex lexical items with *self-* prefixes. The correspondence between these is no mere coincidence. If a verb will not enter into a reflexive construction, then there is also no adjective with a *self-* prefix. Thus parallel to our paradigm (15)–(22) of grammatical sentences is the paradigm (23)–(30) of ungrammatical sentences.

(23) * This is a woman who hesitates herself.
(24) * This is a woman who is self-hesitating.
(25) * This is a woman who runs herself.
(26) * This is a woman who is self-running.
(27) * This is a woman who steals herself.[1]
(28) * This is a woman who is self-stealing.
(29) * This is a woman who drops herself.
(30) * This is a woman who is self-dropping.

The verbs *steal* and *drop* are transitive verbs which are exceptional in that they do not enter the reflexive paradigm; and the verbs *hesitate* and *run* do not enter into a reflexive paradigm because they are intransitive.

[1] With the sense of *steal* that is implied in the sentences *He stole the money, John stole Bill's wife.*

What remains to be explained is the parallel between the *self*-plus-participle adjective constructions and this reflexive paradigm. In a grammar where the lexical items are inserted as syntactic units before any transformations take place, it is not obvious how the required generalisation can be captured, for the regularity about *self*-plus-participle adjective constructions would not be captured by the reflexive transformation, but would be stated as a regularity in the lexicon quite separate from the transformation itself. On the contrary, however, if sentences containing *self*-plus-participle adjective constructions were derived from a deep structure identical to that of the corresponding reflexive construction, then the grammar can account naturally for the parallel between these two types of construction – the rule of reflexivisation would apply in both cases, capturing the similarity of the constraints in both cases, followed by an optional rule transforming a verb-plus-reflexive pronoun into the corresponding *self*-plus participle adjective construction. The theoretical claim that such a grammar incorporates is that syntactic processes such as reflexivisation play an intrinsic part in characterising the internal structure of at least some lexical items. These *self*-plus participle adjective constructions are not an isolated case. Consider also (31)–(42).

(31) Marijuana can be obatined freely.
(32) Marijuana is freely obtainable.
(33) This door cannot be locked.
(34) This door is not lockable.
(35) This dog cannot be managed/trained.
(36) This dog is not manageable/trainable.
(37) This passage cannot be translated.
(38) This passage is not translatable.
(39) * This girl can be hesitated.
(40) * This girl is hesitateable.
(41) * This man can be existed.
(42) * This man is existable.

For those verbs which undergo the passive transformation, there is a corresponding construction with the verb plus an *-able* suffix. Those verbs such as intransitives which do not have a passive form have no corresponding verb-plus-*able* construction. Moreover, those transitive verbs which are exceptional in not having a passive form, also have no corresponding verb-plus-*able* construction. For example, the verb *weigh* is ambiguous. The verb *weigh* in *He weighed the salt* has a passive form; the verb *weigh* in *He weighs 60 kilos* does not. *Sixty kilos is weighed by him* is ungrammatical. This second sense of *weigh* has no verb-plus-*able* construction. *This salt is not weighable* has only the interpretation of the first sense of *weigh*. Similarly *Our baby is unmeasurable* does not mean that the baby has no measurement, but merely that it is not possible for someone to measure her (because she won't keep still long enough, etc.). This parallel between whether a verb can enter a passive construction and whether it can enter a verb-plus-*able* construction can be naturally captured in a grammar which derives this latter, morphologically complex construction from the same deep structure as the corresponding passive construction: if a verb has to be marked as not undergoing the passive transformation, it will then follow as an automatic consequence that there will be no such -*able* construction. It is not obvious how such a correspondence could be captured in a grammar which explains the distribution of the passive construction by means of a transformational rule, but which characterises lexical items such as *manageable, trainable, readable, sellable, translatable, understandable, likeable* as syntactically simple items, inserted at the level of deep structure, with the identical constraint to the constraint on the passive construction captured by means of an entirely unrelated semantic rule. In these cases of *self*-plus-participle adjective constructions and verb-plus-*able* constructions, it appears then that we have evidence that the syntactic transformational processes of reflexivisation and passive are required to account for the internal structure of lexical items. But this step immediately commits us to accepting a deep structure more abstract than that of the standard 1965 theory, and closer to a deep structure identical to the semantic representation of the sentence.

10.5 Syntax and semantics: the issue reviewed

On the one hand, we have seen evidence in favour of a more abstract deep structure corresponding much more closely to a level of semantic representation: the ambiguity in sentences such as *A hundred students shot twenty professors* seems to lead to this conclusion, and so too does the existence of the verb-plus-*able* and *self*-plus-participle constructions. There are also the arguments concerning the structural nature of semantic representation and ambiguity involving *almost*, but, as we saw, these were comparatively weak. On the other hand we considered evidence which suggested the opposite conclusion – that semantic representation, far from being stateable at an extremely abstract level, had to make reference to certain aspects of surface structure. It is this conflict which accounts for what has been one of the major disagreements among generative grammarians in recent years. On the one hand, Chomsky and his followers argued that the justification of deep structure as the level at which lexical items are inserted and the level at which subject–object relations are explicitly characterised remains intact,[1] but that the semantic interpretation of sentences depends in part on information specified at the independent syntactic level of deep structure, and in part on information such as word order and stress assignment which is specified at surface structure. Furthermore, the statement of semantic rules is argued to be separate from, and different in kind from, the rules of syntax. On the other hand, a group of Chomsky's early pupils argued that if syntactic processes are to be stated most generally, the level of deep structure has to be much more abstract and identical to semantic representation. Since the deep structure of a sentence is postulated to account for the syntactic properties of that sentence, it follows from the generative semanticists' position that the syntactic properties of a sentence are predicted to be always dependent on its meaning. Now this disagreement is not a terminological one, a parochial disagreement between members of the same camp. On the contrary, it has considerable general significance. The disagreement turns on the nature of the interdependence between syntactic facts and semantic facts, a problem which is fundamental to any linguistic theory. This is not an area in which one would anticipate that grammars of individual languages would differ. In attempting to formulate within a theory the precise nature of the interdependence of syntactic and semantic generalisations, linguists are, on the contrary, concerned with a linguistic universal of the strongest kind, one which is predicted to hold of all languages by virtue of being a necessary property of a system which underlies a human language. This particular disagreement within transformational grammar therefore concerns all linguists, whatever their affiliation.

How then do these alternative theories solve the paradox implicit in the conflicting data we considered earlier? First we considered data where the syntactic account (captured by the transformational rule of

---

[1] More recently, the entire justification of deep structure as a syntactic construct has been radically altered by Chomsky: cf. Chomsky 1975.

conjunction reduction) seemed homogeneous, but the semantic account was not (sometimes synonymy was involved, sometimes not). Secondly we considered ambiguity data which suggested that the syntactic account of sentences had to be more abstract than had previously been considered. Finally we considered data where the syntactic and semantic accounts seemed to correspond one to another, leading to the same conclusion as the second set of arguments, that the syntactic account of sentences has to be more abstract – indeed identical to semantic structure. Which of these sets of data provide the strongest arguments? Recall first, sentences (1)–(12) (repeated here for convenience).

(1) John is an informal kind of guy and John is easy to get on with.
(2) John is an informal kind of guy and easy to get on with.
(3) The men who planted the bomb were known to the police and the men who planted the bomb were careful to conceal their identity.
(4) The men who planted the bomb were known to the police and were careful to conceal their identity.
(5) The group went to the shop and the group bought themselves some new gear.
(6) The group went to the shop and bought themselves some new gear.
(7) Many people are married and many people are happy.
(8) Many people are married and happy.
(9) No number is even and no number is odd.
(10) No number is even and odd.
(11) Some cakes are fruity and some cakes are not fruity.
(12) Some cakes are fruity and not fruity.

(1)–(6) are those examples where there is synonymy between the members of the pair, (7)–(12) are those where there is not. Now it is clear that this set of examples provides no problem in principle for the view that syntactic properties are independent of semantic properties, for there is no expectation that syntactic homogeneity will correspond to semantic homogeneity. Thus Chomsky's 1965 position, though it demands revision to allow for an interdependence between surface structure and semantic representation, is not seriously incompatible with the data. But what of generative semantics, where syntactic generalisations are predicted to correspond to semantic ones? Some have tried to argue that the syntactic data are not as homogeneous as they look. Consider (1)–(12) again. In sentences (1), (3) and (5), the subject noun phrase in the first conjunct sentence is interpreted as referring to the same person (or set of people) as the subject of the second conjunct sentence. This is not so in sentences (7), (9) and (11). On the basis of this difference, it has been argued (G. Lakoff 1970a) that the rule of conjunction reduction itself depends on the two subject noun phrases in question being interpreted as being co-referential. In other words, though (1) and (2), (3) and (4), (5) and (6) have an identical deep structure source for each pair, (7) and (8), (9) and (10), (11) and (12) do not. (8), (10) and (12) have, as their deep structures, structures similar to (7), (9) and (11) but where the interpretation is specified as involving co-referential subjects of the two sentence conjuncts. That is to say, on this view the syntactic facts do correspond to a single semantic generalisation despite a superficial indication that they do not. The validity of this alternative characterisation depends on requiring of conjunction reduction that it only apply where two subject noun phrases are co-referential: but this requirement is quite unsatisfactory. Consider example (9), which I have so far glossed over. There is no sense in which the two subject noun phrases can be said to refer to the same set of objects: they do not refer at all. And this is not an isolated example:

(43) No-one other than us has a hundred dalmatians and no-one other than us has six fox cubs.

(44) No-one other than us has a hundred dalmatians and six fox cubs.

(45) An indeterminate number of seeds were crushed and an indeterminate number of seeds were wasted.

(46) An indeterminate number of seeds were crushed and wasted.

In (43)–(46), no condition of co-reference could ever be met: (43) is like (9) in that the subject carries no reference implication at all; in (45) the subject is interpreted as referring to a non-determinate group of individuals so it would be impossible to state co-reference between the individuals of that set and some other equally ill-determined set. Yet if conjunction reduction did indeed depend on a condition of identity of reference, (10), (44) and (46) would never be generated by the grammar. Since they are grammatical, and *are* generated by the grammar, they must have been generated by the rule of conjunction reduction, for the syntactic process involved is clearly the same as that in (2), (4) and (6).

But for these reasons, the condition of identity of reference on the two subject noun phrases involved in conjunction reduction cannot be maintained. Since the claim of consistency between syntactic and semantic generalisation depended on this co-reference condition it appears that the claim cannot be upheld. So this entire set of sentences does indeed exemplify a lack of correspondence between syntactic facts and semantic facts, thus suggesting that the generative semantics position cannot be maintained. At the very least, these sentences provide an anomaly for generative semantics to which there is no obvious explanation.

What of the conflicting data concerning *self*-plus-participle and verb-plus-*able* constructions which appeared to provide an anomaly for the position we have just been endorsing? In this case, there *did* appear to be a correspondence between the syntactic constraints on reflexive and passive formations and the constraints on the intra-lexical problems of *self*-constructions and *-able* constructions. In this case then, it will be the linguists supporting Chomsky's concept of deep structure who will seek to explain away the data. Their move is thus to question just how close is the correspondence between reflexive constructions and *self*-plus-participle constructions. This counter-move is more convincing than the generative semanticists' counter-move in the conjunction reduction examples. For indeed the correspondence is not as close as examples (15)–(22) suggest. In the first place, there are verbs which have no corresponding *self*- construction, though they do allow reflexive forms. There are no adjectives *self-killed, self-sold, self-talked*. Thus though it might appear that *self*- constructions share some of the constraints of the reflexive constructions they are not identical to them. There are also *self*- constructions formed with nouns which have no corresponding verb, despite the fact that, if they were explained in the same way as other *self*- constructions, they would have to be derived from a structure containing some such verb. Thus there is *self-portrait*, but not *self-portrayed*. Perhaps more serious than this are the difficulties involved in capturing the required distributions within a generative semantics position, which the data apparently support. In particular, the semantic parallel is not as striking as it first appears. For example, though *self-locking, self-adjusting, self-effacing* correspond to *X locks self*, *X adjusts self*, *X effaces self* respectively, there is no consistency as to which verbs enter a past participle construction and which a present participle construction. Most verbs either form one type of construction or the other, a few enter both: there is no form *self-effaced*, though perhaps we can accept *self-adjusted* as a well-formed English word. And though we have *self-taught*, *self-employed*, *self-inflicted*, there is conversely no *self-teaching*, *self-employing*, *self-inflicting*. Furthermore, the semantic interpretation is not consistent within a single type of form. Quite to the contrary, the *self*-plus-participle constructions display considerable semantic variety. Though a self-taught man is one who taught himself, a self-addressed envelope is not an envelope which addressed itself, according to the pattern of *self-taught*, but is rather an envelope which has been addressed to oneself. A self-determined girl is neither a girl who determined herself, nor a girl who is determined by oneself: the paraphrase relation in this case is different yet again. Even within the more regular forms, the semantic relationship is not the same. A self-taught philosopher is someone who taught himself philosophy but a self-employed man is not a man who employed himself, in the past, but (unlike the interpretation of *self-taught*) is a man who is currently employing himself. So if a generative semantics position is adopted, not only will separate rules of *self*-plus-participle construction insertion have to be set up for the derivation of forms such as *self-addressed* and *self-determined*, but also quite distinct rules will have to be set up for the derivation of the apparently regular forms *self-taught* and *self-employed*, because the semantic source of each is distinct. This is not the end of the problems, for once having set up such distinct rules, the grammar has to guarantee that, though there is a rule for deriving *self*-plus-past-participle constructions from present tense verbs (in order to account for *self-employed*), the rule must not apply to a verb such as *teach*. Conversely for *employ*: despite there being a separate rule deriving *self*-plus-past-participle constructions from past tense verbs, the rule must *not* apply to a verb such as *employ*. Thus, far from giving a uniform homogeneous explanation of the data, the generative semantics position is forced to set up large numbers of transformational rules to characterise the single set of *self-* constructions, each rule operating under rather different conditions and only applying to a very small set of verbs. These problems are only difficulties for a grammar which seeks to capture the relationship between *self-denying* and *denies self* by means of the reflexive transformation. In a grammar such as that containing a deep structure in which lexical items are inserted as units, no such problems arise precisely because the grammar does not seek to capture the relation directly by means of the transformational rule. All *self*-plus-participle constructions are, like all other lexical items, listed in the lexicon, together with their syntactic, phonological and semantic properties. Whatever relation there may be between the forms of the lexicon is captured by redundancy rules (cf. 6.2.3); and since there is a relation between these forms and their corresponding verb, this could be captured by a redundancy rule. That is to say, it appears that a Chomskian linguist has to admit that the parallel between *self*-plus-participle constructions and reflexive constructions remains unexplained, at least directly, within a model with a standard syntactically defined level of deep structure. But in this case, it is arguable that this is defensible, for the regularities involved are not in fact sufficient to justify the complication to the grammar that would be the consequence of a syntactic account of the data.

Similar kinds of arguments can be put forward in the case of the parallel between verb-plus-*able* adjectives and the passive construction. Like the *self*-plus-participle constructions, the semantic relation is not constant. *Manageable* might correspond to *able to be managed* (cf. pp. 172–3 above), but *preferable* does not correspond to *able to be preferred*, but rather to *is preferred*. *Valuable* corresponds to neither of these paraphrase forms but to *is highly valued*. Similar problems arise with *despicable, detestable, likeable*, etc. Moreover some *-able* adjectives have no root: *amicable, amiable, miserable, sociable*. In more general terms, forms such as *self*-plus-participle items and verb-plus-*able* items display the idiosyncrasy and variability which is characteristic of lexical processes, and unlike syntactic processes. For this reason, it can be argued that they do not provide as strong evidence as at first appeared against a grammar which generates lexical items as syntactically simple items, given as a list in the lexicon.

What of the other arguments in favour of a more abstract level of deep structure than that represented by a grammar in which lexical items are inserted at deep structure? The first of these was the ambiguity in a sentence such as *A hundred students shot twenty professors*, a characterisation of which can only be given in terms of the two logical forms of the sentence, i.e. their semantic representations. The second of these was that since semantic representations in general involve hierarchic structure, they should be generated by phrase structure rules, this guaranteeing that the output of these rules, deep structure, be identical to semantic representation. The third argument concerned the alleged ambiguity of a sentence such as *John almost killed the hostages*, an account of which would demand access to a level of structure in which *kill* is represented as the complex *cause to die*, and not merely as a unitary lexical item. We have already seen that two of these three arguments are extremely weak. On the one hand, sentences containing *almost* are not ambiguous, so no conclusion follows from arguments based on such ambiguity data. And on the other hand, it does not follow from the requirement of character- ising the semantic representation of a sentence in terms of a hierarchical structure that this structure is identical to the structure required for a syntactic account of that sentence. What of the first argument, con- cerning the ambiguity of the quantified sentence *A hundred students shot twenty professors*? First of all, it is not certain that this sentence is ambiguous in the required way, rather than having a single semantic representation specifying a disjunction of all the possible ways in which such a sentence could be true. However, even if we assume that it is indeed ambiguous, what consequences does such an ambiguity have for the level of deep structure? Given that ambiguity is accepted as evidence of the deep structure of a sentence, then of course the ambiguity of this sentence must lead to the setting up of a more abstract deep structure. But recall the original motivation for the level of deep structure. This was that such a level was required in order to account for syntactic generalisations about the language. Ambiguity however is a semantic phenomenon. It follows that ambiguity data are not in themselves evidence for setting up such a level as deep structure. However in some cases, the ambiguity involved has different syntactic consequences depending on the interpretation given to the sentence. Thus for example, it is not the ambiguity in the sentence *Visiting relatives can be a nuisance* which is itself evidence for setting up two deep structures for this sentence: it is the fact that the two interpretations of this sentence have different syntactic properties, in one the *-ing* form being a gerundive verb form with *relatives* as the object of that verb, in the other the *-ing* form being a non-finite present participle with *relatives* as the subject of the verb. Now all the examples of ambiguity used by Chomsky as evidence for his 'standard' concept of deep structure are of this kind: their contrastive semantic interpretations have different syntactic properties. In general then, the defining condition on deep structure concerning ambiguity is not simply that deep structure is the level at which ambiguity is characterised, but that deep structure is the level at which an ambiguous sentence is given two (more than one) characterisa- tions if the interpretations of the sentence have different syntactic properties. It follows from this revised condition that the ambiguity in *A hundred students shot twenty professors* will only be evidence for a more abstract deep structure if the syntactic characterisation of the sentence differs according to which interpretation is involved. However it does not: in both cases we have quantified noun phrases as subject and object linked by a transitive verb. Under both interpretations the syntactic account is identical. So it appears that even if we grant the ambiguity of the sentence *A hundred students shot twenty professors*, this has no consequences for a syntactically defined level of deep structure. A sentence such as this would simply be an example where a single deep structure representation has to be mapped onto two semantic representations. While the details of this mapping process need a formal statement, this does not pose a problem of principle.

10.6 Summary

The over-all question raised in this chapter has been the inter-relation between syntactic generalisations and semantic generalisations. Within the framework of transformational grammar, this question can be posed particularly clearly, because the syntactic account attributed to languages involves the level of deep structure which has been given a precise characterisation. Thus we considered the detailed definition of deep structure accepted in about 1965. As we saw however, it appears that not all of these defining conditions can be maintained; and linguists are divided as to which of these should be relinquished. Some no longer claim that deep structure is the level on which the characterisation of semantic representations is based, or solely based, others no longer claim that deep structure is a level giving a hierarchical characterisation to a string of lexical items. For this latter group of linguists, deep structure as the semantic representation of a sentence is a hierarchical structure relating a complex of semantic components.

The evidence that I have considered in this chapter has tended to suggest the correctness of the former view which alone is compatible with the traditional view that the syntactic and semantic structures of languages are two independent systems, albeit with relations between them. However it is important to bear in mind that this issue concerns a much wider range of arguments than I have been able to consider in this chapter. The problem concerns the nature of semantic representations, about which there is virtually no agreement, and the concept of deep structure, which even in its revised form remains a controversial level, not accepted by many linguists working within transformational grammar. Thus the problem of the inter-relation between syntax and semantics remains an ever-present issue: as our understanding of both syntax and semantics increases, so our understanding of the relation between these two systems changes. All that can be achieved by a brief discussion such as this is an indication of the pattern which arguments have taken, and the reason why these arguments have taken the form they have. For the rest, the issue remains an open one, subject to linguists' conflicting interpretation of the subject they are studying.

RECOMMENDED READING

10.1 The problem of providing a formal statement of the relation between the syntactic structure of a sentence and its semantic interpretation, though by no means ignored by other linguists (see for example Leech *Towards a Semantic Description of English*), has been most emphasised by transformational linguists in recent years. For an account of deep structure, see the references listed in the recommended reading for chapter 7. This 1965 concept of deep structure was attacked by G. Lakoff in 'Instrumental adverbs and the concept of deep structure', *Irregularity in Syntax*, 'On generative semantics', and 'Repartee', by McCawley in 'The role of semantics in grammar', 'Concerning the base component of a transformational grammar', and 'Lexical insertion in a transformational grammar without deep structure', by Postal in 'On the surface verb "remind"' (reprinted in Fillmore and Langendoen (eds.) *Studies in Linguistic Semantics*), by Bach in 'Nouns and noun phrases', and by Ross in 'Auxiliaries as main verbs'. Of these articles, perhaps the most useful for students as an introduction to the generative semantics position is Postal 'On the surface verb "remind"', as it gives a summary of the two opposing theoretical positions. All of the arguments presented in the articles listed above led to the conclusion that the deep structure of a sentence was much more abstract than had previously been thought. Arguments leading towards the other conclusion, that aspects of surface structure are relevant to an interpretation of the sentence were presented by Jackendoff *Semantic Interpretation in a Generative Grammar*, Dougherty 'An interpretive theory of pronominal reference', 'The syntax and semantics of *each other* constructions', Hall-Partee 'Negation, conjunction and quantifiers', and Bresnan 'Sentence stress and syntactic transformations'. Two particularly good over-view articles of the theoretical controversy have been written by Hall-Partee 'Linguistic metatheory' (reprinted in Harman (ed.) *On Noam Chomsky*) and 'On the requirement that transformations preserve meaning'. Chomsky's 'Some empirical issues in the theory of transformational grammar' is a clear defence of his own position, criticising the attacks made by those arguing for generative semantics. The argument for the relevance of surface structure to semantic interpretation concerning the rule of conjunction reduction was presented by Hall-Partee in 'Negation, conjunction and quantifiers', to which Lakoff aptly replied with 'Repartee, or a reply to negation, conjunction and quantifiers'. The evidence is given a further brief consideration in Hall-Partee 'On the requirement that transformations preserve meaning'. The purported ambiguity of sentences such as *A hundred students shot twenty professors* is discussed by G. Lakoff in 'Linguistics and natural logic', and in 'On generative semantics', and by Hall-Partee in 'Linguistic metatheory' and, briefly, in 'On the requirement that transformations preserve meaning'. That lexical items such as *kill* require a description in terms identical to mechanisms for describing syntactic structure was first argued by McCawley in 'Lexical insertion in a transformational grammar without deep structure', to which Fodor responded with 'Three reasons for not deriving "kill" from "cause to die"'. A whole section of Kimball (ed.) *Syntax and Semantics I* is devoted to the relation between *kill* and *cause to die*, with Kac and Shibatani criticising McCawley, and McCawley replying to them: see Kac 'Action and result: two aspects of predication in English', Shibatani 'Three reasons for not deriving "kill" from "cause to die" in Japanese' and McCawley 'Kac and Shibatani on the grammar of killing'. See also however Wierzbicka 'Why "kill" does not mean "cause to die": the semantics of action sentences'. The purported ambiguity of sentences containing *almost* is used as an argument by McCawley who claims that *John almost killed Fred* is three-ways ambiguous: Kac in response argues that it is two-ways ambiguous. The morphological data concerning the prefix *self-* and the suffix *-able* were first discussed by Chapin *On the Syntax of Word-Derivation in English* and later by Chomsky in 'Remarks on nominalization' (reprinted in *Studies on Semantics in Generative Grammar*), whose defence of his so-called lexicalist position I have presented here. For further reading on the generative semantics position, Seuren (ed.) *Semantic Syntax* is a useful collection. Since the late sixties, when the arguments I have used were aired, the positions of the two contending groups of linguists have changed considerably. See for example Chomsky *Reflections on Language*, and G. Lakoff and Thompson 'Introducing cognitive grammar' and 'Dative questions in cognitive grammar'.

I I

The state of the art and prospects for the future

It must have become increasingly obvious during the course of this book that there is almost no aspect of semantics over which there is any degree of certainty: there is considerable disagreement over the basic assumptions of a semantic theory, the nature of semantic representations is contentious, and there is no agreement about the relation of semantics either to logic or to other parts of a grammar. To increase the confusion, many of the problems are interdependent, a solution to one problem thereby depending on a solution to another. Consider for example the choice to be made between a truth-conditional semantics and a speech act semantics. In chapters 3 and 5, I argued that, of these two, a truth-based semantics was to be preferred; but in criticising speech act theories of semantics I assumed that the task in semantics is to explain the basis of the interpretation of sentences, and not the interpretation of utterances, the individual uses to which those sentences might be put, on the basis that an account of sentence use is a task for a theory of performance. If however it is argued that the distinction between competence and performance is an idealisation which can no longer be maintained, at least in the form that Chomsky presented it in 1965 (and that I have assumed here), then it might be argued that the restriction of semantics to a characterisation of sentence meaning is mistaken. The distinction between semantics and pragmatics too depends on the assumptions that there are properties intrinsic to sentences and that an explanation of factors of use in utterances depends on a prior explanation of the inter-pretation of sentences. So the problems of distinguishing between semantics and pragmatics, distinguishing between competence and performance, or evaluating truth-conditional semantics and speech act semantics, are all inter-related. This is by no means the end of the interaction of problem areas. We saw in chapter 9 that a presupposition-based analysis of semantics differed from an entailment-based analysis in that it purported to provide an explanation within semantics of speakers' assumptions in using sentences, distinguishing between what is presupposed and what stated. To be consistent with an entailment-based analysis, generalisations about speakers' assumptions in using sentences would have to be part of an explanation of utterance meaning – pragmatics. Thus even this controversy is interdependent with the others. Furthermore many of the disagreements involved in the issues we have considered in this book turn on ambiguity evidence. The purported ambiguity of negation is a central point of dispute in the presupposition v. entailment disagreement, and ambiguity plays a large part too in the controversy of the interdependence of syntax and semantics, the evidence we considered in chapter 10 including the purported ambiguity of such sentences as *John almost killed Bill* and *A hundred students shot twenty professors*. So we have very considerable uncertainty both at the level of deciding upon the nature of the data, deciding for example whether a given sentence is ambiguous or not, and at the level of deciding upon the theoretical account best able to explain the given data.

11.1   **Linguistic semantics v. logical semantics?**

Not only is there this pervasive uncertainty in almost every aspect of semantics, but there is also a dichotomy in the way the subject is approached by linguists and logicians (cf. pp. 76–9 above). Many linguistic accounts of semantics assume the validity of specifying some form of componential representation as an account of the semantic interpretation of a sentence, and discuss in detail only the exact nature of this specification. On the other hand, those logicians who are concerned with specifying semantic properties of natural language see their task as specifying logical forms of sentences, and giving a semantic interpretation of those forms in terms of rules (called functions) stating the relation between those forms and the non-linguistic objects, events, etc., which a language is used to describe. This dichotomy is mirrored in this book. The relation between the discussion of a truth-conditional semantics in chapter 3 and, on the one hand, the outline of a component-based semantics in chapters 6 and 7 and, on the other, the discussion of the syntax–semantics interdependence within a component-based framework must have seemed at best tenuous. Why is this dichotomy so severe if, as I have argued in this book, the specification of semantic representations within a linguistic theory should involve, as logicians assume, the specification of a set of logical forms together with rules (functions) stating explicitly the relation between these and the objects, events, etc., of the world they describe? The gap is, I suggest, created by two factors, one of which is a matter of terminology: these are the problem of analyticity, and the different concepts linguists and logicians have of syntax. To take the terminology problem first, the specification of the syntax of a logic is a specification of the logical forms from which all inferences relevant to logical truth can be deduced. In dealing with natural languages, logicians commonly assume that the syntactic account of a language will be, like that of logic, a specification of the logical forms of a language. That is to say, to a logician it is a sine qua non of the syntax of formal languages and correspondingly of natural languages, that it be a vehicle from which semantic generalisations can be stated. However this is certainly not assumed by linguists. For a linguist on the contrary, a syntactic account of a language must provide (at least) an explanation of the regularities of structure in the arrangement of lexical items to form sentences. The syntax of a grammar is not, or not principally, designed to account for generalisations in the interpretation of sentences, but to account for generalisations in the structure of sentences. It is a matter of argument to establish whether such syntactic regularities correspond to the regularities involved in specifying the logical forms of sentences (as is argued by linguists supporting the generative semantics position). As we shall see shortly, this disagreement over terminology makes the disagreement over the nature of semantic representation appear more extreme than it is.

Even so, the difference between a logician's specification of logical form, with the accompanying interpretive functions, and a linguist's semantic representation is not slight. And this difference, whether only implicitly recognised or whether explicitly drawn attention to, can be traced to the attack of circularity and vacuousness that Quine raised against the terms *analytic, meaning, synonymy*, etc. (cf. 3.3 above). It is a standard move for logicians, following Quine, to treat entities of meaning as so contentious as to be avoided in a theory of meaning for natural language at all costs.[1] In any case, logics are set up to account for inferences relating to logical truth and not to analytic truth (cf. 3.4 above), and in line with these the logical forms of natural languages are set up to account only for these inferences, and not to account for those inferences relative to analytic truth. Yet I have argued (cf. 3.3 above) that the problem presented by Quine's attack of circularity has to be

---

[1] Cf. Foster 1976 as a representative of this view.

bypassed if we are to make the correct predictions about sentence relatedness: it is not sufficient for a semantic theory to predict only that a sentence such as *John killed the warden and Bill was later arrested* entails *John killed the warden*, and *Bill was later arrested*, and other such sentences, none of which involves a decomposition of the lexical items of the entailing sentence. It should also predict that the conjoined sentence entails the further sentences *John caused the warden to die* and *The warden died* (on the basis of the first conjunct *John killed the warden* entailing these sentences). It is this further prediction which a linguist's semantic representation in terms of semantic components is set up to fulfil. Thus one main reason why a linguist's specification of the semantic representation of a sentence seems radically different from a logician's specification of the logical form of that sentence is that the set of inferences to be predicted from a linguist's semantic representation is of greater range than the set of inferences to be predicted from a logician's.

Even with this difference accounted for, there are two omissions in an account of the interpretation of sentences merely in terms of semantic representations. If, as I have argued (cf. 3.4 above), these representations are indeed the logical forms of sentences, then there should be a logic characterising them and there should also be a set of functions interpreting them in terms of the objects, concepts, etc., that they are used to talk about. But there is no such logic and there are no such functions; for all that linguists have been interested in, at least until recently,[1] is stating the semantic representations themselves, and not the principles which account for those semantic representations. Thus even if a specification of semantic representations in terms of components can be justified, there remain the tasks of devising a logic with sufficient structure to account for all the entailments in question and then specifying the entire set of functions necessary to interpret the infinite set of logical forms characterised by this yet-to-be-written logic.

One reason why this task has not attracted the attention of logicians[2] is the scepticism with which logicians view linguists' semantic representations. As Lewis has cogently expressed it (Lewis 1972: 169–70):

Semantic markers are *symbols*: items in the vocabulary of an artificial language we may call *Semantic Markerese*. Semantic interpretation by means of them

---

[1] The collection of papers in Keenan (ed.) 1975 demonstrate the increasingly converging interests of logicians and linguists.

[2] One notable exception is Reichenbach 1947.

amounts merely to a translation algorithm from the object language to the auxiliary language Markerese. But we can know the Markerese translation of an English sentence without knowing the first thing about the meaning of the English sentence: namely, the conditions under which it would be true. Semantics with no treatment of truth conditions is not semantics. Translation into Markerese is at best a substitute for real semantics, relying either on our tacit competence (at some future date) as speakers of Markerese or on our ability to do real semantics at least for the one language Markerese. Translation into Latin might serve as well.

Now this scepticism is not altogether justified, for, as we have seen, there is a certain misunderstanding about the nature of syntactic structures. No logician doubts the need for specifying logical forms, but he sees this as the task of syntax. If those linguists who hold to the independence of syntactic and semantic generalisations are correct (cf. chapter 10), then what the logician sees as the extra level of analysis called semantic representation is none other than the level of logical form. The level that is additional to the logician's characterisation of language is thus not the much-derided level of semantic representation but the level of syntactic structure.

This being said, there remains the deep mistrust of semantic components as a form of explanation. To explain the meaning of the English word *adult* in terms of the universal component '[ADULT]' is after all not much of an explanation. The question that we must finally consider is whether, as linguists concerned to characterise analytic truths, we are bound to defend such components, or whether there is any alternative.

11.2 Meaning postulates

The most celebrated alternative to componential analysis is an analysis in terms of so-called meaning postulates, an analysis which is due, at least in its original formulation, to Carnap (cf. Carnap 1947). One of the reasons why componential analysis often seems unconvincing is the assumption implicit in a componential analysis of lexical items that a total account of the meaning of a lexical item can be given by a componential analysis of that item. The aim of an analysis of lexical meaning in terms of meaning postulates is rather weaker: a meaning postulate is an explicit generalisation of relations of hyponymy (cf. 6.2 above), in the form

$$(x) (A_x \rightarrow B_x)$$

which may be understood in a preliminary way as meaning

Anything if it is A will also be B[1]

and if this form of generalisation is adopted as a means of formulating lexical meaning, it allows a full statement of lexical relations without making the further requirement that this be a complete characterisation of lexical meaning in any single case. Take the well-worn example *bachelor* under the interpretation of this word as a man who has never been married. While a componential analysis is committed to fully specifying this interpretation of the word *bachelor*, an analysis in terms of meaning postulates allows in principle for partial specifications of lexical meaning, giving a formal statement of the fact that if someone is a bachelor (in the required sense) he will be male, adult, and unmarried, without making any commitment as to whether or not this be the total semantic content of the lexical item. In the case of *bachelor*, it is arguable that these implications do constitute the total contribution that this item *bachelor* makes to the meaning of sentences in which it occurs. But there are very, very many cases where this is not so. It may not have gone unnoticed in chapter 6 that the extent to which componential analysis can give a formalisation of the full variety of hyponymic relations is extremely restricted (cf. 6.2 above). What universal, language-independent semantic components distinguish the following pairs of lexical items: *skip, move*; *yellow, coloured*; *bathroom, room*; *dog, animal*; *cabbage, vegetable*; *toffee, sweet*; *waitress, woman*; *sculptor, artist*; *toddler, child*; *bible, book*; *chat, talk*? In view of such large areas of vocabulary where componential analysis does not appear to be even feasible as a means of encapsulating the precise interpretation of each lexical item, it is arguable that a weaker account of lexical meaning, in terms of partial specification, is all that should be required of a semantic theory.

I have so far introduced the concept of meaning postulate quite informally, but the interpretation of the formalism

$$(x) (A_x \rightarrow B_x)$$

must be made more precise. There are two principal ways in which it has been interpreted: the predicate letters *A* and *B* have been interpreted as ranging over lexical items on the one hand and as ranging over language-independent representations of universal concepts on the other. But one of these options is untenable if meaning postulates are to

---

[1] For a more rigorous account of what the variables *A* and *B* range over, see below.

provide an alternative formulation to semantic components of lexical meaning. For if componential analysis can be criticised on the basis of the dubiousness of postulating large numbers of universal components, such a criticism is even more pressing against an analysis in terms of meaning postulates between universal concepts, for such an analysis would account for the relations of hyponymy between lexical items such as *waitress* and *woman*, *bible* and *book*, and *cabbage* and *vegetable* in terms of the universal language-independent concepts of 'waitress', 'bible', 'cabbage', 'vegetable', 'book' and 'woman'.[1] So it seems that for those who are suspicious of the universal status accorded to semantic components, the meaning postulate formalism must be interpreted in terms of the lexical items themselves.

However this use of meaning postulates is not without its problems. In the first place, the adoption of meaning postulates to account for lexical meaning is not sufficient in itself as the basis for a theory of meaning, for we still have to explain the relation between lexical meaning and sentence meaning, and this problem the meaning postulate formalism does not purport to account for. Secondly, meaning postulates are language specific: so unless some extra formulation is included within the theory, there is no way of relating the meaning postulates for English to corresponding meaning postulates in other languages.[2] If however we build into such a theory both a mechanism for relating lexical meanings and sentence meanings, and an explicit account of the cross-language relationships between the lexical items of the individual languages, both of which seem essential to an adequate account of semantics as part of a universal linguistic theory, then it is not obvious that any substantial distinction remains between this revised form of the meaning postulate approach and a componential analysis approach. For on the one hand, relating the interpretation of lexical items to the interpretation of sentences to show the compositional nature of sentence meaning involves some statement of the inter-relation between the syntactic structure of the sentence and the meanings of the lexical items in the sentence in the manner of a projection rule. And on the other hand, isolating what is common to meaning postulates across languages involves some statement of that common element and is therefore

[1] I have used single quotation-marks for the specification of universal concepts in order not to prejudge the issue as to whether such specifications are in fact non-distinct from semantic components.

[2] It is arguable that such cross-language generalisations can only be stated from sentences, but this does not affect the argument in question.

equivalent in effect to identifying universal, language-independent concepts or components of meaning. So it seems that despite the superficial contrast between a meaning postulate approach and a semantic representation approach, the difference is not so great, when the former approach is modified to meet certain basic conditions of adequacy. The difference lies in the fact that a meaning postulate formalism allows for only a partial account of lexical meaning: it does not follow from

horse → animal
animal → physical object

that the explanation of the meaning of *horse* is exhausted by these postulates. A semantic analysis of lexical meaning in terms of a componential semantic representation does however imply that a full statement of the meaning of a lexical item can in principle be given. Now it is arguable that the former position is correct. Yet, though the emphasis is different in this respect in particular, both formulations of lexical meaning require the use of semantic components or their theoretical equivalent if they are to characterise the entailments relevant to analytic truth within a semantic component[1] that is part of a general linguistic theory. So it appears that even though the meaning postulate approach may be adopted, there is no option but to accept the methodological validity of at least some semantic components.

11.3 Outlook for the future

11.3.1 *Semantics*

Despite the uncertainty which hangs over the entire subject, I do not think we need conclude that semantics is a non-empirical discipline, not open to falsifiable argument. Indeed, this book has been written in the hope of demonstrating quite the contrary. If even some of the arguments that I have presented here are valid, then the outlook for the future of the subject is bright: what I have argued for is a truth-based theory of semantics which specifies logical forms from which all inferences relevant to analytic truth can be deduced, and this provides a real point of contact with work currently being done in the field of formal logic. Logicians are working on many semantic problems that I have ignored in this book, extending the concept of logical truth to include inferences contributed by time expressions, adverbs, modality and

---

[1] I am here using *semantic component* in the sense of a section of the over-all grammar.

belief expressions – each of which in so far as it provides an adequate explanation of the data will have to be taken account of in the linguist's semantic theory. And as the domain of logical truth is further and further extended, the goal of writing a logic with complexity sufficient for all the entailments of sentences of a natural language becomes an increasingly realistic one.

The message of this book then, if it is to be interpreted as having such an evangelical aim, is that linguists cannot afford to be ignorant either about problems in the philosophy of language or about formal logic (and conversely that logicians cannot afford to be ignorant about the linguistic concepts of syntax and semantics). For what is needed in my view, if the contact between linguists, logicians and philosophers is to be fruitful, is sufficient sophistication in both the subject of linguistics and the subjects of logic and philosophy of language to be able critically to assess hypotheses put forward in each of these disciplines.

11.3.2 *Pragmatics*

There is little doubt that the Cinderella of this book has been the area of pragmatics, for all those phenomena which I have argued should be accounted for within this domain have been subsequently ignored. The reason for this has been solely exegetical: an introduction to semantics is an introduction to semantics. This omission should not be taken as a dismissal of these problem areas as not of interest to linguists. On the contrary, it is an investigation of these areas which may provide the testing-ground for the restrictive truth-based semantics which excludes them. Within the domain of pragmatics, according to the position adopted in this book, fall topics such as metaphor, stylistics, rhetorical devices in general, and all the phenomena relating what we might call thematic structure – the way in which a speaker presents his utterance. There has been a considerable body of work written on each of these subjects, and I cannot do more here than point out their significance.

Take for example the phenomenon I have called thematic structure, relating to what the speaker of a sentence assumes is the focus of information in that utterance of his sentence (in the case of an indicative sentence)[1] as opposed to what he assumes is background knowledge.[2]

---

[1] This is of course an approximation. See chapter 5 p. 62 for cases where indicative sentences are not used to convey information.

[2] *Topic-comment, focus-presupposition* are other labels which have been used

In English, this is not in general reflected in the syntactic structure[1] but by the use of stress and intonation. Consider the difference between the sentence *Harriet tickled Mavis in the conservatory* said with varyingly placed heavy stress (indicated by small capital letters):

(1) Harriet tickled Mavis in the CONSERVATORY.
(2) Harriet tickled MAVIS in the conservatory.
(3) Harriet TICKLED Mavis in the conservatory.
(4) HARRIET tickled Mavis in the conservatory.

One way in which this might be interpreted is that in (1) the speaker would be assuming that the hearer already knows that Harriet tickled Mavis somewhere but that in saying (1) he is informing the hearer that it took place in the conservatory, in (2) the speaker would be assuming that the hearer already knows that Harriet tickled someone in the conservatory and that in saying (2) he is informing the hearer that it was Mavis that Harriet tickled in the conservatory (notice my use of the cleft structure), that in (3) the speaker would be assuming that Harriet did something to Mavis in the conservatory and that the point of new information in his saying (3) is that what Harriet did to Mavis in the conservatory was tickle her, and in (4) the speaker would be assuming that someone tickled Mavis in the conservatory and that the point of new information in his saying (4) is that it was Harriet who did so. Accordingly we might say as a property of the *sentence*, that with the stress assignment as in (1) the sentence invariably implies that it is already known to a hearer of this sentence that Harriet tickled someone in the conservatory, etc. This being so, we might incorporate an analysis of thematic structure along these lines into our semantic theory as part of the interpretation of sentences. We would then have to relinquish the hypothesis that the semantics of natural language is exclusively truth-conditional in favour of a weaker analysis in terms of a partially truth-conditional semantics. In my view, this move is not justified by data such as we have just considered. It certainly seems to be the case that speakers draw attention by stress or intonation to those parts of their utterance of a sentence that they feel are important in some way, but this cannot I think be reduced to the simple division between what is

in describing phenomena of this kind. Linguists differ as to how many different parameters should be isolated at this level: see for example Halliday 1967/8 for the greatest number of distinctions.

[3] A possible exception to this are structures such as in *It is John that Mabel kissed*, known as cleft sentences.

assumed by the speaker to be known by the hearer, and what is assumed by the speaker to be new to the hearer. However there are languages where this distinction seems to be structurally more clear-cut. In a number of languages – for example Latin, Greek, Russian and Czech – the word order allowable in a sentence is extremely free; and in these languages there appears to be a systematic correspondence between linear order and thematic structure, left-most elements of the sentence tending to be assumed to be part of the background knowledge shared by speaker and hearer and right-most elements tending to be understood as new elements of information. And in some languages, this distinction between given background information and new information is said to be unambiguously marked structurally.[1]

The question that is relevant at this stage is whether this information structure is best handled at the level of the structure of the language itself (i.e. as part of the competence model) or whether it is better handled at the level of performance analysing the phenomenon in terms of factors such as perceptual ease and the pragmatic matter of speaker–hearer interaction. A performance account of the interaction of linear order, stress and intonation, and thematic structure might be formulated, as a first rough approximation, along the lines that items at the end of a sentence are naturally more prominent to a hearer than those which occur initially. Any part of a sentence which is made deliberately prominent by its speaker (either in this way or by stress) is likely to be construed as of especial significance by its hearer and hence a focal point of the communication (in the case of questions as the part being questioned, in the case of negative sentences as the part being negated, in positive indicatives as the part being new information).[2] Now in languages such as English where there is little formal marking of thematic structure, it is arguable in my view[3] that a pragmatically based performance account is to be preferred, but a language which incorporates such a distinction within its formal structure provides strong evidence to the contrary. Indeed on the strength of such languages, it has been argued that thematic structure is relevant to language typology (Li and Thompson 1976). But if, in the light of these arguments, we

---

1   These languages include Tagalog and Genoese.
2   Cf. p. 192 n. 1.
3   That this view is by no means generally held should perhaps be stressed. For a wide range of analyses incorporating this kind of data within linguistic theory, cf. Firbas 1962, 1964, Halliday 1967/8, Chomsky 1971, Jackendoff 1972, Sgall 1967, and the articles in Li (ed.) 1976.

draw the conclusion that the account of the inherent properties of a language as a formal system should include an account of thematic structure, then we have to review again the network of problems that we have considered in this book – the restriction of semantics to a truth-based account, the distinction between semantics and pragmatics, and between competence and performance, and also the restriction of our truth-based account to an entailment-based analysis. This I must leave the reader to do for himself. However, even this brief reference to the problem of the status of an analysis of thematic elements should leave the reader in no doubt that phenomena which are in a preliminary way dubbed as pragmatic are not thereby excluded as of little theoretical interest. On the contrary their detailed investigation remains an essential task.

And so we have seen yet another problem in the investigation of the interpretation of sentences whose solution is interdependent with the solutions given to those other problems we have considered. There are still others which could be discussed. But at this stage, I wish only to urge the readers of this book not that they feel bound to agree with what I have argued but that in assessing the detailed arguments presented in the literature (including those of this book), they do not lose sight of the consequences of either agreeing or disagreeing with the arguments in question. For on these consequences, often unstated, may hang the fate of the subject of semantics.

RECOMMENDED READING

In connection with the problem of distinguishing *sentence* and *utterance*, see Kasher 'Sentences and utterances reconsidered'. For suggested reading on linguists' use of semantic components to give an account of the semantic interpretation of a sentence, see the recommended reading for ch 6. For work by logicians who are concerned with specifying semantic properties of natural language see for example work by Davidson (see the recommended reading for ch 3), the articles in Keenan (ed.) *Formal Semantics of Natural Language*, and in particular Lewis 'General semantics' and Montague 'English as a formal language'.

11.2   The concept of meaning postulate is due to Carnap's 'Meaning postulates' in *Meaning and Necessity*, and it was introduced by him in an attempt to account for analyticity. On this basis it was attacked by Quine in 'Two dogmas of empiricism'. It has been discussed and criticised in detail by Katz and Nagel 'Meaning postulates and semantic theory'. See also Bar-Hillel 'Dictionaries and meaning rules'. Despite the criticisms of Katz and Nagel, an analysis in terms of meaning postulates has been invoked by Fodor, Fodor and Garrett as the only possible solution to the problem of semantic represent- ation in 'The psychological unreality of semantic representations'. This article is interesting for the additional reason that the authors argue that the level of semantic representation does not exist. It is significant though that they do not extend this scepticism to the concept of logical form.

11.3 For references on non-standard logics, see the recommended reading for 3.4.2 above. For references on metaphor and style see the recommended reading for 5.4 above. The problem of thematic structure as I have called it has been much studied by the Prague school of linguists under the term *functional sentence perspective*. See in particular Firbas 'Notes on the function of the sentence in the act of communication', 'On defining the theme in functional sentence analysis', and Sgall 'Functional sentence perspective'. An analysis of sentences in terms of functional sentence perspective within a transformational framework has been made by Kuno in 'Functional sentence perspective'. Halliday's most detailed work in this area is 'Notes on transitivity and theme in English'. An analysis of the interdependence of linear order, stress assignment and the interpretation of sentences in terms of thematic structure and *focus* v. *presupposition* has been made by Jackendoff *Semantic Interpretation in a Generative Grammar* and Chomsky 'Deep structure, surface structure and semantic interpretation'. For a most useful collection of articles on problems of information structure, and related subjects, see Li (ed.) *Subject and Topic*.

Bibliography

Akmajian, A. and Heny, F. (1975) *An Introduction to the Principles of Transformational Grammar*. MIT Press.

Allen, J. and Van Buren, P. (eds.) (1971) *Chomsky: Selected Readings*. Oxford University Press.

Alston, W.P. (1963) 'Meaning and use', *Philosophical Quarterly* 13, 107–24.

(1964) *Philosophy of Language*. Prentice-Hall.

(1974) 'Semantic rules' in Munitz, M. and Unger, P. (eds.) *Semantics and Philosophy*, 17–48. New York University Press.

Åqvist, L. (1965) *A New Approach to the Logical Theory of Interrogatives*. Uppsala.

(1971) 'Revised foundations for imperative-epistemic and interrogative logic', *Theoria* 37, 33–73.

Austin, J.L. (1962) *How to Do Things With Words*. Clarendon Press.

(1963) 'Performative-constative' in Caton, C. (ed.) *Philosophy and Ordinary Language*. University of Illinois Press.

Bach, E. (1968) 'Nouns and noun phrases' in Bach, E. and Harms, R. (eds.) *Universals in Linguistic Theory*. Holt, Rinehart, Winston.

(1974) *Syntactic Theory*. Holt, Rinehart, Winston.

Bach, E., Bresnan, J. and Wasow, T. (1975) ' "Sloppy identity": an unnecessary and insufficient criterion for deletion rules', *Linguistic Inquiry* 6, 515–31.

Baker, A. (1956) 'Presupposition and types of clause', *Mind* 65, 368–78.

Bar-Hillel, Y. (1954) 'Indexical expressions', *Mind* 63, 359–79.

(1967) 'Dictionaries and meaning rules', *Foundations of Language* 3, 409–14.

Barrett, R. and Stenner, A. (1971) 'On the myth of the exclusive "or" ', *Mind* 79, 116–21.

Bartsch, R. and Vennemann, T. (1972) *Semantic Structures*. Athenäum Verlag.

Bazell, C.E. (1955) 'Logical and linguistic syntax', *Litera* 2, 32–4.

Bendix, E. (1969) *Componential Analysis of General Vocabulary*. Mouton.

Bennett, D. (1975) *Spatial and Temporal Uses of English Prepositions*. Longman.

Berlin, B. and Kay, P. (1970) *Basic Color Terms*. University of California Press, Berkeley.

Bever, T. (1970) 'The cognitive basis for linguistic structures' in Hayes, J. (ed.) *Cognition and the Development of Language*, 279–362. Wiley, New York.

Bickerton, D. (1969) 'Prolegomena to a linguistic theory of metaphor', *Foundations of Language* 5, 34–52.

Bierwisch, M. (1967) 'Some semantic universals of German adjectives', *Foundations of Language* 3, 1–36.

(1969) 'On certain problems of semantic representation', *Foundations of Language* 5, 153–84.

(1970) 'Semantics' in Lyons, J. (ed.) *New Horizons in Linguistics*, 166–84.

(1971) 'On classifying semantic features' in Steinberg, D. and Jakobovits, L. (eds.) *Semantics*, 410–35. Cambridge University Press.

Black, M. (1962) *Models and Metaphors.* Cornell University Press.

Bloomfield, L. (1933) *Language.* Holt, Rinehart, Winston.

Botha, R. (1973) *The Justification of Linguistic Hypotheses.* Mouton.

Bresnan, J. (1973) 'Sentence stress and syntactic transformations' in Hintikka, J., Moravcsik, J. and Suppes, P. (eds.) *Approaches to Natural Language.* Reidel.

Brooke-Rose, C. (1958) *A Grammar of Metaphor.* Secker and Warburg.

Burling, R. (1970) *Man's Many Voices.* Holt, Rinehart, Winston.

Campbell, R. and Wales, R. (1970) 'The study of language acquisition' in Lyons, J. (ed.) *New Horizons in Linguistics*, 242–60.

Carden, G. (1973) *English Quantifiers: Logical Structure and Linguistic Variation.* Taishukan.

Carnap, R. (1947) *Meaning and Necessity.* University of Chicago Press.

Carroll, J. (ed.) (1956) *Thought and Reality: Selected Writings of Benjamin Lee Whorf.* Chapman and Hall.

Cartwright, R. (1962) 'Propositions' in Butler, R. (ed.) *Analytical Philosophy*, 81–103. Blackwell.

Cassin, C. (1970a) 'Russell's discussion of meaning and denotation: a re-examination' in Klemke, E. (ed.) *Essays on Bertrand Russell*, 256–72. University of Illinois Press.

(1970b) 'Russell's distinction between the primary and secondary occurrence of definite descriptions' in Klemke, E. (ed.) *Essays on Bertrand Russell*, 273–84. University of Illinois Press.

Catlin, J.C. and Catlin, J. (1972) 'Intentionality: a source of ambiguity in English', *Linguistic Inquiry* 3, 504–8.

Caton, C. (1959) 'Strawson on referring', *Mind* 68, 539–44.

Chapin, P. (1967) *On the Syntax of Word-Derivation in English.* MIT Ph.D.

Chihara, C. (1975) 'Davidson's extensional theory of meaning', *Philosophical Studies* 28, 1–15.

Chomsky, N. (1957) *Syntactic Structures.* Mouton.

(1959) Review of Skinner, B., *Verbal Behavior* in *Language* 35, 26–58.

(1965) *Aspects of the Theory of Syntax.* MIT Press.

(1969) 'Quine's empirical assumptions' in Davidson, D. and Hintikka, J. (eds.) *Words and Objections: Essays on the Work of W. V. Quine.* Reidel.

(1970) 'Remarks on nominalization' in Jacobs, R. and Rosenbaum, P. (eds.) *Readings in English Transformational Grammar*, 184–222. Ginn and Co.

(1971) 'Deep structure, surface structure and semantic interpretation' in Steinberg, D. and Jakobovits, L. (eds.) *Semantics*, 183–216.

(1972a) 'Some empirical issues in the theory of transformational grammar' in Peters, S. (ed.) *Goals of Linguistic Theory*, 63–130. Prentice-Hall.

(1972b) *Studies on Semantics in Generative Grammar.* Mouton.

(1975) *Reflections on Language.* Temple Smith, London.

Chomsky, N. and Halle, M. (1968) *The Sound Pattern of English.* Harper and Row.

Clifford, J. (1966) 'Tense logic and the logic of change', *Logique et Analyse* 34, 219–30.

Cohen, D. (1973) 'On the mis-representation of presuppositions', *Glossa* 7, 21–38.

Cohen, L.J. (1964) 'Do illocutionary forces exist?', *Philosophical Quarterly* 14, 118–37.

(1971) 'Some remarks on Grice's views about the logical particles of natural language' in Bar-Hillel, Y. (ed.) *Pragmatics of Natural Languages*, 60–8. Reidel.

Cohen, L.J. and Margalit, A. (1972) 'The role of inductive reasoning in the interpretation of metaphor' in Harman, G. and Davidson, D. (eds.) *The Semantics of Natural Language*, 722–40. Reidel.

Cole, P. and Morgan, J. (eds.) (1975) *Syntax and Semantics 3: Speech Acts*. Academic Press.

Conklin, H. (1962) 'Lexicographical treatment of folk taxonomies' in Householder, F. and Saporta, S. (eds.) *Problems in Lexicography*, 119–41. Mouton.

Dahl, Ö. (1973) 'On so-called "sloppy identity" ', *Synthese* 26, 81–112.

Davidson, D. (1967a) 'Truth and meaning', *Synthese* 17, 304–23.

(1967b) 'The logical form of action sentences' in Rescher, N. (ed.) *The Logic of Decision and Action*.

(1970) 'Semantics for natural languages' in *Linguaggi Nella Societa e Nella Tecnica*, 177–88. Milan.

Dougherty, R. (1969) 'An interpretive theory of pronominal reference', *Foundations of Language* 5, 488–519.

(1974) 'The syntax and semantics of *each other* constructions', *Foundations of Language* 12, 1–48.

Drange, T. (1967) *Type Crossings*. Mouton.

Ducrot, O. (1972) *Dire et ne pas Dire*. Hermann.

Dummett, M. (1973) *Frege: Philosophy of Language*. Duckworth.

(1976) 'What is a theory of meaning? (II)' in Evans, G. and McDowell, J. (eds.) *Meaning and Truth*, 67–137.

Evans, G. and McDowell, J. (eds.) (1976) *Meaning and Truth*. Oxford University Press.

Fillmore, C.J. (1969) 'Types of lexical information' in Kiefer, F. (ed.) *Studies in Syntax and Semantics*, 109–37. Reidel.

(1971) 'Verbs of judging: an exercise in semantic description' in Fillmore, C.J. and Langendoen, D.T. (eds.) *Studies in Linguistic Semantics*, 273–89.

(1972) 'On generativity' in Peters, S. (ed.) *Goals of Linguistic Theory*. Prentice-Hall.

Fillmore, C.J. and Langendoen, D.T. (eds.) (1971) *Studies in Linguistic Semantics*. Holt, Rinehart, Winston.

Firbas, J. (1962) 'Notes on the function of the sentence in the act of communication', *Sbornik Praci Filos. Fak. Brnenské University* 11, A10, 133–48.

(1964) 'On defining the theme in functional sentence analysis', *Travaux Linguistiques de Prague* 1, 267–80.

Firth, J.R. (1951) *Papers in Linguistics 1934–51*. Oxford University Press.

Fodor, J.A. (1970) 'Three reasons for not deriving "kill" from "cause to die" ', *Linguistic Inquiry* 1, 429–37.

(1972) 'Troubles about actions' in Harman, G. and Davidson, D. (eds.) *Semantics of Natural Language*, 48–69. Reidel.

Fodor, J.A., Bever, T. and Garrett, M. (1974) *The Psychology of Language*. McGraw-Hill.

Fodor, J.A., Fodor, J.D. and Garrett, M. (1975) 'The psychological unreality of semantic representations', *Linguistic Inquiry* 6, 515–31.

Fodor, J.A. and Garrett, M. (1966) 'Some reflections on competence and performance' in Lyons, J. and Wales, R. (eds.) *Psycholinguistics Papers*, 135–54.

Fodor, J.D. (1970) 'Formal linguistics and formal logic'. In Lyons, J. (ed.) *New Horizons in Linguistics*, 198–214.

Foster, B. (1976) 'Meaning and truth theory'. In Evans, G. and McDowell, J. (eds.) *Meaning and Truth*, 1–32.

Fraser, B. (1971) 'An analysis of "even" in English' in Fillmore, C.J. and Langendoen, D.T. (eds.) *Studies in Linguistic Semantics*, 151–78.

(1974) Review of Searle, J., *Speech Acts* in *Foundations of Language* 11, 433–46.

Frege, G. (1892) 'Über Sinn und Bedeutung'. Translated in Geach, P. and Black, M. (1966) *Translations from the Philosophical Writings of Gottlob Frege*, 56–78. Blackwell.

Fromkin, V. and Rodman, R. (1974) *An Introduction to Language*. Holt, Rinehart, Winston.

Gale, R. (1970) 'Negative statements', *American Philosophical Quarterly* 7, 206–17.

Garner, R. (1971) ' "Presupposition" in philosophy and linguistics' in Fillmore, C.J. and Langendoen, D.T. (eds.) *Studies in Linguistic Semantics*, 23–42.

Geach, P. (1958–9) 'Russell on meaning and denoting', *Analysis* 19, 69–72.

Geiss, M. and Zwicky, A. (1971) 'On invited inferences', *Linguistic Inquiry* 2, 561–6.

Goodenough, W. (1956) 'Componential analysis and the study of meaning', *Language* 32, 195–216.

Gordon, D. and Lakoff, G. (1975) 'Conversational postulates' in Cole, P. and Morgan, J. (eds.) *Syntax and Semantics 3: Speech Acts*, 83–106.

Green, G. (1974) *Semantics and Syntactic Regularity*. Indiana University Press.

(1975) 'How to get people to do things with words' in Cole, P. and Morgan, J. (eds.) *Syntax and Semantics 3: Speech Acts*, 107–42.

Greimas, A. (1966) *Sémantique Structurale*. Larousse, Paris.

Grice, H.P. (1957) 'Meaning', *The Philosophical Review* 66, 377–88.

(1968) 'Utterer's meaning, sentence-meaning, and word-meaning', *Foundations of Language* 4, 225–42.

(1969) 'Utterer's meaning and intentions', *The Philosophical Review* 78, 147–77.

(1975) 'Logic and conversation' in Cole, P. and Morgan, J. (eds.) *Syntax and Semantics 3: Speech Acts*, 41–58.

Grice, H.P. and Strawson, P.F. (1956) 'In defence of a dogma', *The Philosophical Review* 65, 141–58.

Grinder, M. and Elgin, S. (1973) *Guide to Transformational Grammar*. Holt, Rinehart, Winston.

Hacker, I. (1975) *Why Does Language Matter to Philosophy?* Cambridge University Press.

Hall-Partee, B. (1970) 'Negation, conjunction and quantifiers: syntax *vs.* semantics', *Foundations of Language* 6, 153–65.

(1971a) 'On the requirement that transformations preserve meaning' in Fillmore, C.J. and Langendoen, D.T. (eds.) *Studies in Linguistic Semantics*, 1–21.

(1971b) 'Linguistic metatheory' in Dingwall, W. (ed.) *A Survey of Linguistic Science*, University of Maryland Press.

(1972) 'Opacity, coreference and pronouns' in Harman, G. and Davidson, D. (eds.) *Semantics of Natural Language*, 415–41. Reidel.

(1974) 'Opacity and scope' in Munitz, M. and Unger, P. (eds.) *Semantics and Philosophy*, 81–102. New York University Press.

(1975) 'Deletion and variable binding' in Keenan, E. (ed.) *Formal Semantics of Natural Language*.

Halliday, M. (1967/8) 'Notes on transitivity and theme in English', *Journal of Linguistics* 3, 37–81, 199–244; and 4, 179–215.

(1970) 'Language structure and language function' in Lyons, J. (ed.) *New Horizons in Linguistics*, 140–65.

Harman, G. (1972a) 'Logical form', *Foundations of Language* 9, 38–65.

(1972b) 'Deep structure as logical form' in Harman, G. and Davidson, D. (eds.) *Semantics of Natural Language*, 25–47. Reidel.

(1974a) 'Meaning and semantics' in Munitz, M. and Unger, P. (eds.) *Semantics and Philosophy*, 1–16. New York University Press.

(ed.) (1974b) *On Noam Chomsky*. Anchor Press, New York.

Harrah, D. (1961) 'A logic of questions and answers', *Philosophy of Science* 28, 40–46.

Hempel, C. (1966) *Philosophy of Natural Science*. Prentice-Hall.

Herzberger, H. (1970) 'Truth and modality in semantically closed languages' in Martin, R. (ed.) *The Paradox of the Liar*, 25–46. Yale University Press.

Hintikka, J. (1962) *Knowledge and Belief*. Cornell University Press.

(1969a) 'Semantics for propositional attitudes' in Davis, J. et al. (eds.) *Philosophical Logic*, 21–45. Reidel.

(1969b) *Models for Modalities*. Reidel.

(1972) 'The semantics of modal notions and the indeterminacy of ontology' in Harman, G. and Davidson, D. (eds.) *Semantics of Natural Language*, 398–414. Reidel.

(1973) 'Grammar and logic: some borderline problems' in Hintikka, J., Moravcsik, J. and Suppes, P. (eds.) *Approaches to Natural Languages*, 197–214. Reidel.

(1974a) 'Quantifiers *v.* quantification theory', *Linguistic Inquiry* 5, 153–79.

(1974b) 'Questions about questions' in Munitz, M. and Unger, P. (eds.) *Semantics and Philosophy*, 103–59. New York University Press.

Holdcroft, D. (1964) 'Meaning and illocutionary acts', *Ratio* 6, 128–43.

Hook, S. (ed.) (1969) *Language and Philosophy*. New York University Press.

Householder, F. (ed.) (1972) *Syntactic Theory*. Penguin.

(1973) 'On arguments from asterisks', *Foundations of Language* 10, 365–75.

Hudson, R. (1975) 'The meaning of questions', *Language* 51, 1–31.

Hughes, G. and Cresswell, M. (1968) *An Introduction to Modal Logic*. Methuen.

Hull, R. (1975) 'A semantics for superficial and embedded questions'. In Keenan, E. (ed.) *Formal Semantics of Natural Language*, 35–46.

Hundsnurscher, F. (1971) *Neuere Methoden der Semantik*. Tübingen.

Hymes, D. (1970) 'On communicative competence' in Gumperz, J. and Hymes, D., (eds.) *Directions in Sociolinguistics*. Holt, Rinehart and Winston.

Jackendoff, R. (1972) *Semantic Interpretation in a Generative Grammar*. MIT Press.

Jacobs, R. and Rosenbaum, P. (eds.) (1969) *Readings in English Transformational Grammar*. Ginn and Co.

(1971) *Transformations, Style and Meaning*. Xerox College Publishing.

Jacobson, A. (1970) 'Russell and Strawson on referring' in Klemke, E. (ed.) *Essays on Bertrand Russell*, 285–308. University of Illinois Press.

Jakobson, R. (1970) 'On the verbal art of William Blake and other poet-painters', *Linguistic Inquiry* 1, 3–25.

Jardine, N. (1975) 'Model-theoretic semantics and natural language' in Keenan, E. (ed.) *Formal Semantics of Natural Language*.

Kac, M. (1972) 'Action and result: two aspects of predication in English'. In Kimball, J. (ed.) *Syntax and Semantics I*, 117–24.

Karttunen, L. (1969) 'Pronouns and variables' in Binnick, R. et al. (eds.) *Papers from the Fifth Regional Meeting of the Chicago Linguistics Society*, 108–16. University of Chicago.

(1971a) 'Some observations on factivity', *Papers in Linguistics* 4, 55–70.

(1971b) 'Definite descriptions with crossing coreference', *Foundations of Language* 7, 157–82.

(1973) 'Presuppositions of compound sentences', *Linguistic Inquiry* 4, 169–93.

(1974) 'Presupposition and linguistic context', *Theoretical Linguistics* 1, 181–94.

Bibliography

Kasher, A. (1972) 'Sentences and utterances reconsidered' *Foundations of Language* 8, 312–45.

(1974) 'Mood implicatures: a logical way of doing generative pragmatics', *Theoretical Linguistics* 1, 6–38.

Katz, J.J. (1966) *The Philosophy of Language*. Harper and Row.

(1967) 'Recent issues in semantic theory', *Foundations of Language* 3, 124–94.

(1970) 'Generative semantics versus interpretative semantics', *Foundations of Language* 6, 220–59.

(1972) *Semantic Theory*. Harper and Row.

(1973) 'On defining presupposition', *Linguistic Inquiry* 4, 256–60.

(1975) 'Logic and language: an examination of recent criticisms of intensionalism' in Gunderson, K. (ed.) *Language, Mind and Knowledge*, 36–130. University of Minnesota Press.

Katz, J.J. and Fodor, J.A. (1963) 'The structure of a semantic theory', *Language* 39, 170–210.

Katz, J.J. and Langendoen, D.T. (1976) 'Pragmatics and presupposition', *Language* 52, 1–17.

Katz, J.J. and Nagel, R. (1974) 'Meaning postulates and semantic theory', *Foundations of Language* 11, 311–40.

Katz, J.J. and Postal, P. (1964) *An Integrated Theory of Linguistic Descriptions*. MIT Press.

Keenan, E. (1971) 'Two kinds of presupposition in natural language' in Fillmore, C.J. and Langendoen, D.T. (eds.) *Studies in Linguistic Semantics*, 45–54.

(1972) 'On semantically based grammar', *Linguistic Inquiry* 3, 413–61.

(ed.) (1975) *Formal Semantics of Natural Language*. Cambridge University Press.

Keenan, E. and Hull, R. (1973) 'The logical presuppositions of questions and answers' in Franck, D. and Petöfi, J. (eds.) *Präsuppositionen in der Linguistik und der Philosophie*. Athenäum Verlag.

Kempson, R.M. (1975) *Presupposition and the Delimitation of Semantics*. Cambridge University Press.

Kimball, J. (ed.) (1972) *Syntax and Semantics I*. Seminar Press.

Kiparsky, P. and Kiparsky, C. (1971) 'Fact' in Steinberg, D. and Jakobovits, L. (eds.) *Semantics*.

Kooij, J. (1971) *Ambiguity in Natural Language*. North-Holland.

Kripke, S. (1972) 'Naming and necessity' in Harman, G. and Davidson, D. (eds.) *Semantics of Natural Language*, 253–355. Reidel.

Kuno, S. (1972) 'Functional sentence perspective', *Linguistic Inquiry* 3, 269–320.

(1974) 'Lexical and contextual meaning', *Linguistic Inquiry* 5, 469–77.

Kuroda, S-Y. (1969) 'Remarks on selectional restrictions and presuppositions' in Kiefer, F. (ed.) *Studies in Syntax and Semantics*, 138–67. Reidel.

Labov, W. (1971) 'Methodology' in Dingwall, W. (ed.) *A Survey of Linguistic Science*. University of Maryland Press.

Lakatos, I. and Musgrave, A. (eds.) (1970) *Criticism and the Growth of Knowledge*. Cambridge University Press.

Lakoff, G. (1968) 'Instrumental adverbs and the concept of deep structure', *Foundations of Language* 4, 4–29.

(1970a) 'Repartee, or a reply to negation, conjunction and quantifiers', *Foundations of Language* 6, 389–422.

(1970b) *Irregularity in Syntax*. Holt, Rinehart, Winston.

(1970c) 'A note on ambiguity and vagueness', *Linguistic Inquiry* 1, 357–9.

(1971a) 'On generative semantics' in Steinberg, D. and Jakobovits, L. (eds.) *Semantics*, 232–96.

(1971b) 'Presupposition and relative well-formedness' in Steinberg, D. and Jakobovits, L. (eds.) *Semantics*, 329–40.

(1971c) 'The role of deduction in grammar' in Fillmore, C.J. and Langendoen, D.T. (eds.) *Studies in Linguistic Semantics*, 63–72.

(1972) 'Linguistics and natural logic' in Harman, G. and Davidson, D. (eds.) *Semantics of Natural Language*, 545–665. Reidel.

Lakoff, G. and Thompson, H. (1975a) 'Introducing cognitive grammar' in Cogen, C. et al. (eds.) *Proceedings of the First Annual Meeting of the Berkeley Linguistics Society*, 295–313. University of California.

(1975b) 'Dative questions in cognitive grammar' in Grossman, R. et al. (eds.) *Papers from the Parasession on Functionalism, Chicago Linguistics Society*, 337–50. University of Chicago.

Lakoff, R. (1971) 'If's, and's, and but's about conjunction' in Fillmore, C.J. and Langendoen, D.T. (eds.) *Studies in Linguistic Semantics*, 115–50.

(1972a) 'Language in context', *Language* 48, 907–27.

(1972b) 'The pragmatics of modality' in Peranteau, P. et al. (eds.) *Papers from the Eighth Regional Meeting of the Chicago Linguistic Society*, 229–47. University of Chicago.

(1974) 'What you can do with words', *Berkeley Studies in Syntax and Semantics* 1.

Leech, G. (1969) *Towards a Semantic Description of English*. Longman.

(1970) 'On the theory and practice of semantic testing', *Lingua* 24, 343–64.

(1975) *Semantics*. Penguin.

Lehrer, A. (1974) *Semantic Fields and Lexical Structure*. North-Holland.

Lehrer, K. and Lehrer, A. (eds.) (1970) *Theory of Meaning*. Prentice-Hall.

Lemmon, E. (1965) 'Deontic logic and the logic of imperatives', *Logique et Analyse* 29.

(1966) 'Sentences, statements and propositions' in Williams, B. and Montefiore, A. (eds.) *British Analytical Philosophy*, 87–107. Routledge and Kegan Paul.

Lewis, D. (1969) *Convention: A Philosophical Study*. Harvard University Press.

(1972) 'General semantics' in Harman, G. and Davidson, D. (eds.) *Semantics of Natural Language*, 169–218. Reidel.

(1973) *Counterfactuals*. Blackwell.

(1975) 'Adverbs of quantification' in Keenan, E. (ed.) *Formal Semantics of Natural Language*, 3–15.

Li, C. (ed.) (1976) *Subject and Topic*. Academic Press.

Li, C. and Thompson, S.A. (1976) 'Subject and topic: a new typology of language' in Li, C. (ed.) *Subject and Topic*, 457–90.

Linsky, L. (ed.) (1971) *Reference and Modality*. Oxford University Press.

Loewenberg, I. (1975) 'Identifying metaphors', *Foundations of Language* 12, 315–38.

Lounsbury, F. (1964) 'The structural analysis of kinship semantics' in Lunt, H. (ed.) *Proceedings of the Ninth International Congress of Linguists*. Mouton.

Lyons, J. (1963) *Structural Semantics*. Blackwell.

(1966) 'Firth's theory of "meaning" ' in Bazell, C. et al. (eds.) *In Memory of J. R. Firth*. Longman.

(1968) *Introduction to Theoretical Linguistics*. Cambridge University Press.

(ed.) (1970) *New Horizons in Linguistics*. Penguin.

(1977) *Semantics*. 2 vols. Cambridge University Press.

Lyons, J. and Wales, R. (eds.) (1966) *Psycholinguistics Papers*. Edinburgh University Press.

McCawley, J. (1968a) 'Lexical insertion in a transformational grammar without deep structure' in Darden, B. et al. (eds.) *Papers from the Fourth Regional Meeting of the Chicago Linguistics Society*, 71–80. University of Chicago.

(1968b) 'The role of semantics in grammar' in Bach, E. and Harms, R. (eds.) *Universals in Linguistic Theory*, 125–69. Holt, Rinehart, Winston.

(1968c) 'Concerning the base component of a transformational grammar', *Foundations of Language* 4, 243–69.

(1971a) 'Meaning and the description of languages' in Rosenberg, J. and Travis, C. (eds.) *Readings in the Philosophy of Language*, 514–33.

(1971b) 'Where do noun phrases come from?' in Steinberg, D. and Jakobovits, L. (eds.) *Semantics*, 217–31.

(1971c) 'Interpretative semantics meets Frankenstein', *Foundations of Language* 7, 285–96.

(1972) 'Kac and Shibatani on the grammar of killing' in Kimball, J. (ed.) *Syntax and Semantics I*, 139–50.

McNeill, N. (1972) 'Colour and colour terminology', *Journal of Linguistics* 8.

Magee, B. (1973) *Popper*. Fontana.

Martin, R. (1969) 'Sommers on denial and negation', *Nous* 3, 219–26.

(1971) 'Some thoughts on the formal approach to the philosophy of language' in Bar-Hillel, Y. (ed.) *Pragmatics of Natural Languages*, 120–44. Reidel.

Mates, B. (1973) 'Descriptions and reference', *Foundations of Language* 10, 409–18.

(1975) 'On the semantics of proper names' in Abraham, W. (ed.) *Ut Videam*, 191–207. The Peter de Ridder Press.

Matthews, R. (1971) 'Concerning a "linguistic theory" of metaphor', *Foundations of Language* 7, 413–25.

Mistler-Lachman, J. (1973) 'Comments on vagueness', *Linguistic Inquiry* 4, 549–51.

Montague, R. (1970) 'English as a formal language' in *Linguaggi Nella Societa e Nella Tecnica*, 189–223. Milan.

Moore, G.E. (1936) 'Is existence a predicate?', *Proceedings of the Aristotelian Society*, Suppl. Vol.

Morgan, J. (1969) 'On the treatment of presuppositions in transformational grammar' in Binnick, R. et al. (eds.) *Papers from the Fifth Regional Meeting of the Chicago Linguistics Society*, 169–77. University of Chicago.

(1975) 'Some interactions of syntax and pragmatics' in Cole, P. and Morgan, J. (eds.) *Syntax and Semantics 3: Speech Acts*, 289–304.

Morris, C. (1938) 'Foundations of the theory of signs' in *International Encyclopaedia of Unified Science* 1, no. 2. University of Chicago Press.

(1946) *Signs, Language and Behavior*. Prentice-Hall.

Nerlich, G. (1965) 'Presupposition and entailment', *American Philosophical Quarterly* 2, 33–42.

Nida, E. (1975) *Componential Analysis of Meaning*. Mouton.

Ohmann, R. (1967) 'Generative grammars and the concept of literary style' in Steinmann, M. (ed.) *New Rhetorics*. Scribner.

Olshewsky, T. (ed.) (1969) *Problems in the Philosophy of Language*. Holt, Rinehart, Winston.

Osgood, C. (1964) 'A behavioristic analysis of perception and language as cognitive phenomena' in Harper, R. et al. (eds.) *The Cognitive Processes*, 184–210. Prentice-Hall.

Parkinson, G. (ed.) (1968) *The Theory of Meaning*. Oxford University Press.

Parsons, T. (1972) 'Some problems concerning the logic of grammatical modifiers' in Harman, G. and Davidson, D. (eds.) *Semantics of Natural Language*, 127–41. Reidel.

Pears, D. (1963) 'Is existence a predicate?', *Aquinas Paper* 38. Aquin Press.

Popper, K. (1963) *Conjectures and Refutations*. Routledge and Kegan Paul.

Postal, P. (1964) *Constituent Structure: A Study of Contemporary Models of Syntactic Description*. Bloomington.

    (1970) 'On the surface verb "remind" ', *Linguistic Inquiry* 1, 37–120.

Pottier, B. (1962) *Systématique des Éléments de Relation*. Klincksieck.

Potts, T. (1975) 'Model theory and linguistics' in Keenan, E. (ed.) *Formal Semantics of Natural Language*.

Prior, A.N. (1967) *Past, Present and Future*. Clarendon Press.

    (1968) *Time and Tense*. Clarendon Press.

Quine, W.V. (1953a) *From a Logical Point of View*. Harvard University Press.

    (1953b) 'The problem of meaning in linguistics' in *From a Logical Point of View*, 47–64.

    (1953c) 'Two dogmas of empiricism' in *From a Logical Point of View*.

    (1960) *Word and Object*. MIT Press.

    (1967) 'Russell's ontological development' in Schoenman, R. (ed.) *Bertrand Russell, Philosopher of the Century*, 304–14. Allen and Unwin.

    (1969) 'Reply to Chomsky' in Davidson, D. and Hintikka, J. (eds.) *Words and Objections: Essays on the Work of W. V. Quine*. Reidel.

    (1970) *Philosophy of Logic*. Prentice-Hall.

    (1972) 'Methodological reflections on current linguistic theory' in Harman, G. and Davidson, D. (eds.) *Semantics of Natural Language*, 442–54.

Reeves, A. (1975) 'Ambiguity and indifference', *Australasian Journal of Philosophy* 53, 220–37.

Reich, P. (1969) 'The finiteness of natural language', *Language* 45, 831–43.

Reichenbach, H. (1947) *Elements of Symbolic Logic*. Dover.

Rescher, N. (1966) *The Logic of Commands*. Dover.

    (ed.) (1967) *The Logic of Decision and Action*. Pittsburgh.

    (1968) *Topics in Philosophical Logic*. Reidel.

Richards, T. (1975) 'The worlds of David Lewis', *Australasian Journal of Philosophy* 53, 105–18.

Roberts, G. (1969) 'A problem about presupposition', *Mind* 78, 270–71.

Robins, R.H. (1964) *General Linguistics: An Introductory Survey*. Longmans.

Rosenberg, J. and Travis, C. (eds.) (1971) *Readings in the Philosophy of Language*. Prentice-Hall.

Ross, J.R. (1969) 'Auxiliaries as main verbs' in Todd, W. (ed.) *Philosophical Linguistics* 1.

    (1970) 'On declarative sentences' in Jacobs, R.A. and Rosenbaum, P.S. (eds.) *Readings in English Transformational Grammar*, 222–72.

    (1972) 'Act' in Harman, G. and Davidson, D. (eds.) *Semantics of Natural Language*, 70–126. Reidel.

    (1975) 'Where to do things with words' in Cole, P. and Morgan, J. (eds.) *Syntax and Semantics 3: Speech Acts*, 233–56.

Russell, B. (1902) 'On denoting', *Mind* 14, 479–93.

Sadock, J. (1970) 'Whimperatives' in Sadock, J. and Vanek, A. (eds.) *Studies Presented to R. B. Lees by His Students*, 223–38. Edmonton.

    (1974) *Towards a Linguistic Theory of Speech Acts*. Academic Press.

Sampson, G. (1973) 'The concept "semantic representation" ', *Semiotica* 7, 97–134.

    (1975) *The Form of Language*. Weidenfeld and Nicolson.

Sapir, E. (1921) *Language*. Harcourt, Brace and World.

Saussure, F. de (1916) *Cours de Linguistique Générale.* Paris. (Translated by Baskin, W. as *Course in General Linguistics,* New York, 1959.)

Schiffer, S. (1972) *Meaning.* Oxford University Press.

Schmerling, S. (1975) 'Asymmetric conjunction and rules of conversation' in Cole, P. and Morgan, J. (eds.) *Syntax and Semantics 3: Speech Acts,* 211–32.

Schnitzer, M. (1971) 'Presupposition, entailment, and Russell's theory of descriptions', *Foundations of Language* 7, 297–9.

Schreiber, P. (1972) Style disjuncts and the performative analysis', *Linguistic Inquiry* 3, 321–48.

Searle, J. (1965) 'What is a speech act?' in Black, M. (ed.) *Philosophy in America,* 221–39. Allen and Unwin.

   (1968) 'Austin on locutionary and illocutionary acts', *Philosophical Review* 77, 405–24.

   (1969) *Speech Acts.* Cambridge University Press.

   (ed.) (1971) *The Philosophy of Language.* Oxford University Press.

   (1975a) 'A taxonomy of illocutionary acts' in Gunderson, K. (ed.) *Language, Mind and Knowledge,* 344–69. University of Minnesota Press.

   (1975b) 'Indirect speech acts' in Cole, P. and Morgan, J. (eds.) *Syntax and Semantics 3: Speech Acts,* 59–82.

Sellars, W. (1954) 'Presupposing', *Philosophical Review* 63, 197–215.

Seuren, P. (1972) 'Autonomous versus semantic syntax', *Foundations of Language* 8, 237–65.

   (ed.) (1974) *Semantic Syntax.* Oxford University Press.

Sgall, P. (1967) 'Functional sentence perspective', *Prague Studies in Mathematical Linguistics* 2, 203–25.

Shibatani, M. (1972) 'Three reasons for not deriving "kill" from "cause to die" in Japanese'. In Kimball, J. (ed.) *Syntax and Semantics I,* 125–38.

Shibles, W. (1971) *Metaphor: An Annotated Bibliography and History.* Whitewater, Wisconsin.

Skinner, B. (1957) *Verbal Behavior.* Appleton-Century-Crofts.

Sommers, F. (1963) 'Types and ontology', *Philosophical Review* 72, 327–63.

   (1965) 'Predicability' in Black, M. (ed.) *Philosophy in America.* Allen and Unwin.

Sosa, E. (ed.) (1975) *Causation and Conditionals.* Oxford University Press.

Stalnaker, R. (1968) 'A theory of conditionals' in Rescher, N. (ed.) *Studies in Logical Theory.* Blackwell.

   (1972) 'Pragmatics' in Harman, G. and Davidson, D. (eds.) *Semantics of Natural Language,* 380–97. Reidel.

   (1974) 'Pragmatic presuppositions' in Munitz, M. and Unger, P. (eds.) *Semantics and Philosophy,* 197–214. New York University Press.

Stampe, D. (1975) 'Meaning and truth in the theory of speech acts' in Cole, P. and Morgan, J. (eds.) *Syntax and Semantics 3: Speech Acts,* 1–40.

Steinberg, D. and Jakobovits, L. (eds.) (1971) *Semantics.* Cambridge University Press.

Steiner, G. (1974) *After Babel: Aspects of Language and Translation.* Oxford University Press.

Strawson, P.F. (1950) 'On referring', *Mind* 59, 320–44.

   (1952) *Introduction to Logical Theory.* Methuen.

   (1954) 'A reply to Mr Sellars', *Philosophical Review* 63, 216–31.

   (1964a) 'Intention and convention in speech acts', *Philosophical Review* 73, 439–60.

   (1964b) 'Identifying reference and truth values', *Theoria* 30, 96–118.

   (ed.) (1967) *Philosophical Logic.* Oxford University Press.

   (1971a) *Logico-Linguistic Papers.* Methuen.

(1971b) 'Meaning and truth' in *Logico-Linguistic Papers*, 170–89.

Sumner, L. and Woods, J. (eds.) (1969) *Necessary Truth*. Random House.

Tarski, A. (1933) 'Projecie prawdy w językach nauk dedukcyncych'. Translated as 'The concept of truth in the languages of the deductive sciences' in *Logic, Semantics, and Metamathematics*.

(1943) 'The semantic conception of truth', *Philosophy and Phenomenological Research* 4, 341–75.

(1956) *Logic, Semantics, and Metamathematics*. Oxford University Press.

Taylor, B. (1976) 'States of affairs' in Evans, G. and McDowell, J. (eds.) *Meaning and Truth*, 263–84.

Teller, P. (1969) 'Some discussion and extension of Manfred Bierwisch's work on German adjectivals', *Foundations of Language* 5, 185–217.

Thomason, R. (1972) 'A semantic theory of sortal incorrectness', *Journal of Philosophical Logic* 1, 209–58.

Thomason, R. and Stalnaker, R. (1973) 'A semantic theory of adverbs', *Linguistic Inquiry* 4, 195–220.

Thomson, J. (1963) 'Is existence a predicate?', *Aquinas Paper* 38. Aquin Press.

Thorne, J. (1970) 'Generative grammar and stylistic analysis' in Lyons, J. (ed.) *New Horizons in Linguistics*.

Ullmann, S. (1962) *Semantics*. Blackwell.

(1973) *Meaning and Style*. Blackwell.

Van Fraassen, B. (1968) 'Presupposition, implication and self-reference', *Journal of Philosophy* 65, 136–52.

(1969) 'Presuppositions, super-valuations, and free logic' in Lambert, K. (ed.) *The Logical Way of Doing Things*, 67–91. Yale University Press.

(1970) 'Truth and paradoxical consequences' in Martin, R. (ed.) *The Paradox of the Liar*, 13–23. Yale University Press.

Vassilyev, L. (1974) 'The theory of semantic fields: a survey', *Linguistics* 137, 79–93.

Vermazen, B. (1966) Review of Katz, J.J. and Postal, P. *An Integrated Theory of Linguistic Descriptions* and Katz, J.J. *The Philosophy of Language*, *Synthese* 17, 350–65.

Von Wright, G. (1963) *Norm and Action: A Logical Inquiry*. Routledge and Kegan Paul.

Walker, R. (1975) 'Conversational implicatures' in Blackburn, S. (ed.) *Meaning, Reference and Necessity*. Cambridge University Press.

Weinreich, U. (1962) 'Lexicographic definition in descriptive semantics' in Householder, F. and Saporta, S. (eds.) *Problems in Lexicography*, 25–43. Mouton.

(1963) 'On the semantic structure of language' in Greenberg, J. (ed.) *Universals of Language*. MIT Press.

(1966) 'Explorations in semantic theory' in Sebeok, T. (ed.) *Current Trends in Linguistics* 3, 395–477. Mouton.

White, A. (1970) *Truth*. Macmillan Press.

Wierzbicka, A. (1972) *Semantic Primitives* (translated by Wierzbicka, A. and Besemeres, J.). Athenäum Verlag.

(1975) 'Why "kill" does not mean "cause to die": the semantics of action sentences', *Foundations of Language* 13, 491–528.

Wiggins, D. (1971) 'On word-sense, sentence-sense and difference of word-sense. Towards a philosophical theory of dictionaries' in Steinberg, D. and Jakobovits, L. (eds.) *Semantics*, 14–34.

Wilson, D. (1975) *Presuppositions and Non-Truth-Conditional Semantics*. Academic Press.

Bibliography

Wotjak, G. (1971) *Untersuchungen zur Struktur der Bedeutung*. Berlin.
Ziff, P. (1960) *Semantic Analysis*. Cornell University Press.
   (1964) 'About ungrammaticalness', *Mind* 73. 204–14.
   (1966) *Philosophic Turnings*. Cornell University Press.
   (1967) 'On H. P. Grice's theory of meaning', *Analysis* 28, 1–8.
   (1974) 'The number of English sentences', *Foundations of Language* 11, 519–32.
Zwicky, A. and Sadock, J. (1975) 'Ambiguity tests and how to fail them' in Kimball, J.
   (ed.) *Syntax and Semantics 4*. Academic Press.

INDEX

act: *see* speech act
adjective, 13, 14, 113, 116, 171–3, 177–9
adverb, 6, 13, 14, 191
Akmajian, 121
all, 35, 37
Alston, 20, 55, 56,
ambiguity, and *and*, 151, 152, 153, 155;
    and deep structure, 109, 160, 165,
    168, 180–1; and generative semantics,
    164, 165, 168–9, 173, 185; and
    negation, 120, 128, 132–5, 138, 146–7,
    148–9, 152–5, 185; and quantifiers,
    136–8, 164–5, 173, 179–80, 183; and
    speech act semantics, 58–9; and
    vagueness, 120, 124, 128–38; lexical,
    3, 4, 16, 44, 80–3, 86, 165; of
    sentences, 3–4, 7, 9, 63, 69, 81–2,
    106, 118, 120, 123–38, 155–6, 168–70,
    175, 179–80, 183, 185; of words, 3–4,
    103, 123–8, 131–2, 135–8; structural,
    3, 165, 168; tests, 128–37, 148–9, 164;
    truth-conditional definition of, 40,
    128–9, 135
analytic: *see* truth, analytic
and, 13, 17, 34, 37, 111, 141, 143, 144,
    157; and presuppositional logic,
    149–54, 158
anomaly, 71, 73, 112–17 (*see also*
    meaningless)
anthropology, 96 (*see also* kinship terms)
antonymy, 84–6, 88, 89, 91; converse,
    85, 86, 89; gradable, 84–5
appropriacy condition, 51–3, 54, 57,
    58–61, 64
Åqvist, 45
argument, in predicate calculus, 89, 90;
    in semantic representation, 90, 91,
    120, 170 (*see also* variable in semantic
    representation); logical, 33–7
assertion, 53, 118, 133, 145, 150–3
assumptions, speaker's, 42, 70–2, 74,
    100, 142, 150–2, 185, 192–4 (*see also*
    belief, speaker's; presupposition,
    speaker's)

Bach, 10, 121, 130, 138, 182
Baker, 156
Bar-Hillel, 68, 195
Barrett, 138
Bartsch, 103
Bazell, 83
behaviorism, 47–50, 55
belief, speaker's, 42–54, 60–1 (*see also*
    assumptions, speaker's; logic,
    doxastic; presupposition, speaker's);
    verbs of, 66–7
Bendix, 21, 90, 104
Bennett, 95
Berlin, 104
Bever, 32, 45, 55, 73, 75
Bickerton, 71, 75
Bierwisch, 19, 91, 94, 103, 104, 109–11,
    114, 120–2
Black, 75
Bloomfield, 47–9, 55
Botha, 9
Bresnan, 130, 138, 182
Brooke-Rose, 75
Burling, 21, 104
but, 53, 57

Campbell, 57
Carden, 138
Carnap, 91, 188, 195
Cartwright, 45
Cassin, 156
Catlin, 138
Caton, 157
Chapin, 183
Chihara, 43
Chomsky, 4, 8–10, 50, 54–6, 73–4, 78,
    92, 96–7, 103–7, 109, 113–14, 121–2,
    138, 157, 160–1, 174–5, 177, 182–4,
    194, 196
Clifford, 45
Cohen, D., 157
Cohen, L.J., 41, 45, 56, 75
command, 41–2, 45 (*see also* imperative)
communication, 8, 9, 11, 12, 43, 47, 50,

Index